ISSUES OF
WORLD COMMUNISM

by
ANDREW GYORGY
Boston University

NEW PERSPECTIVES
IN
POLITICAL SCIENCE

D. VAN NOSTRAND COMPANY, INC.

PRINCETON, NEW JERSEY

TORONTO   NEW YORK   LONDON

To The Memory of

ROBERT P. BENEDICT

D. VAN NOSTRAND COMPANY, INC.
120 Alexander St., Princeton, New Jersey
(*Principal Office*)
24 West 40 Street, New York 18, New York

D. VAN NOSTRAND COMPANY, LTD.
358, Kensington High Street, London, W.14, England

D. VAN NOSTRAND COMPANY (Canada), LTD.
25 Hollinger Road, Toronto 16, Canada

Published simultaneously in Canada by
D. VAN NOSTRAND COMPANY (Canada), LTD.

PRINTED IN THE UNITED STATES OF AMERICA

Preface

IT IS THE PURPOSE OF THIS BOOK TO PRESENT IN A SERIES OF carefully selected essays various facets and issues of Marxism-Leninism. A survey of these complex problems may then give the reader a sharper insight into the intricate theoretical processes and practical strategies of world Communism.

The major political ideologies of our era are so murky and imprecise that they provide practically no safe and sound criteria of standardization or selection. Capitalism, Communism, Nazism, Fascism, the "new" nationalism, colonialism, anticolonialism, imperialism, and anti-imperialism are all-powerful human and institutional motivating forces, and yet none of them is sufficiently clearcut and definable to constitute a self-contained social and political belief system. The selection of individualized problem areas may facilitate further observation for more effective theoretical analysis.

Issues of World Communism focuses on 12 specific incidents or developments in the broad field of international Communism. In presenting a historic fact, event, or circumstance, each essay is based on a unique and nonrecurring situation; however, all of our studies are also applicable to the evolving and testing of Communist theory and to a further understanding of the broad field of world Communism. On the whole, the studies in this volume fall into four major categories. As variations on the common theme of international Communism, these are:

1. An analysis of a diplomatic incident, crisis, or controversy, including the observations of participants. This pattern is illustrated by the essay on the complex Gomulka story in Poland, the continuing tightrope-walking of Kádár in Hungary, the Rumanian and Albanian controversies within the Communist world, as well as reflections on the original (1948) and the more recent (1958) Soviet-Yugoslav disputes;

2. A portrayal of a long-term political, social, or military conflict stressing the pressures which generated it and the tangible and

intangible factors which have influenced it. This type is illustrated by the study of bipolarity in world Communism in the 1953-1960 period, the essay on the current polycentric phase centered on the continuing disarray of the "world Communist system," and the survey of Communist revolutionary strategies;

3. An examination of a specific agency, institution, or movement. This is illustrated by the selection on the monolithic, single-institution, and single-leadership stage of world Communism in the 1945-1953 period, the discussion of the strength of a flexible strategy, and the gathering impact of de-Stalinization as a Soviet and Eastern European "counter-institution" of recent vintage; and

4. A consideration of a specific theoretical problem (national Communism, military and economic integration, the Sino-Soviet dispute, revolutions, both successful and abortive) which can be effectively isolated and pinpointed, thus offering a *single* useful insight into some broader and more general problem of world Communism. This is illustrated also by the first three studies that present consecutively the theoretical aspects of monolithism, bipolarity, and polycentrism in the recent structural evolution of Communism, and by the interesting analytical survey focusing on the rationale and the chronology of unsuccessful Communist revolutionary attempts.

The 12 essays in this volume are divided into four main parts. Each part is preceded by a brief, factual introduction that summarizes the historic highlights and the more significant long-term political, diplomatic, and social facets of the individual selections. In turn, each essay is introduced by a summary prepared by the editor, which calls attention to the fundamental problems involved in the specific selection and to its author's principal conclusions.

Because each contributor was asked to stress four principal areas in his particular problem or specialized field of interest, the reader's attention is called to the following aspects of each essay:

1. The way in which the basic issue arose;

2. The manner in which various policy makers (actors on the political conflict stage) perceived the central problem;

3. The policy alternatives which were available to them, whether on a theoretical or practical level; and

4. The portrayal of the decision-making process, the implemen-

tation of the actual decision, and the presentation of conclusions that bridged the gap between theory and practical application.

Each essay is followed by a "Suggested Reading" list consisting of four or five leading books and a few selected and representative articles that are designed to whet the reader's appetite. They are not to be considered definitive or exhaustive, but merely convenient "jumping off" points for purposes of further reading in a specific field.

The challenging essay by Betty Burch reviews the goals in a Communist system and draws pertinent conclusions from the surveys in this book of the highlights of world Communism. Her article represents the over-all evaluation and conclusion of the 12 essays that constitute the four parts of this book.

ACKNOWLEDGMENTS

Issues of World Communism has been a collaborative venture from its inception. It has relied on the friendly cooperation of a number of contributors. The editor gratefully thanks all the contributors who cheerfully coped with the lengthy and intricate editorial processes and cooperated loyally in this study of the various contemporary facets of world Communism.

The editor expresses his particular appreciation to William G. Andrews, Coeditor of the New Perspectives Series, for his patient and wise counseling; to Marilyn Dexheimer for excellent editorial help and for the writing of the introduction to Part III; to Mrs. Helena Lothrop for patient typing of the manuscript; and to Jean Rex Gyorgy for able editorial assistance.

ANDREW GYORGY

Boston, Massachusetts

Contents

Part II

NATIONAL VARIATIONS ON A WORLD COMMUNIST THEME

Part III

WORLD COMMUNIST AREAS OF STRENGTH

Evolution and Change in the Structure of World Communism

Introduction to Part I

PART I PRESENTS THE POST-WORLD WAR II STAGES OF INTERNATIONAL Communism in three chronologically distinct phases of its evolution.

The first stage of modern Communism covers the immediate postwar era, from the triumphant days of victory in Europe and over Japan in 1945 to the death of Stalin in 1953. This eight-year period witnessed the greatest political and geographic extension of the Communist system. The "takeover" of Eastern European countries was matched by the rise of Communism in China. The Cold War began and displayed itself in the practically continuous struggle between East and West.

What were the principal distinctive features of this Communist empire? We stress the dates 1945 to 1953 because so much of this Communist realm depended on Stalin's character and personality. When he died in 1953 the nature and type of rule over the Communist countries changed almost immediately. Thus, this first stage was characterized by the single and highly centralized direction of *one man,* Joseph Stalin, whose domain stretched from the Elbe River in Central Europe to the Black Sea, across Siberia to Outer Mongolia and the Pacific. This period saw the domination of *one country,* the Soviet Union, over the "satellites" and the control of *one single party,* the Communist Party of the U.S.S.R., over all other Communist Parties behind the Iron Curtains of Europe and Asia, with the exception of that of Yugoslavia.

Political scientists, borrowing from geology, portray this first period as the *monolithic* stage of world Communism. "Monolith" suggests the absence of cracks, fissures, openings, or rifts. Politically speaking, it implies the absence of disagreement, challenge, or even back-talk. It points to one focal area of authority and leadership without any major opposition or even hesitation on the part of the followers. It underlines the absolute nature of Soviet leadership throughout the Communist bloc from 1945 to 1953.

Viewing it more closely, this Soviet bloc appears as an interesting mixture of strong and weak points. From the Communist perspective, the lack of political opposition helped to strengthen the leader's hand. In a few years this discipline made it possible for the Soviet leadership to transplant and establish Soviet institutions and ideas, both political and cultural, among the defenseless captive peoples of the Communist world. Thus, there appeared the small-scale replicas of both the Soviet Communist Party and Russian institutions on European and Asian soil. Determination and terror were the twin instruments by which Stalin succeeded in keeping his empire together.

The second stage, extending from Stalin's death in 1953 to about 1960, is generally described as one of Communist *bipolarity*. By "bipolarity" we mean the existence of two centers of power opposing each other, which by definition implies the end of the single center or monolithic stage of Communism—a stage that collapsed with the death of Stalin. The historic emergence of Peking as an increasingly obvious parallel center to Moscow initiated the new, bipolar phase of world Communism. Moscow was still the senior partner in the arrangement: Soviet aid was essential to Chinese economic development, and Russia was able to keep some special, privileged positions in China, although the phenomenon of bipolarity in the Communist world actually reflected advances by Red China along several fronts. Primarily, it implied Peking's search for equality in prestige and recognition. A subtle indication of this process was a change in the Communist world leaders' travel directions between the two major capital cities. Beginning with Nikita Khrushchev's journey to Peking in late 1954, Soviet delegations had to travel to China rather than Chinese officials to Moscow for advice and consultation. In several cases lower-ranking Chinese Communists returned the state trips that had been undertaken by higher-ranking members of the Soviet leadership. In an Asian world where prestige is all-important and "losing face" is considered a disaster, this exchange of visits became quite meaningful. It was China's way of expressing that the Soviets needed them more than they needed Russian support.

Equally interesting was a newly developed Chinese concern with Russia's Eastern European empire. In Stalin's lifetime it would have been impossible for Communist China to interfere with the political life of the heavily iron-curtained satellite world. Yet, by the fall of 1956 there was firm evidence that the Chinese Communists had encouraged Poland to act independently of the Russians, even promising aid to the Poles in their determined resistance to Soviet pressure. Following the Hungarian revolution of 1956, Premier Chou En-lai personally traveled to Budapest and used his political influence to smooth and ease relationships between Hungary and the Soviet Union. Thus, as a significant criterion of the age of bipolarity, the Asian world of Communism could not remain immune from Russian intervention, and—in a parallel manner—European Communism could not remain immune to repeated interventions from Asia.

The third, or *polycentric,* stage implies the presence of many competing forces and areas of challenge within the once harmonious Communist family. The year 1960 was the period of time when the seeds of disunity, sown during the Stalinist period and quietly growing during the early Khrushchev years, suddenly burst into the open. In April of that year the Chinese Communists attacked Moscow's policy on international Communism, and in June an important conference was called to try to maintain some unity in the Communist world. The conference was held in Bucharest—capital of Rumania—a city safely located behind the Iron Curtain. At this meeting, the disagreement, which had been smoldering since 1958 between Soviet Russia and Communist China, exploded into the open. Bitter accusations were made and angry charges were hurled by these two "partners in dispute," although not directly at each other, but indirectly through a third party. This was how the basically unimportant country of Albania entered the conflict. China denounced the Soviets through the voice of the Albanian Communist leaders, and in turn the Russians criticized Mao and his colleagues by angrily turning on the Albanians. The Bucharest conference thus acted as a political catalyst of Communism's current and significant phenomenon: "Polycentrism." It isolated the opponents, clarified the issues, and brought Communist disunity into greater evidence. "We have succeeded in washing our dirty linen in public," ruefully observed a Communist leader in the late summer of 1960.

The term polycentrism was first used in 1956 by the late Palmiro Togliatti, then leader of the Italian Communist Party, who prophetically forecast a growing diversity in the Communist "bloc." His phrase suggested not one, not two, but many areas or centers of Communism replacing the simpler early phases of single and dual leadership. Polycentrism thus implied that different conditions required different leadership and operational situations for the world's diverse Communist Parties and leaders—what may suit the Soviet Union and European Communists may be wholly repulsive to China and to Asian Communists. It meant that around the two principal centers of world Communism there now emerged other Marxist-Leninist forces of note, although of different size and sharply varying political importance.

Since 1956 this diversity in Communism tended toward an organizational and structural dissolution of the Communist family of nations and grouping of parties. The principal difference between bipolarity and polycentrism lies precisely in the fact that since the Bucharest Conference of June 1960 and the Moscow Conference of November 1960 (which unsuccessfully tried to patch up the increasing areas of divergence) the Communist camp has been rent asunder by a multiplicity of challenges and by the emergence of a surprisingly large number of self-styled interpreters of Marxism-Leninism. Consequently, there has been a Yugoslav "road to socialism" matched by the Hungarians', the Poles', the Rumanians', and even the Outer Mongolians' search for their own roads to socialism.

Nor is polycentrism confined to the two Communist giants and to their European and Asian satellites. Challenge to senior leadership and differing interpretations of the basic ideology have increasingly characterized other Communist parties and groups, namely, such important forces as the Indonesian and Indian parties and the various Southeast Asian nuclei of Communism. Towering above these fundamental policy disagreements there is the threatening "superstructure" of the Sino-Soviet dispute which itself has contributed considerably to the growing diversity of international Communism. By splitting individual parties and groups into Chinese and Soviet factions, the Sino-Soviet rift has gradually set the stage for a truly runaway form of Polycentrism: the total disappearance of even the last vestige of that monolithic unity which had once characterized the world Communst bloc. As an Italian Communist recently observed: "If there is a Communist center in Moscow, another center in Peking, why would there not be a center in Rome or in Paris or in Djakarta to direct the Communist parties of these various countries?" At this point we begin to witness a new chapter and the end of an international Communism which not so long ago was primarily the instrument of Soviet policy.

The three essays in Part I portray the recent stages in the structural and ideological evolution of international Communism. They progress from the Monolithic to the Bipolar, and finally to the Polycentric stage of world Communism.

1. The Monolithic Stage of World Communism (1945-1953)

by Massimo Salvadori*

In his excellent analysis of the postwar expansion of Communism, Massimo Salvadori reaches the following conclusion: "By the end of 1949, the Communist movement, which fifty years before was only an idea in the minds of a few hundred . . . radicals, had achieved complete power over one-fourth of the land area of the globe, inhabited by one-third of the world's population." In order to understand this frightening expansion of world Communism, a close study of the eight-year period of monolithic Stalinism is essential. Communism, in this stage, was either forcefully imposed upon Russia's neighbors such as the Eastern European countries, or encouraged by subversive tactics in such Free-World countries as France and Italy. Thus, the author clearly distinguishes between postwar Communism in Communist-controlled areas and the sweep of Communism outside Communist-controlled areas.

In the latter category two geopolitical regions loom as particularly significant: the Middle East and Southeast Asia. In the Middle East, as Salvadori notes, the Soviets have failed to create a system of Communist-directed buffer states (particularly in Turkey, Iran, and the Arab countries), while in the vulnerable countries of Asia the Moslem religion has served as a strong barrier against the spread of Communism. In 1953 these two areas seemed to be at least temporary exceptions to the author's distressingly accurate final assessment: "After a quarter of a century of Stalinism, Communism had truly become a world-wide movement."

* From *The Rise of Modern Communism*, Revised Edition, by Massimo Salvadori, Copyright 1952, © 1963, by Holt, Rinehart and Winston, Inc. All rights reserved. Pp. 86-115.

1. THE POSTWAR EXPANSION OF COMMUNISM:
COMMUNIST-CONTROLLED AREAS

The end of World War II in Europe found much of the Continent in a state of anarchy. Fascist rule had been the equivalent of a revolution. Millions of people had been killed, tens of millions uprooted; for years, suffering had been part and parcel of life. Political and economic institutions had collapsed. Beliefs, values, ideas around which the social structure of many European nations had been organized, had either disappeared or their influence had lessened considerably. Nazi-fascism had suffered a crushing military defeat; there were still plenty of individual fascists, but they were isolated units and hence incapable of action. Conservatism and capitalism as organized social forces were weakened by the fall of fascism. Liberalism had withered to an extent unthinkable a generation earlier. Liberal parties, whether of the right or the left, were only a faint reflection of what they had been. The liberal animus had largely vanished and the liberals' sense of justice and aspiration toward equality, which make liberty meaningful, had declined. Because of this, attachment to what used to be liberal institutions had become an expression of conservatism. Democratic socialism was still numerically important but its inability to check the advance of authoritarianism in the previous twenty years had exposed its fundamental lack of energy. This lack was largely the result of the conflict, not yet resolved by socialists, between (a) the desire to establish collectivism, which requires an authoritarian framework, and (b) a genuine attachment to liberty, which requires at least some degree of autonomy in the pursuit of economic activities. Nationalism was still a powerful emotion, if less so than in the recent past, but had little organization in the form of parties. In nations predominantly Roman Catholic or Orthodox, the postwar political vacuum was only partially filled by several varieties of Christian socialism or Christian democracy. Under conditions of disorder, poverty, confusion, deluded hopes, and intense hatreds, Communism found an atmosphere conducive to its further development.

From a Communist viewpoint, the most important result of the war was the strengthening of the Soviet Union. In May 1945 Soviet troops were in total occupation of what, before 1938, had been eight independent states in Europe: Estonia, Latvia, Lithuania, Poland, Czechoslovakia, Hungary, Rumania, and Bulgaria. Parts of Germany, Austria, Finland, Norway, and the Danish island of Bornholm were also occupied by forces of the USSR. In addition some Soviet troops were stationed in Yugoslavia and Albania, where power was firmly held by the Communist leaders Tito and Hoxha.

Soviet troops were soon withdrawn from northern Norway and Bornholm. The annexations of 1939 and 1940 were confirmed through agreements among the big powers that were reached at Teheran, Yalta, and Potsdam. To them were added sections of northeastern Germany and southeastern Czechoslovakia. This represented a total of about 185,000 square miles with over 23 million inhabitants, of which about 40,000 square miles with nearly 8 million inhabitants had never belonged to imperial Russia. In the Far East, no one objected to the formal annexation in 1944 of the former Chinese territory of Tannu Tuva, *de facto* a Soviet area since 1921. Manchuria, Korea north of the 38th parallel, southern Sakhalin, and the Kurile islands were occupied by the Soviets, who annexed the two last-named territories (about 20,000 square miles and 500,000 inhabitants). A Soviet-supported regime ruled Mongolia. The wealth of the annexed territories largely compensated for the economic losses the Soviet Union suffered in the war.

The Impact of World War II

During the war there had been considerable talk among people who did not understand the dynamics of the Communist movement about a possible "liberalization" of the Soviet regime—in the sense of allowing some intellectual and political freedom—and about the concession of real self-government to the sixteen republics of the Union. There had been mention of differences between the Communist party, the bureaucracy, and the armed forces, of tension between the ruling oligarchy and the new middle class of managers and professional people (accounting for 9 or 10 percent of the population), of dissensions within the higher levels of the Communist oligarchy, of a desire for freedom of expression among the intelligentsia. The fact that out of several million prisoners of war possibly as many as 200,000 Ukrainians and 80,000 Moslems from the Caucasus and Soviet Central Asia had agreed to fight for the

Germans had been interpreted to mean that the Soviet Union's cohesiveness was not as great as had been supposed in the late 1930's.

With the war's end, however, there was no indication that the internal solidity of the Soviet Union had declined or that the authority of its leaders was challenged. Not everyone in the Union was happy about the development of socialism. The official line nevertheless remained the nation's line and the masses confidently expected the realization of their leaders' promise that standards of living would soon equal those of the Americans. Seven ethnic groups were deprived of what the Soviets call national and cultural autonomy, because of the sympathy which a majority of their people had shown toward the German invaders. Measures were taken in 1946 to stamp out what appeared to be a recrudescence of nationalism in the Ukraine. When elections took place, the customary plebiscite went to the candidates chosen by the Communist organizations.

After 1945 the backing of the Soviet Union was, even more than before 1939, instrumental in guaranteeing the influence of Communist parties in every corner of the globe. It is reckoned that the Soviet Union lost over 7 million dead in the war against Germany and spent on the war effort, at the official rate of exchange, nearly $200 billion (corresponding in real value to approximately $60-$80 billion). In spite of these losses, the Soviet Union was stronger than ever. Internationally, the Soviet Union enjoyed a better position than Russia had ever had. In 1914 there had been seven great powers in the Eastern Hemisphere; in 1945, besides the Soviet Union, only one remained—a considerably weakened United Kingdom. Militant Communism was encouraged by the first postwar five-year plan, with an emphasis on heavy industry that could be interpreted as a willingness to use violent methods if peaceful ones failed.

The Soviet Take-Over Process

In Europe, Soviet military occupation was the prelude to the establishment of Communist dictatorships. European states not annexed by the Soviet Union but included at the end of the war in the Soviet sphere of influence cover an area of about 400,000 square miles and have a population of over 100 million, with total national incomes equivalent to nearly one third of the official national income of the Soviet Union. Since 1945 they have been referred to as the satellites. Postwar developments in these countries followed a similar pattern.

When, as the result of Soviet military victories, the Germans were compelled to evacuate or surrender, the victorious Russians or their allies (such as the Yugoslav partisans) put power in the hands of a coalition government composed of representatives of the groups that had participated in the anti-Nazi national fronts during the war. The main feature of these coalition governments was the appointment of a Communist as minister of the interior who, in European countries, has direct control over the police. Noncoalition parties, on the pretext—sometimes untrue, as in the case of Poland —that they had aided and abetted fascism, were outlawed or prevented from exercising any influence by being deprived of using means of communication (press, radio, cars, meeting places, and so forth), all strictly controlled by the government. At the same time a fairly considerable section of the economy was nationalized in order to make producers more dependent on the government. Having acquired full control of the police, the Communists proceeded to the second phase: the weakening, through arrests and threats, of non-Communist members of the coalition who showed signs of independence. This phase occupied most of 1946 and part of 1947.

The third phase was characterized by the structural reorganization of the state and the consolidation of Communist political monopoly. The appearances of the coalitions were usually kept up, with a few well-chosen crypto-Communists (such as Cyrankiewicz in Poland, Dinnyés in Hungary, Fierlinger in Czechoslovakia) representing non-Communist groups. All organized opposition was liquidated. Fundamental liberties were abolished or restricted to the point of suppression. Rapid advances were made in collectivization, transforming most citizens into wage or salary earners whose livelihood was dependent on the government. State monopoly was established over education, the press, and all other means of communication. Forced-labor camps were opened or expanded. Recalcitrant or potentially recalcitrant citizens were arrested. A few were sentenced to death and shot or hanged, in order to intimidate those who still harbored resentment against the Communist dictatorship. This final phase was reached in Albania, Bulgaria, Rumania, and Yugoslavia by the end of 1947. Poland, Czechoslovakia, and Hungary reached it in 1948, East Germany in 1949.

A fourth phase was a purely internal Communist affair. It corresponded to Stalin's purges and concerned the elimination of actual or potential opposition to the dominant faction within the Communist parties. It began in 1948 and ended in 1952. Only a few hundred people were executed, but this was enough to inspire the fear that acts as a prime deterrent of oppositional activities. By the end of 1952 each party seemed, on the surface, to have achieved the monolithic unity that is a basic Leninist principle.

The speed of the Communist advance was partly regulated by internal conditions. In Czechoslovakia there was a relatively high standard of living and education, lively nationalism and, in large sections of the population, fairly strong democratic feeling. In East Germany strong nationalism remained, but twelve years of ruthless Nazi repression had weakened all democratic forces to the point of near extinction. In the other countries there was little democratic strength or tradition. Poland and Hungary had been ruled, in the period between the two wars, by the corrupt and weak descendants of what had once been a virile and responsible feudal class; Bulgaria, Rumania, Yugoslavia and Albania by despots who had little root among the peasant population of their countries. Once the old political structure had been swept away, the only political force that could have checked the advance of Communism was agrarian socialism. This was represented in Poland by the Polish Peasant party led by Mikolajczyk, in Hungary by the Smallholders party under ineffectual leadership, in Rumania by the followers of Maniu; in Yugoslavia by those of Macek, and in Bulgaria by the movement led by D. Dimitrov and N. Petkov. Agrarian socialism had numbers but lacked organization. The Communists were efficiently organized and were helped by the presence of Soviet troops. The struggle could hardly be called such, as agrarian socialism was nowhere able to put up serious opposition. It collapsed as easily in these countries in 1945-1947 as its Russian counterpart, the Socialist Revolutionary party, had done in 1918-1919.

In four countries, either a majority (as in Poland, Czechoslovakia, and Hungary) or a large minority (in Yugoslavia) of the people had been reared in the beliefs and institutions of Roman

Catholicism. In these countries the Catholic Church was the only organization that seriously tried to put up a certain amount of resistance. But it fought a rapidly losing battle. The arrest and trial of a few members of the hierarchy (cardinals, archbishops, and bishops) was enough to intimidate a good many of the clergy. Through the nationalization of wealth, the clergy were reduced to the servile position of all bureaucrats in authoritarian regimes. Their cohesion was weakened by the presence of a few pro-Communist clerics. By the end of 1952 it seemed as though Catholicism in Soviet-controlled Europe (with the possible exception of Poland) might soon lose all political, and possibly also intellectual, significance. Other religious bodies offered even less resistance than the Catholic Church, and accepted, on the whole, the position of obedient cogs in the new dictatorial machinery.

The Soviets Reorganize Eastern Europe

Events in the Soviet zone of Germany followed a somewhat similar pattern. At first, as in other zones, four political parties had been authorized by the victors: Social Democratic, Christian Socialist, Communist, and Liberal Democratic. Taking advantage of the usual socialist split between those who gave priority to democracy and those who gave priority to collectivism, the Soviet authorities were able to bring about a fusion of the latter with the Communists, under Wilhelm Pieck and Walter Ulbricht. This led to the establishment of the Unified Socialist party. The Social Democratic party, which anti-Communist socialists would have liked to organize, was outlawed. At the end of 1947, Jakob Kaiser and other Christian socialists were forced to abandon the leadership of the Christian socialists and were replaced with pro-Communists. Liberal democrats, unwilling to accept the Communists' orders, were compelled to find refuge in the Western zones of Germany. Whatever the appearances, four and a half years after the end of the war, East Germany was solidly in the grip of the Communists.

The close relationship between all these countries and the Soviet Union was made clear in June-July 1947, when they were compelled to reject the invitation sent by the British and French governments to participate in a common effort for the economic recovery of Europe through the Marshall Plan. Under the leadership of the Soviet Union, steps were taken toward economic integration of

Communist-controlled states through a system of trade agreements, then called the Molotov Plan. The Molotov Plan took concrete shape in the Mutual Assistance Organization (Comecon) consisting, since 1961, of the Soviet Union, six European satellites, and Mongolia.

What the Molotov Plan was supposed to achieve on an economic level the Cominform aimed to realize on intellectual and political levels. The central control established by Stalin's group in the 1920s over the Communist movement, as a whole, had weakened during World War II. This weakening could easily lead to the development of heresies, or "deviations," in the Communist parties outside the Soviet Union. To maintain orthodoxy and conformity, central power had to be institutionalized, and at the same time supplied with the means to enforce its control. This led to the establishment (September 1947) of the *Cominform* (Communist Information Bureau), organized at a meeting in which the leaders of eight European parties, including those of Italy and France, participated.

It is probable that when the Cominform was established, the Soviet authorities already had misgivings about Tito, the leader of Yugoslav Communists. For over a quarter of a century he had been a loyal party official; then the accidents of war made him a leader strong in his own right. The withdrawal and surrender of the Germans had left him in complete control of Yugoslavia—a country lying on the western border of the Soviet sphere of influence, and thus enjoying the possibilities of direct relations with the Western powers. Moreover, Yugoslavia was endowed with natural defenses and considerable resources. Distrust of Tito led the other members of the Cominform to accept the Yugoslav capital, Belgrade, as the headquarters of the organization—the best place from which to keep an eye on a potential rebel. We do not yet know the exact reasons leading to the rupture between Tito and the Cominform in 1948 when, in view of the forthcoming struggle with the Western powers, greater discipline was demanded of all Communists. But whatever the reason, the break occurred. Tito and his advisers found it necessary to formulate a Communist ideology different from Soviet ideology. Stalinist Communism was based on the twin concepts of total centralization and power from above. Yugoslav Communists, in self-defense, began to stress the concepts of decentralization and power from below, thus moving one step toward the fundamental Western democratic concept of the individual's autonomy and responsibility. Decentralization and power from below meant, politically, rendering Yugoslav federalism effective; economically, it meant replacing a hierarchically organized economy with considerable autonomy and responsibility in the hands of local bodies and workers' organizations.

Hopes connected with a large-scale development of Titoist nationalist and federalist Communism were high among non-Communists in 1948 and the following years. The American government subsidized Tito to the tune of over $3 billion in a period of fifteen years to give him the possibility of resisting Soviet threats and blandishments. Results, however, fell considerably short of hopes. The effect of Titoism on the Communist movement outside Yugoslavia was slight. A few purges were enough to deter would-be imitators. Furthermore, in the Yugoslav case there was no cogent formulation, and Titoist national-Communism remained an expression without clear ideological content.

As long as Stalin lived, the mutual hatred he and Tito felt for each other was a deciding factor in the making of Yugoslav policy. After Stalin's death and for several years thereafter, the deciding factor for Yugoslav Communists was a desire for national independence, and for Tito the ambition to play an autonomous role in world affairs. In 1954 the attempt to formulate a schismatic Communist ideology was abandoned.

Communism in Asia

In Asia, the Soviet attempt in the immediate postwar period to create a system of buffer states controlled by local Communist groups, either kept in hand by Russian leadership or simply affiliated with Soviet Communism, met with varying success. It failed in the west (in Turkey, Iran, and the Arab nations) and succeeded in the east.

Afghanistan and what used to be called outlying regions of China (such as Sinkiang, Mongolia, Manchuria) border on the Soviet Union. No attempt was made by Soviet representatives to stimulate the growth of a Communist organization in Afghanistan. Long-range considerations of foreign policy prevailed over immediate party interests. An excess of Communist activities would have disturbed the good relations that had existed since 1919 between Afghanistan and the Soviet Union. Furthermore, according to the Marxist-Leninist historical scheme, the traditional authoritarian regime of Afghanistan was more acceptable to Communists than a democratic or social-democratic regime.

Farther east, in Sinkiang, the largest and westernmost province of China, the USSR had exercised a good deal of influence over local tribes during the greater part of the 1930s. There was a withdrawal during World War II, when Soviet leaders sought to inspire confidence in the members of the nationalist government which, at that time, ruled most of non-occupied China and was bent on fighting Germany's ally in the Far East. At the end of 1947 Soviet influence was reestablished through the support of anti-Chinese tribes whose kinsmen lived in Soviet central Asia. After the proclamation of the People's Republic in China, Soviet officials and troops withdrew from Sinkiang, which came under direct Chinese Communist control. Still farther east, Mongolia, closely linked to the Soviet Union since 1921, remained within the Soviet sphere of influence and was in reality as much a part of the Soviet Union as the five Soviet republics of central Asia. Most of Manchuria had been occupied by Soviet troops in 1945; their subsequent withdrawal was effectuated so as to leave the country and its considerable resources in the hands of Chinese Communists.

As the result of an agreement between the American and the Soviet governments at the end of the war, Soviet troops occupied Korea north of the 38th parallel. Under the supervision of Soviet agents and led by Kim Il-sung, Korean Communists acted as their colleagues in the European satellite countries had done. Opponents and potential opponents were destroyed. Power was concentrated in the hands of the hierarchically organized Communist party. State monopoly was imposed over means of communication and education. Much of the wealth was nationalized. A few reforms were introduced in order to give the inhabitants the impression that from now on they would be properly looked after by the state. A People's Republic was proclaimed in 1948; immediately, with feverish activity and good results, a relatively large army of probably not less than 200,000 men in fighting units was organized, commanded by Soviet officers and by Koreans who had been trained militarily either by the Japanese or by the Chinese Communists.

The Korean War

Encouraged by an American statement in January 1950 that seemed to exclude Korea from the American line of defense, the Communist government of North Korea attacked South Korea on June 25, 1950. The Korean war soon became, whatever its appearances, a war between the United States and China. During one year of major fighting and nearly two years of minor fighting, it brought untold suffering to the Korean people. The war had far-reaching effects as well. At the time it convinced the American nation that force was an important factor in Communist expansion and that force had to be checked by force. It was a major factor, at the end of 1952, in the formulation of Stalin's policy—since followed by Soviet Communists—of avoiding a military clash with the United States while maintaining all-out aggressiveness. The Korean war strengthened internal unity in China, and for three years weakened the pressure of Chinese Communism on southeast Asia and of Soviet Communism on western Europe and the Middle East.

By far the most important event of the immediate postwar period was the victory of the Chinese Communists and the establishment of a Communist state in the "closed continent," the home of the oldest great civilization still in existence. As in the case of eastern Europe, the Communist success in China was due mainly to the intelligent use of violence by a strongly integrated and highly cohesive minority group endowed with a fanatical belief in the righteousness of its cause. To this factor, inherent in the Communist movement, must be added others that had nothing to do with the Chinese Communists. The Japanese aggression had dislocated China, exhausted large sections of the population, and had prevented the nationalists from concentrating all their efforts on unifying the country. The occupation of Manchuria by Soviet troops made possible the transfer to the Chinese Communists, at a critical moment, of large stocks of Japanese arms and ammunition. Partly because of unwillingness and partly because of inefficiency, the nationalist regime failed to carry out a badly needed agrarian reform and to maintain law and order—which were sadly lacking in many areas under their control.

The pressure exercised by the United States Government over the nationalists to induce them to collaborate with the Communists was another element that should not be ignored or minimized. This pressure was based on the assumption of a fundamental difference between Russian and Chinese Communism. Chinese Communist leaders had always held that they were Marxist-Leninist. The faction in power since 1932 had conducted itself loyally according to the Stalinist line. But American experts insisted that Chinese Communism was not Leninist, and even less Stalinist, but extreme agrarian reformism. In the state of chaos in which China found itself, power was bound to fall into the hands of the best organized minority. Only foreign intervention could have kept in power a divided and inefficient minority such as that represented by the Kuomintang.

Throughout the war against Japan, which lasted, with brief intervals of peace, for fourteen years (1931-1945), relations between nationalists and Communists in China had remained strained in spite of several attempts at collaboration. During the last stages of the war, the nationalists had insisted on unification of the armed forces as the price for eventual collaboration in the government with the Communists. While the war was in progress, the Communists were concerned about building up their own strength and had no intention of giving up what they knew to be the most important element in the struggle for final success. In the summer of 1945, the Communists had about 1 million men under arms and were in control of large areas in northern China. Their guerrillas took over districts evacuated by the Japanese in the eastern provinces before the nationalists had time to arrive.

The Triumph of Communism on Mainland China

The occupation of Manchuria by Soviet troops in August 1945 influenced the course of events more than anything else. A considerable economic expansion had been effected by the Japanese in Manchuria, severed from China in 1931 and *de facto* independent even before then. In August 1945, a treaty had been rashly signed between the Chinese government (which was under the impression that it was implementing American policies) and the Soviet government. The treaty recognized on the one hand the end of Chinese sovereignty over Outer Mongolia and limited Soviet rights in Manchuria and, on the other, it recognized Chinese sovereignty over Manchuria. When the Soviet troops withdrew, most of the vacated areas were handed over to the Communists. Two years after V-J Day, the Communist forces numbered 2 million well-trained and well-equipped men.

Fighting between nationalists and Communists varied in intensity, but never stopped entirely. At first there were nationalist offensives, such as the one that led to their temporary occupation of Yenan (March 1947), the capital of the Communist area. When fresh and newly equipped Communist divisions took the offensive, the nationalist military leaders made the strategic blunder of trying to hold Manchuria, a region far from China proper. Their best troops were encircled and compelled to surrender. Defeat followed defeat, peasant dissatisfaction led to a general anti-nationalist jacquerie, and by the end of 1949 the whole of mainland China was in the hands of the Communists. A People's Republic had been proclaimed on September 21, with its capital at Peiping. Under nationalist control remained the island of Formosa—technically, until the signing of the peace treaty with Japan in 1951, a Japanese possession, and then the refuge of the nationalist government.

Following the example set by the states of Eastern Europe, Communist China had a nominal coalition government. In reality it was a one-party police state run by the highly centralized and hierarchically organized Communist party. No opposition or dissent was tolerated. Class liquidation was carried out as efficiently as in the Soviet Union thirty years before. All media of communication were strictly controlled by the government. Parts of the economy were nationalized immediately; the rest was rigidly controlled by the government, which held the monopoly of economic initiative. It was reported that in 1950 executions of so-called counter-revolutionaries had claimed nearly 1 million victims. In Marxist-Leninist jargon the people executed were either monopolists (businessmen and landlords) or lackeys of imperialism (democrats). In 1951 the liquidation of counter-revolutionaries continued. Early in the year Tibet was occupied. All educational, cultural, charitable, and religious foreign institutions were nationalized; all Chinese Christian churches were ordered to sever relations with foreign missions. The following year saw the end of all organized opposition, the intensive "re-education" of pro-Western intellectuals, and the establishment of a complete network of state trusts, trading corporations, and cooperatives for the control of all aspects of the economy. Extensive economic agreements with the Soviet Union accompanied the launching, early in 1953, of the first five-year plan.

Although the masses in China cared little for Communism or anti-Communism (and had no voice or possibility of expressing their views), Communism appealed to a larger minority of the population than democracy ever had. The concept of liberty and the accompanying value of individual responsibility and dignity were never strong in the Chinese tradition; traditional Chinese society had possessed an excellent system for the control of the human mind and had developed political despotism to a fine art. The Communist regime took over where China had left off in 1842, adding economic control to political and intellectual control.

By the end of 1949, the Communist movement, which fifty years before was only an idea in the minds of a few hundred or a few thousand radicals, had achieved complete power over one fourth of the land area of the globe, inhabited by one third of the world's population. The extraordinary success of Communism in just a few years could be compared to the Roman conquest of the Mediterranean in the second century B.C., to the Islamic expansion of the seventh century, to the empires conquered in a few years by Attila, Genghis Khan, and Timur.

2. POSTWAR COMMUNISM OUTSIDE
   COMMUNIST-CONTROLLED AREAS

Until the last year of the Stalinist era, control over as many as possible of the advanced industrial nations of continental Europe and the disruption of those which could not be controlled remained major Communist goals. The priority given to the Communization of industrial Europe had been inherited from nineteenth-century socialism and from Leninism. There was, however, growing resistance west of the Iron Curtain against internal and external Communist pressures—at least partly as a result of

American aid and the stiffening of American anti-Communism. Because of this, a major change in Communist global tactics was decided on by Stalin and his collaborators in 1952. Free Europe would no longer have priority in Communist efforts to seize power. This priority would be transferred to the underdeveloped areas. Communist efforts should aim at isolating western Europe and the United States from the rest of the world, at stimulating internal tensions, at strengthening anti-Americanism everywhere.

In the immediate postwar years, the greatest Communist successes were achieved in France and Italy. This was partly the result of the excellent organization built up by the Communists during the period of German occupation and of their activity in the resistance movements of those countries. In the first postwar French elections held in 1945, the Communist party, which used to receive about one vote in seven before World War II, improved its position considerably and obtained the support of more than one fourth of the voters. Party members numbered nearly 1 million. During the following years its voting strength increased to 29 percent; in the elections of 1951 it still drew more than 25 percent of the vote, in spite of economic recovery and the reorganization of anti-Communist forces. In the 1951 parliament the Communists formed the second largest group. For nearly three years after the liberation of the country they participated in coalition governments, except for the short-lived government led by the socialist Léon Blum (December 17, 1946-January 22, 1947). In May 1947 the socialists—accusing the Communists of sabotaging the efforts of the government from the inside and of making use of their position to strengthen their own party, and supported by the Catholics of the *Mouvement Républicain Populaire* and by the liberals of the Radical Socialist Party—decided to form a government without Communist participation. Later in the year an anti-Communist rightist movement was organized by General de Gaulle. It received a plurality of votes in the municipal elections of 1947, and in 1951 sent to the parliament the largest single block of deputies. From then on Communist influence declined, although a large minority of the French remained loyal to Marxism-Leninism.

In Italy, Communist ministers sat in coalition governments April 1944-May 1947. At the general elections of June 2, 1946, the first free elections since 1921, the Communists received just under one fifth of the votes. Under the leadership of Togliatti, the Italian Communist party then became the largest outside the Communist empire with a membership that already totaled more than 2 million. In May 1947, the leader of the Christian democrats resigned as premier and, entrusted with the formation of a new cabinet, formed a homogeneous one of Christian democrats and independents. This was strengthened at the end of the year by the inclusion of representatives of small democratic groups. Contrary to what was happening in France, a majority of Italian socialists decided in favor of close collaboration with the Communist party, from which they became almost indistinguishable. At the national elections of April 1948, and again at the local elections of 1951, Communists and socialists voted together. It is supposed that the strictly Communist vote increased by about 50 percent, from 4 to 6 million voters. In the parliament the Communists formed the second largest group. "Deviation" was kept firmly under control. Some intellectuals left the party and a few deputies were expelled. This caused a number of speculations concerning "Titoism," but only a negligible influence was exercised at first by the dissidents over the masses of the faithful. In April 1951 the party leadership announced a total membership of over 2½ million.

Communism in Other European Countries

The collapse of Nazism had brought about a limited revival of the Communist movement in the non-Soviet zones of Germany, where more than seven tenths of the German people lived. In 1932 the Communist party had been the third largest, ranking after the Nazis and the social-democrats. After the defeat of 1945 the Communists were competing with the Christian democrats, the social-democrats, and the liberals. Under conditions of freedom of vote guaranteed by the occupying forces of the United States, Great Britain and France, the Communists could nowhere obtain more than a small fraction of the vote. In the *länder* of the three zones, the largest percentage of votes was received by the Christian democrats in predominantly Catholic areas, elsewhere by the social-democrats. The Communists made a determined effort to forge ahead, but with remarkably little success. They were able to recruit less than 200,000 members and at the first postwar elections in 1949, polled a little over 1 million votes. The local elections of

1952 showed that they had lost ground, and that their voting strength was not more than 2-4 percent of the electorate.

In the Austrian general elections that took place in 1949 and again in 1953, the Communists received less than one vote in twenty. The prestige of the small Austrian Communist party was at first strengthened by the presence of the Soviet army of occupation. This prestige later declined almost to the vanishing point.

In the Scandinavian countries, in Holland, Belgium, and Luxemburg Communist parties at first improved their position in comparison with the prewar period. But they soon lost what extra influence they had gained, and remained small and relatively unimportant. Political leadership was retained in the hands of social-democrats and liberals in Scandinavia, of Christian democrats in the Benelux countries. In Finland and Iceland, the Communists were proportionately more numerous but failed to gain the upper hand. In Switzerland and in the British Isles as well, the Communists remained small noisy minorities with little weight in political affairs. In Spain and Portugal they existed then only as small underground groups.

In Greece there had been little or no evidence of Communist participation in the war between Greece and the Axis. After the Nazi attack on the Soviet Union, the Communists, together with other groups, took active part in the resistance. After the withdrawal of the Germans in October 1944, they attempted to overthrow the Greek coalition government of which they had been members. The revolt was put down by the combined efforts of British troops and Greek anti-Communist forces. The Communists and various pro-Communist groups refused to participate in the elections of March 1946. Allied observers—British, American, and French—expressed the opinion that, had the Communists participated in the elections, they and their fellow-travelers would have received less than one third of the votes. They decided instead on guerrilla activities, favored by the mountainous nature of the country and by its extensive frontier with Bulgaria, Yugoslavia, and Albania, all controlled by Communists. By the end of 1946, considerable guerrilla activity had been carried out under the military leadership of Markos Vafiades. During 1947, attacks were made against many towns and villages in the northern provinces. A commission sent by the United Nations to investigate the situation reported that the Communist-led guerrillas, then estimated at

15,000 men, were receiving help from the Communist dictatorships of Bulgaria, Yugoslavia, and Albania.

The deterioration of the situation in Greece and the possibility that the conflict between Communists and anti-Communists would lead to further complications and to the establishment of a Communist regime caused the United States Government, in March 1947, to take a direct interest in the internal affairs of the country. The Communist party was outlawed. At the end of December 1947 a provisional government was formed by the Communists in the area of Mount Grammos. The reorganization of the Greek forces under the supervision of American experts and Tito's defection from the Soviet camp contributed toward bringing the civil war to an end early in 1949. At the 1952 general elections only a small section of the population showed itself to be in favor of Communism.

As already mentioned, the Soviet attempt to create a system of buffer states controlled by local Communists failed in western Asia, that is, Turkey, Iran, and the Arab countries. During World War II and periodically after, there were Soviet threats against Turkey. Pressure against Turkey was also exercised through Bulgarians (there were serious frontier incidents) and Soviet Armenians clamoring for Turkish provinces once inhabited by Armenians. As a result of the severe anti-Communist policy followed by Turkish nationalists since 1919, there was no organized group in Turkey capable of lending support to the activities of native or foreign Communists, and Soviet attempts to intimidate the Turkish republic failed.

During World War II, Soviet troops occupied the northern provinces of Iran, and the British occupied the southwestern section of the country. The Soviet troops were to have left Iran a few months after the end of the hostilities, as the British did, but when the time came they did not move. Combined British-American pressure, exercised through the United Nations, induced the Soviet Government to order the evacuation of Iran in 1946. This was done in such a way as to leave behind in Azerbaijan—the most populous province, inhabited by people akin to those of Soviet Azerbaijan— a Communist-controlled provincial administration. A few months later, the central government of Iran sent an expeditionary force and after brief fighting reestablished its authority. Subsequently, waves of nervousness swept Iran each time Soviet troops moved along the border. To this was added, from time to time, the agitation of Kurdish tribesmen, acting under Communist influence both in Iran and Iraq. In contrast to what happened in Turkey, a section of the Iranian intelligentsia embraced Communism and the Iranian Communist party, in spite of the lack of any sizeable mass following, was able to maintain a fairly efficient underground organization.

Communism in the Middle East and in Asia

In general, postwar Communist progress was considerably slower in Islamic nations than in other parts of the world. By the time World War II ended, there were active, but small, Communist groups in French North Africa, mostly in Algeria, in some of the states of the Middle East (Syria, Lebanon, Iran), and farther east in Indonesia. Religion was a strong barrier against the spread of Communism. Moreover, the influential groups of the population were then either fanatically traditionalist, or (in the case of most of the intelligentsia) fanatically nationalist. In some Arab nations, particularly, the combination of extreme nationalism and vague socialism has produced movements more akin to European fascism than to Soviet Communism.

The Communist leaders' attempt to create a pro-Soviet attitude in the Moslem countries by allowing Soviet Moslems to travel outside the USSR did not give appreciable results. And in 1947, on the pretext of danger of epidemics, Soviet Moslems were again forbidden to make their pilgrimage to Mecca. In Syria the Communist party was outlawed at the end of 1947. At times, however, some Arab governments flirted with the idea of agreements with the Soviet Union for nationalistic reasons. Since acquiring independence in 1932, Iraq had been governed by a Westernized minority. A few intellectuals called themselves Communists; Kurds in the north were, for tribal reasons, open to Soviet overtures; but Communism was yet hardly a political factor. The same can be said of Egypt, even before the 1952 revolution that put a nationalist socialist dictatorship in power. There were active Communists in Lebanon and among Palestinian Arabs, but few in the other independent or near-independent Arab nations. In Pakistan, a minor Communist agitation, which was mainly connected with Indian Communism, existed only in the eastern section of the country. In Malaya, Communism failed to penetrate the Moslem section of the population.

Only in Indonesia, the most populous Moslem state, did Communists have a strong organization before 1952. There, Dutch and Indonesian Communists had been active for several decades. They took advantage of the chaotic conditions that followed the end of Japanese occupation and the proclamation of independence by a group of Japanese-sponsored nationalists to strengthen their organization. Attempts at open revolt in October 1949 were crushed by the nationalists; in the fighting the Communist leader Muso died, as did also the former leader Tan Malaka. After riots in Jakarta in August 1951, many Communists were arrested. Shortly afterwards came a *coup de scène:* nationalists and Communists made common cause against the moderates and the socialists. From then on Communist influence increased rapidly.

Since the end of World War II, a main area in the Communist struggle for power has been the easternmost peninsula of southern Asia. Three to four years of Japanese occupation had created a political vacuum propitious for Communist activities. For centuries, Burma, Annam, and to a lesser extent Thailand, Laos, and Cambodia had gravitated within the orbit of Chinese civilization. In Malaya, Chinese immigrants formed the largest group of the population. Direct or indirect European control had been disrupted by the Japanese invasion and occupation during World War II and traditional social structures had weakened. These factors, together with the impetus provided by small groups of active and dedicated Communists, had combined to make Communism, in which most radical aspirations were confluent, a primary problem.

The revolt against the French and against native traditional authorities in Vietnam was organized by Ho Chi Minh, one of the ablest Asian Communists and a disciple of French Communism. A common boundary with Mao's China after the end of 1949 gave the Vietnamese Communists a considerable advantage over their opponents. In Burma and Malaya the Communists were fewer than in Vietnam. What they lacked in numbers they made up in energy and activity. As soon as they had mustered adequate forces, they started civil wars that lasted several years. Less tense in the immediate postwar period was the situation in Cambodia and Laos. In Thailand, Thai nationalism and a military dictatorship checked the diffusion of Communism, which found followers only among the intelligentsia of the Chinese minority.

In Japan, Communism had been repressed almost to the point of extinction during the period following the end of party rule in 1932.

Just 1200 party members formed the nucleus of the postwar Communist movement. Their main assets were the fellow-traveling leanings of a large section of the Socialist party (which for a while was divided into two independent organizations, one pro-Communist and the other anti-Communist), the leadership they immediately established in the labor movement, and the deep hatred that sections of the population at first felt against the Americans. Guided by Nozaka, Communists received 2 million votes in elections in 1946 and 3 million in 1949. Growing resistance on the part of the socialists, growing opposition in the labor unions, diminishing antagonism against Americans, and factionalism between groups headed respectively by Nozaka and Tokuda, led to a loss in influence. In the elections of October 1952, the Communist vote had dropped to well below 1 million.

To summarize, we must stress that at the beginning of 1953, on the eve of Joseph Stalin's death, there were throughout the world approximately 24 million members in the various Communist parties, 6 million of which were outside the Communist empire. In countries where free elections had taken place, the total voting strength of the Communists was a little over 20 million, of whom most were to be found in France, India, Italy, and Japan. After a quarter of a century of Stalinism, Communism had truly become a world-wide movement.

SUGGESTED READING

Books:

Daniels, Robert V., *The Nature of Communism,* New York: Random House, 1962.

Deutscher, Isaac, *Stalin: A Political Biography,* London: Oxford University Press, 1949.

Hunt, R. N. Carew, *The Theory and Practice of Communism,* New York: The Macmillan Company, 1951.

Shulman, Marshall D., *Stalin's Foreign Policy Reappraised,* Cambridge: Harvard University Press, 1963.

Articles:

Byrnes, Robert F., "Climax of Stalinism: 1950-1953," *Annals,* May 1958, pp. 8-11.

Crankshaw, Edward, "A Long Look at Stalin, Ten Years After," *The New York Times Magazine,* May 2, 1963, pp. 30 *et seq.*

Schwartz, Harry, "Stalin and Stalinism Five Years After," *The New York Times Magazine,* May 2, 1958, pp. 13 *et seq.*

2. The Bipolar Stage of World Communism (1953-1960)

by John S. Gibson

This stage of world Communist development serves as a bridge, a transition point between the monolithic period of all-out Stalinism and the full-fledged challenge of Soviet leadership by Communist China, from 1960 onward. John Gibson stresses the important erosion process which had been developing imperceptibly behind the sturdy façade of the world Communist monolith. With Stalin's death and the Korean armistice, both in 1953, "two of the main pillars supporting Sino-Soviet solidarity were knocked down."

The bipolar stage increasingly revealed the personality conflict between Khrushchev and Mao. Beginning with his runaway pattern of de-Stalinization, Khrushchev had introduced new, and to the Maoist leadership, frightening and unpalatable policies. This essay enumerates some of the theoretical (ideological) and practical arguments proffered by the Chinese Communist elite in its repudiation of at least two of Khrushchev's major policy-lines: the "peaceful coexistence" stress in foreign policy and the anti-Stalin campaign in domestic affairs. The exciting events of 1960, culminating in the 81 party-meeting in Moscow in December, are rightly seen here as the watershed between the phases of Communist bipolarity and polycentrism.

THE COMMUNIST WORLD IN 1953

The death of Joseph Stalin on March 5, 1953, was an event of signal importance for the destiny of world Communism. For almost three decades, the Soviet dictator had held a tight monopoly on the manifold operations of the global Communist movement. He shaped the theory of Marxism-Leninism to meet the crises of his era and to fortify his and Russia's pre-eminent position in the Communist bloc. He dominated the Communist Party of the Soviet Union, and either officially or without portfolio, directed the affairs of the government of the U.S.S.R.

Soviet national policy was Stalin's policy, a force which he considered to be the spearhead of international Communism. His orders and Soviet national policy were obediently carried out within most of the Communist parties throughout the world. With one exception, Stalin was the master of that massive monolith called world Communism. In less than eight years after the Kremlin despot's death, however, the monolith was shattered and today the multiplicity of schisms in world Communism is one of the most explosive features of contemporary international relations.

What were the cracks in the iron wall of Communism in 1953? Obviously, one Communist state, Marshal Tito's Yugoslavia, preferred to go it alone in striving toward the presumed goal of Communism, the classless society. Tito's defiance of Stalin's power tentacles and party line, and his defection from the Soviet-led Communist bloc by June 1948, produced the first major breach in Stalin's carefully constructed ideological edifice. The master of the Kremlin raged at Tito, accused him of joining the Western camp, and vowed to crush him and all those who sympathized with the Yugoslav "renegade."

Tito, unlike most of the other leaders in the Eastern European satellites, felt little obligation to follow Stalin's directives on key questions of domestic and foreign policy, noting that he seized control of Yugoslavia at the end of World War II without the assistance of Soviet military power. Claiming that Communism could be "national" in design and application rather than suffocate in the confines of Stalin's "international" network, Tito spun his revisionist doctrine of "national Communism." With material support from some Western nations for his partial blocking of the Soviet forward movement in Europe, Tito was able to ignore the death warrants addressed to him by Stalin. In March 1953, therefore, Tito's Yugoslavia represented the one sharp and painful break in the once-solid Communist bloc.

In the Far East, there was another Communist-controlled state which was destined to cause much greater havoc in the world Communist movement than the ideological mischief hatched by Tito.

But few people would have ventured to predict in the Spring of 1953 that within eight years, Mao's China and Khrushchev's Russia would be at opposite ends of the ideological pole of Communism.

It was clear in 1953 that the Chinese style of Communism with its agrarian foundations hardly paralleled the urban-oriented brand of Marxism-Leninism found in the Soviet Union and Eastern Europe. Mao and his associates had, on many occasions, emphasized the differences between their ideological perspective and that embraced by the Kremlin elite. A comparison between Communist China and Tito's Yugoslavia was also a factor in assessing the status of China in the international Communist camp in 1953. Like Tito, Mao did not come to power riding on the coat-tails of the Red Army as was the case with most other satellite leaders in eastern Europe. Actually, Stalin rarely took Mao seriously and extended only token support to his movement until the People's Republic of China completed its sweep of the mainland in October 1949. The long and frequently turbulent history of Sino-Russian relations and the striking dissimilarity in culture and world outlook between the two massive nations also provided ready evidence that China and Russia did not spring from the same mold. However, these fundamental differences between the two Communist superpowers were not emphasized in March 1953, when the People's Republic of China, along with the other Soviet satellites, publicly mourned the passing of Joseph Stalin.

Regardless of the false or true ring of Mao's lamentations, his clique in Peking in all probability pondered long and hard on the future course of the world Communist movement. Mao had admired the authority and orthodoxy of Stalin's Communism and hailed the Moscow dictator's stress on a militant approach to Communist goals. But on March 5, 1953, the towering tyrant was no longer at the helm. Without Mao even realizing it, Stalin's death marked a quiet and almost unnoticed transition to the bipolar stage of international Communism.

KHRUSHCHEV, SOVIET COMMUNISM AND PEACEFUL COEXISTENCE (1953-1957)

Following the death of Stalin there emerged in Russian ruling circles a unique form of government known as "collective leadership." Although veteran party war horse Georgi Malenkov was given the reins of government and, for a short period, the key position as First Secretary of the Party, clustered around him and guiding his hand were such eminent survivors of the Stalin regime as Beria, Molotov, Bulganin, Kaganovich, Mikoyan, Voroshilov and Khrushchev. An April 1953 article in Pravda hailed this new era of collective directorship as: "one of the fundamental principles of party leadership of collectivity in deciding all important problems of party work. It is impossible to provide genuine leadership if inner party democracy is violated in the party organization, if genuine collective leadership and widely developed criticism and self-criticism are lacking. Collectiveness and the collective principle represent a very great force in party leadership."

Malenkov forged ahead in a clumsy manner by stressing a relaxation of economic controls; the Party Presidium was reduced in size; for a brief period the tensions which had been mounting for so many years seemed to ease. However, stationed in the wings was Lavrenti Beria, Minister of the Interior and chief of the dreaded secret police, the MVD; he now began his move to seize the Party and control of the state. The other "collective leaders," sensing that Beria was on the march to liquidate them, trapped him first in a neat arrest-maneuver in July 1953. Accused of being an "adventurer and hireling of foreign imperialist forces," Beria was promptly executed. He was then cast into the role of a scapegoat and held up as the one responsible for all the domestic and foreign problems which the U.S.S.R. had suffered up to the summer of 1953. Stalin, of course, was elevated to this distinctive status two and a half years later.

In the summer and fall of 1953 the pyramid of Soviet power began to sharpen as Nikita Khrushchev assumed the vital position of First Secretary of the Communist Party on September 7, 1953. Actually much earlier in the same year Malenkov's role in the Party had begun to recede, and the star of Khrushchev to rise. Then, during the remainder of 1953 and 1954, Khrushchev formulated and carried out a "virgin lands" program, designed to bring under cultivation vast areas of land in Central Russia and Asia which had never felt the plow. Fortuitously aided by fine weather and the zest of those involved in a new project, Khrushchev's agrarian plan worked, much to the chagrin of Malenkov and some of his colleagues in the Kremlin. Emboldened by his success, Khrushchev then pushed ahead with a concentrated heavy industrial program at the expense of the Soviet consumer, and simultaneously criticized Malenkov for inept leadership.

With Malenkov's prestige on the wane, and his own riding on the tail of sheer good luck, the First Secretary was able to purge the stodgy and lack-luster Premier. In early February 1955, in a grand totalitarian style, Malenkov "resigned," and Marshal Nikolai Bulganin, a man of some military repute but hardly one of brilliance in the echelons of governing, became the Premier of the Soviet government. The real reins of power, however, were now in Khrushchev's hands. Khrushchev, with Bulganin's support, pushed the heavy industrialization program, while both took off on a series of travels which was to alter the entire course of the Communist world.

The first stop for the touring Kremlin leaders was in Belgrade on May 27, 1955. In an obvious attempt to heal old wounds and to unify the Communist world through persuasion and patient cajoling, Khrushchev was the epitome of humility as he greeted Marshal Tito at the Belgrade airport. Placing all the blame for the schism between Yugoslavia and the U.S.S.R. on the convenient whipping boy, Beria, Khrushchev proceeded to assert that "the government of the Soviet Union based its relations with other countries, big and small, on the principle of peaceful coexistence of states." Tito wasn't exactly mesmerized by this candid admission of Soviet wrongdoings in the past and promises for the future. On the other hand, the Yugoslav leader was delighted with the opportunity to witness an acceptance by Khrushchev of his own approach to the goals of Communism. The olive branch was extended, and Tito clasped it lightly.

Khrushchev's Belgrade speech was the touchstone for a new era in the pragmatic application of Communist ideology. Flushed with the success of a dynamic economic program, Khrushchev had undoubtedly come to the conclusion that the U.S.S.R. had much to gain in preserving the material gains and accomplishments of the Soviet economy. Acutely aware of what a World War III might do to Russia, the First Secretary evidently came to the conclusion that the destructive potential of nuclear warheads was the sword of Damocles hanging over his country as well as the rest of the world.

Peaceful coexistence had been a necessary strategy for the security of the Russian state at several stages in the unwinding of Soviet foreign policy. The periods between 1933 and 1939, as well as 1941 and 1945, were ones of relatively peaceful coexistence with the West. In 1955 Khrushchev moved to make peaceful coexistence the keystone of his policies toward other nations. The militant means to the goals of Communism, built into orthodox Communist ideology, had to be subordinated to alternate routes leading to the same goals, as Khrushchev took liberties with the more than century-old dictum of Karl Marx and Friedrich Engels: "(Communists) openly declare that their ends can be attained only by the forcible overthrow of all existing social conditions. Let the ruling classes tremble at a Communist revolution!"

Bulganin and Khrushchev then trooped on to Geneva in July 1955, to attend the meeting of governmental chiefs from the United States, the United Kingdom, France and the U.S.S.R. Bulganin was the official Soviet spokesman, but Khrushchev left no doubt as to who was the puppet and who was the puppeteer. "B and K" journeyed near and far in succeeding months. Their tour to Asia gave them ample opportunity to promote the cause of peaceful coexistence. Within the U.S.S.R., the First Secretary promised a future of peace, progress, and plenty for all his people. He stocked the Party and governmental bureaucracy with his own appointees and proceeded with due dispatch to rise to the highest peaks of power.

For some eight hours on the night of February 24-25, 1956, Khrushchev delivered a speech that must go down in history as one of the most devastating character assassinations ever recorded. In his "secret" address to the Twentieth Congress of the Communist Party of the U.S.S.R., the First Secretary tore into Stalin, the man, and into the late dictator's long administration of Soviet affairs and the Communist Party, in an extraordinarily vicious manner. In seeking to destroy the "cult of personality," which Khrushchev cited as one of Stalin's many crimes, he disclosed that Lenin, before his death, had strongly condemned Stalin. This fact was known in the West, but it had been kept a secret in the Soviet

Union. Proceeding from this attack on Stalin's claim to Party legitimacy, Khrushchev constructed a magnificent case to prove Stalin's guilt in the conduct of Party, governmental, and military affairs.

With his thunderous blast against Stalin in this "closed" session of the Party faithful, Khrushchev took a grave but necessary risk in his bid to lay claim to complete power in the Soviet Union and to reshape the application of Communist ideology. Earlier in the Twentieth Congress sessions, Khrushchev had fully defined and eulogized "the Leninist principle of peaceful coexistence of states with different social systems." He pointed out that this policy was "not a tactical move, but a fundamental principle of Soviet foreign policy." [1] This expression, combined with the launching of the process of "de-Stalinization," had the dual purpose of propping up Stalin as a scapegoat for all previous shortcomings in the U.S.S.R. and transferring the militant approach to Communist ends so implicit in Stalinism to the ambivalent position of "peacefully" pursuing the goals of Communism. The denunciation of Stalin thus gave Khrushchev a clear way, so he hoped, for the molding of Soviet national policy and the spearheading of world Communism.

In stepping out from the long shadow of the iron dictator, Khrushchev found himself in an exceedingly difficult position. He had offended those in Russia who strongly endorsed Stalin's firm handling of Soviet domestic policy and his rigid, militant promotion of Communism in world affairs. Khrushchev had irreparably injured the Stalinists who dominated the governing and Party machinery of the Eastern European satellites. The First Secretary had also shaken the Peking rulers, who, only several days before the Moscow speech, had praised Stalin to the skies. The Chinese were obviously dismayed by the *ex post facto* assassination of Stalin combined with peaceful coexistence as the basis for future foreign policy. Regardless of the "secrecy" of his address, Khrushchev's condemnation of Stalin quickly reached all capitals of world Communism and repercussions were not long in coming.

The uprisings in Poland in June 1956, followed by the riots in October, brought Khrushchev to Warsaw. He placated Gomulka,

---

[1] For the speech at the Twentieth Congress, see G. F. Hudson, Richard Lowenthal and Roderick MacFarquhar, *The Sino-Soviet Dispute* (New York: Praeger, 1961), pp. 42-46.

the Polish Party chief, and extended some concessions which had the effect of diluting Soviet control over Poland. The epidemic of "de-Stalinization" moved at a pace which Khrushchev had never anticipated. The Hungarian Revolution of late October 1956 was of such proportions that Khrushchev was forced to dispatch tanks to Budapest in order to prevent the complete disintegration of Soviet control in Eastern Europe. This militant move was hardly in keeping with the spirit of "peaceful coexistence," but Khrushchev had to place a higher priority on demonstrating Kremlin overlordship than on permitting the effects of "de-Stalinization" to lead to "de-Sovietization."

THE 1957-1960 PHASE

After facing a rough crisis in the Kremlin in the summer of 1957, when Molotov, Bulganin, Shepilov, Malenkov, and Kaganovich nearly forced him out of power, Khrushchev emerged as the new Soviet strong man. The successful launching of Sputnik I in October 1957 skyrocketed the U.S.S.R. to unparalleled levels of world prestige. Basking in his new-found glory, Khrushchev proceeded to expand on his "peaceful coexistence" theme. At a gathering of Communist parties in late November 1957, he took a somewhat firmer line on peaceful coexistence, largely because Mao was present and also because the crises of 1956 were still hovering like ominous clouds over the domestic and foreign affairs of the Soviet Union. At this juncture, Khrushchev undoubtedly communicated with Mao Tse-tung on the emerging differences between the two parties. We may assume that Mao made a strong case for a "tough line" in the international Communist front, while Khrushchev submitted an equally firm brief for emphasizing the nonbelligerent approach to the goals of Communism. The two men parted, undoubtedly trusting that time and events would prove the other's viewpoint wrong.

In 1958, Mao blazed ahead with policies calculated to take the world to the brink of war, assuming that he would receive strong military backing from the Soviet Union. Mao pressed hard on the Nationalist-held off-shore islands of Quemoy and Matsu and might have been successful in routing Chiang's forces, had Khrushchev supplied him with all the military support and material Mao had sought. But while the United States restrained the more ambitious plans of Chiang Kai-shek to attack the mainland of China, Khrushchev muzzled Mao as well. The Soviet leader attempted to make certain that Mao would not provoke a major military engagement in an area where the military might of the United States would be directly involved. Mao therefore turned his attention to Tibet, which he annexed in 1959, and on to India and Nepal, areas in which the United States had no direct commitments. Although Khrushchev could not restrain the militant policies of Communist China, which were closely related to the pursuit of Chinese national interests, he was at least able to prevent Mao's aggressive tendencies from exploding into areas where the United States had a direct concern.

Moscow at this point held the reins. A few of the factors involved were Soviet economic aid to Communist China, Russian technicians working on economic projects as well as the Soviet's military strength and prestige. Although Mao felt that these resources of power should be channeled into an intensive thrust against the non-Communist world, in the years 1958-1959 he was in no position to challenge Khrushchev's broad peaceful coexistence policies.

In September 1959, Khrushchev made his famous visit to the United States, engaged in friendly conversations with President Eisenhower at Camp David, closely inspected American agriculture, and privately debunked Mao Tse-tung's commune system. He then flew to Peking to join in the celebrations of the tenth anniversary of the People's Republic of China. One can imagine that this meeting was not infused with cordiality. The First Secretary undoubtedly criticized Mao's militancy, including his pounding away at the offshore islands, aiding the F.L.N. movement in Algeria, and making preparations for strong-arm action in the Himalayan region. Mao, on the other hand, probably accused Khrushchev of initiating the "spirit of Camp David" and of various other foreign policies not in accord with China's interests. Neither persuaded the other of the logic of his respective position.

In subsequent months, the battle lines between peaceful coexistence and militant Communist action became well defined in official U.S.S.R. and Chinese Communist publications. The U-2 incident in May 1960 and the subsequent Khrushchev explosion at the Paris summit conference convinced many observers that the Soviet

Union was likely to revert to a "tough line" in its foreign policies. However, at the meeting of the Rumanian Communist Party Congress in Bucharest in June 1960 Khrushchev not only re-emphasized his sentiments about peaceful coexistence with some Western leaders (Eisenhower was excluded since the spirit of Camp David was now no more than an unfriendly ghost), but sternly criticized those in the Communist camp who advocated an intransigent and bellicose position vis-à-vis the West. The Chinese delegate, P'eng Chen, made it quite clear in a cool and rigid reply that the People's Republic would not follow in Khrushchev's footsteps, nor would it accept his leadership in delineating the over-all tactics which Communists should pursue. . . .

THE RISE OF MAO TSE-TUNG IN PERSPECTIVE:
COMMUNIST CHINA'S MILITANT COMMUNISM (1953-1957)

In the early 1950's Mao Tse-tung was forced by the weak internal conditions of China and by the logic of world affairs to accept Stalin's leadership of international Communism. Publicly Mao and Stalin, and Russia and China, were united in furthering the goals of Communism. But even at this time, Mao had independent aspirations. He had his eyes on territory that China had long coveted and claimed for itself, but had not, because of its century-old forced subservience to other nations, been able to penetrate. Taiwan had top priority, but there was also Outer Mongolia, Sinkiang to the West, and territories in the Himalayas along the Nepalese and Indian borders. There was Tibet as well. Chinese nationalism and irredentism had been underground for so many decades that few considered China to have any territorial ambitions whatever with respect to the vast and poorly defined territory around its borders. But with the advent of the People's Republic, a new centrifugal force was cut loose, and Stalin was concerned with the possibility of tensions and crises with the new regime in China.

The war in Korea, which brought Mao's troops into conflict with the United Nations' forces in November 1950, hardened the international community's attitude toward the People's Republic. Branded as an "aggressor" by the United Nations General Assembly in February 1951, Mao's Communist China was driven into a closer relationship with the Soviet Union than ever before, and also depended upon the U.S.S.R. for indispensable credits and material economic assistance. The Chinese Communists continued to take the lead from Stalin, and the outside world certainly had the impression that world Communism was a sturdy monolith. However, with Stalin's death in 1953 and with the Korean armistice in the same year, two of the main pillars supporting Sino-Soviet solidarity were knocked down.

At this point in world history the Chinese Communist leaders were not yet ready to upset the unity of the world Communist bloc. Ostracized from the halls of world diplomacy, and particularly from the United Nations, tired and worn from the battles of the civil and Korean war, and uncertain of the outcome of the political turmoil raging in the Kremlin, the elite of the People's Republic was biding its time. In 1953 the Chinese leaders concentrated primarily on internal affairs. A vast program of land reform and agrarian collectivization went into effect, along with Mao's first Five-Year Plan. Continued Soviet economic assistance played a vital role in reconstructing the battered Chinese economy. Bulganin and Khrushchev visited Peking in September 1954, and concluded an extensive aid agreement under which the U.S.S.R. was to grant a long-term credit to China of some 520,000,000 rubles (about $130,000,000). Other agreements called for the withdrawal of Soviet troops from Port Arthur, the construction of new railroads by both states, and cooperation in science and technology.

Along with the bolstering of their economy, the Chinese Communists in 1954 sought to repair their image abroad by devising some peaceful coexistence policies of their own. Chou En-lai and Prime Minister Nehru of India agreed in June 1954 on five principles which were to govern relations between their two countries. These aims included mutual respect for each other's territory, non-aggression, non-interference in each other's internal affairs, equality and mutual benefit in relations between the two states, and peaceful coexistence. At the Bandung Conference of Asian states in April 1955 Chou En-lai reinforced an image of peace and good will.

Within China itself there was a brief and pirmarily oratorical thaw in Mao's overwhelming dictatorship. The main Chinese Communist theoretician (after Mao), Liu Shao-chi, hailed the policy of letting "A hundred flowers bloom together and all schools contend in airing their views," seemingly inviting a less rigid ideological climate. Mao repeated these words saying that "Marxism fears no criticism;" however, he added a stern warning that "revisionism" or "rightist opportunism" would be strongly opposed.

The soft line abroad and evidence of a lightening of tensions within China was a calculated strategy designed to broaden contacts with other nations, and to show cooperation with the Soviet Union in a process of political relaxation. Mao, however, did not alter his blanket condemnation of Tito and his continuous praise of Stalin was certainly at odds with the steady de-Stalinization trend within Russia and Western Communist circles. Furthermore, the evidence of "peaceful coexistence" to be found in Chinese foreign policy was intended only for consumption in the Afro-Asian world and was not to govern relations with Western states. Khrushchev's insistence on de-Stalinization and peaceful coexistence forced Mao to reach a decision on the wisdom of continuing to accept Kremlin leadership in matters of Communist ideology and strategy.

CHINESE COMMUNISM, 1957-1960

In late 1957 and early 1958 the People's Republic of China triggered a "hard" line in both domestic and foreign policy. At home, there was an intense tooling-up for rapid industrialization in order to become as economically self-sufficient as possible. In world affairs, Mao sought to bring the Communist camp back to the orthodox Marxist-Leninist-Stalinist position of placing priority on force and threats of force to gain the goals of Communism. Furthermore, now that the Communist bloc had vastly increased its power in Asia, Mao saw an opportunity to push for the maximization of Chinese prestige.

The "Great Leap Forward," an intensified action to industrialize the Chinese nation, was begun in January 1958. In the spring of that year, the People's Republic supplemented the "Great Leap" with a vast acceleration of new collective community organizations, the "communes." Over 27,000 such communes were organized, with over 500 million Chinese peasants forced into units of agricultural and industrial production designed to produce "instant Communism" in China.

The climate which had earlier produced the "Hundred Flowers" was now rapidly deteriorating. Some flowers had indeed arisen to voice criticism of Mao's regime, but Peking's dictatorship soon went into action, pounded the dissenters, and lopped off their heads. The oppressive nature of Mao's regime became increasingly apparent as the commune system and the hastily conceived economic program fell far short of their targets. The rigid totalitarianism of China in 1959 and 1960 was in distinct contrast to the perceptible relaxation occurring in the Soviet Union.

In foreign affairs Mao also revived the "hard line." The cycle swung from conciliation with India and the "spirit of Bandung" to a policy marked by implacable hostility toward all foes, especially the United States. He proceeded to attack the off-shore islands in the Taiwan Strait, but failed because of strong opposition by the U.S. and lack of support by the U.S.S.R. Tibet was seized and an offensive was launched against the northern parts of India in 1959. Here too the Chinese were disappointed by Khrushchev's reaction. The Soviet Premier declared in 1959 that the U.S.S.R. deeply regretted ". . . the incidents which took place recently on the frontier of two states (China and Russia), both of which are our friends. . . . We would be glad if the incidents on the Chinese-Indian frontier were not repeated and if the existing unsettled frontier questions could be solved by means of friendly negotiations to the mutual satisfaction of both sides."

Not receiving Khrushchev's support in his war with India was undoubtedly a blow to Mao. The Chinese press began to debunk peaceful coexistence almost daily, and continually criticized the U.S.S.R. for its refusal to support the militant approach to advancing Communism. However, Mao was unable to budge Khrushchev or to involve the Soviet Union in China's military crises.

Khrushchev, as we have seen, did not allow the U-2 crisis and the tumultuous summit conference of May 1960 to alter his theory of "peaceful coexistence." This attitude was made clear at the Rumanian Party Congress in Bucharest despite vocal Chinese opposition. During the remainder of 1960 the battle between the two positions was carried on in the party presses of both nations, with threats by Soviet writers to the effect that Russian aid would be cut off to China if Mao continued his tirade against revisionism and pursued his policies calculated to take the world "over the brink" into war. During the fall of 1960 there was a slow but steady departure of Russian technicians from China, at a time when the Chinese economy was on the edge of disaster.

For its part, the Chinese press unleashed torrents of abuse on revisionism, stressing the necessity for all Communists to support the orthodoxy of their movement. At this junction, the Chinese attacks on revisionism were a thin veneer for an outright charge that Khrushchev was the most blatant "revisionist" of all. To have been more explicit would have resulted in the foreclosure of all Soviet aid to China, and as yet this aid was indispensable for the survival of the Chinese Communist economy.

In December 1960, at the Moscow meeting of eighty-one Communist parties, an ambiguous statement sought to reconcile both points of view by diluting the extreme positions of the two sides. By this time, however, the die was cast, and neither Khrushchev nor Mao (who did not even attend the meeting) was prepared to back down. The Chinese left the Moscow sessions in a huff, taking with them tiny Albania which, for its own reasons, had chosen to side with Mao against Khrushchev. In late December 1960 the Communist bloc ceased to convey even the superficial appearance of bipolarity and, by historic evolution, the new era of Communist polycentrism gradually began to emerge.

Two events—Khrushchev's fall from power and China's explosion of a primitive nuclear device—combined to offset somewhat this apparently irrevocable course. In the fall of 1964, Chou En-lai attended a Moscow conference of the Communist World, and indicators were that the new leaders, Breznev and Kosygin would be more polite—though not necessarily more conciliatory—toward the Red Dragon.

SUGGESTED READING

Books:

Crankshaw, Edward, *The New Cold War: Moscow v. Pekin,* Baltimore: Penguin, 1963.

Daniels, Robert V., *A Documentary History of Communism,* New York: Random House, 1963.

Dux, Dieter, *Ideology in Conflict: Communist Political Theory,* Princeton: Van Nostrand, 1963.

Hsieh, Alice L., *Communist China's Strategy in the Nuclear Age,* Englewood Cliffs: Prentice-Hall, 1962.

Hudson, G. F., Richard Lowenthal and Roderick MacFarquhar, *The Sino-Soviet Dispute,* New York: F. A. Praeger, 1961.

Mehnert, Klaus, *Peking and Moscow,* New York: F. A. Praeger, 1963.

Zagoria, Donald S., *The Sino-Soviet Conflict, 1956-1961,* Princeton: Princeton University Press, 1962.

Articles:

Conquest, Robert, Carl Linden, and Thomas H. Rigby, "How Strong Is Khrushchev? Conflict and Authority in the Soviet Union, A Discussion," a Symposium of three articles in *Problems of Communism,* September-October 1963, pp. 27-46.

Gyorgy, Andrew, "The Politics of Peaceful Coexistence: The Internal Political Order," in *Eastern Europe in the Sixties,* Stephen Fischer-Galati, ed., New York: F. A. Praeger, 1963, pp. 159-194.

Schram, Stuart R., "The 'Military Deviation' of Mao Tse-tung," *Problems of Communism,* January-February 1964, pp. 49-56.

3. The Polycentric Stage
of World Communism (1960-):
Change and Struggle in
the Communist Bloc*

by Franz Michael

*Franz Michael's article focuses on the polycentric stage of current
world Communism. This period can probably best be defined by
a series of negative postulates: the absence of a single leader, of
a single party controlling an international movement, of a single
country exerting unchallenged primacy, and hegemony over all
other Communist parties and states. While the emphasis is on the
Maoist challenge of Soviet leadership, it is clear that after 1960
numerous contending voices have been raised in the Communist
world, voices of disagreement and criticism, seriously weakening
"the ideological and political unity of the Communist bloc and
movement."*

*The author considers the ideological disunity of polycentrism as
the most damaging aspect of the contemporary Communist world
development. The combatants' mutual and endless denunciations
of each other as "deviationists" cause bewilderment among the
rank and file and consternation even between the competing party
elites. Yet, we are warned, even throughout its worst trial-and-
error and tribulation periods the Communist movement retains its
close interrelationship between doctrine and strategy. It is this
"doctrinal and political entirety" of the system which poses the
greatest threat to our free-world way of life.*

* Reprinted with permission from the Spring 1963 issue of *Orbis*, a
quarterly journal of world affairs, published by the Foreign Policy Research Institute of the University of Pennsylvania, Vol. VII, No. 1, pp. 49-76.

THE SINO-SOVIET CONFLICT HAS BEEN VIEWED BY MANY AS A SIGN of ideological and political disintegration within the bloc. Where formerly Communist policy was directed from one center—Moscow—there are today, in this view, many centers of Communist authority, and one speaks of a system of "polycentrism."

There is no generally established definition of this term, and its meaning has remained vague. It was first used by the late Italian Communist Togliatti, who meant to express by it not a dissolution of the Communist unity and disobedience to the overall Communist program, but rather a greater autonomy of the parties in adapting to their own areas the overall Communist line. It has now been applied by students of the Communist bloc to describe what they, in different degrees or in different ways, seem to think is a weakening of the ideological and political unity of the Communist bloc and movement as a result of the emergence of a number of independent Communist centers of authority. The reasons for the emergence of these centers are seen in the different histories, ideological climates and national interests of the Communist states, in particular those of the two major Communist states today, Soviet Russia and Communist China. In fact, some scholars, focusing on the Sino-Soviet conflict, speak of the development of two rather than many centers. This concept of "polycentrism," or at least "duocentrism," has led to the assumption that different types of Communism—different "models," based on different histories and backgrounds—are developing, and that these differences in kind explain the different stands taken by Soviet and Chinese Communist leaders on policy issues of the day.

It is the view of this writer that although these different stands on policy within the Communist bloc are to some degree real, and make up the form in which the conflict is expressed, yet the conflict itself is not over the realization of different national policies by different centers, or over deep ideological disagreements, but rather over the right to determine the common policy of the whole movement. What is at stake is not the right to a parting of the ways, but the leadership of the Communist movement as a whole.

In this struggle for leadership Khrushchev and his successors have maintained the monopoly of power, which Mao Tse-tung has challenged by attacking their application of doctrinal principles to the world strategy of Communism. The complex structure of the

Communist movement and the emergence in it of a bloc of countries controlled by Communist parties provided the arena for this battle; the resulting organizational issues are the weapons with which it is fought, and the ideological arguments furnish the ammunition.

Since the Communists claim that, as the vanguard of the proletariat, they represent the decisive historical force of the time, Communist leaders must base their claim to leadership upon their ability to apply the ideological framework correctly to each policy decision. All leadership battles consist, therefore, in the main, in contrasting the opponent's wrong ideology with the attacker's better ideological understanding of the given situation. Neither side must necessarily be consistent, and the stand of either combatant can shift according to the opportunities seen in each situation and according to the opponent's changing ideological claims.

All leadership battles in Communist parties are fought in these "ideological" terms. What distinguishes the present conflict from such local party power struggles is that it is fought in the Communist movement as a whole and reveals a doctrinal and organizational problem that is inherent in the movement, namely, to provide authority in a movement that has no clearly defined theoretical or organizational framework for determining leadership.

Lenin's doctrinal concept of the Communist Party as the vanguard of the international proletariat implied that there was only one world-wide Communist Party, which had its organization or section in each country. Ideally then, there would have to be a decision-making procedure in this world party. Such a procedure was meant to be established through the Communist International, organized in 1919 by Lenin to counter and destroy the socialist international movement and to be the tool of the Communist world revolution. Theoretically, the Comintern was ruled by its Congress, its Executive Committee, and later its Presidium. It established in time its own bureaus and departments to manage the affairs of the movement through the different national parties.

But in practice the Comintern was but an arm of Soviet party power extended to the whole world. This Soviet control of the Comintern and the movement was not based on any organizational theory but simply on the fact that the Communist Party of the Soviet Union was the only party in control of a government and of the resources necessary to promote and control the movement. When this control was criticized in the first years of the Comintern's existence, it was defended by such arguments as: "The Russian comrades on the presidium and the ECCI (Executive Committee of the Communist International) must be accorded the greatest weight, for they have the greatest experience in the field of international class struggle. . . ."

This contrast between fiction and reality in the role of the Comintern destroyed its usefulness, so that by 1943, when Stalin dissolved it as a gesture to his Western allies in the war against Nazi Germany, it had not only become a "discredited symbol of the (Soviet) hegemony," but also had lost some of its importance, since "a large part of its political tasks had long since been transferred to the apparatus of the Soviet foreign ministry and the espionage organizations."

When the *Cominform* was founded in 1947, several parties had gained control, albeit with Soviet help, of the governments in their countries. The fact that many of these parties were mass parties created many problems for the enforcement of central discipline. In theory, therefore, it seemed useful to permit more leeway, to assert the equality of the member parties, and even to imply that "one center" of policy enforcement was no longer needed. The autonomy of the parties was to be combined with a greater theoretical independence of the organization. Thus, although the statutes of the Comintern had provided that the seat of the organization could be in any Communist country, it had remained in Moscow; by contrast, the Cominform had its seat first in Belgrade and, at the end, in Bucharest. But in spite of the location, the admission of the equality of the member parties, and the conciliar form of decision-making, the Cominform, like the Comintern, remained Moscow-directed. Yet, it failed to serve either the fictional or the practical Soviet purpose.

The Soviets' difficulty in enforcing their political control over all other parties at this time was not so much the result of the miscalculations of Stalin and his methods or of the growth in the size of Communist parties in the countries outside the Soviet Union, as of the fact that some of these parties now possessed governments with which they could defy the Soviet authority's attempt to dictate policy. The whole problem of the control of the movement, which remained latent throughout the earlier time, now came to the fore.

Apparently, the Communists did not foresee the problem that would arise after the conquest of power by parties other than the Soviet party. When the Bolsheviks conquered power in Russia and established the Soviet Union, they regarded that Union as the core of a world Communist state. When the name for the new government was discussed, the first proposal was to call it a "Union of Soviet Republics of Europe and Asia." But, as was pointed out by Mikhail Frunze, a comrade-in-arms of Lenin, this name would not do justice to the world revolution, which eventually would involve America, Africa and Australia as well. It was therefore decided to call the new government the "Union of Soviet Socialist Republics," a name that could serve the concept of a new Communist world state. This world state was the goal of the Comintern at the time of its founding, and even when the prospect of the immediate Communist revolution had disappeared, the dream of a federated Soviet state that would introduce the Communist millennium had not faded. Yet when the Communists seized power after the Second World War in a number of states in Europe and Asia, they did not establish Soviet Republics, but semi-autonomous People's Republics.

The resulting bloc had no structural system that would give expression to the unity of the political purpose of the Communist parties in their aim of establishing a world federation. The already existing problem of the absence of an organizational framework to determine leadership and policy-making among the parties of the movement was thus aggravated. Treaties of alliance such as the one concluded between Soviet Russia and Communist China in 1950 hardly provided such a framework. They were patterned after traditional interstate relations and served only a limited purpose. Nor did the slogans of the Communist "bloc" or "camp" or "commonwealth" provide the organizational tool needed.

Until his death, Stalin's authority and prestige as the powerful leader of the Communist movement enabled him to continue his domination over the new Communist bloc, although his authority was already being challenged. But with Stalin's death the authority of his Soviet successors to decide the strategy of the movement could be challenged by any opponent within the bloc who had enough organizational strength and prestige. Mao Tse-tung, in control of a bloc party whose state, largest in population, was most removed from Soviet power, soon posed the challenge to Khrushchev's authority that is at the core of the current Sino-Soviet conflict.

In judging this conflict, it cannot be stressed enough that we are dealing with Communist parties and not with national states of the nineteenth-century variety. It seems necessary to stress this point because when one so often hears that China wants this or Russia wants that, one is prone to forget that the political authority in these countries rests not with the governments but with the parties in control of the governments, and that these parties are constituents of the Communist movement whose policy they represent. There can be no question that the major goal of the policy of the Chinese Communist Party is the Communist world revolution and that its leaders regard their own revolution as a part of this world revolution. . . .

The application of Communist policy has, of course, to be adapted by each party to the conditions of the country in which it operates. The Communists have to deal with national traditions which cannot be ignored; but the Communist purpose differs basically from that of the fulfillment of a national cultural destiny, which was the purpose of the national state. The country of the party is only the setting within which Communist policy is to be applied, and this policy is carried out within the framework of the doctrine and over-all strategy. Conflicts on strategy will therefore concern themselves with the problems of accomplishing the common purpose, not those of serving traditional national interests.

The fact that governments of Communist parties demonstrate territorial ambition does not contradict this view. Expansion at the expense of the non-Communist world serves the Communist cause. It is most unlikely, however, that any such territorial aggression will be carried on by China against the territory of another country of the bloc. The purpose of Communist policy is Communization, not the establishment of national empires at the expense of other bloc countries. The Soviet-Chinese conflict is over the strategy of the advancement of Communism in all parts of the world. The view sometimes expressed in popular writing that a conflict was building up between the Soviet Union and Communist

China over the threat that millions of Chinese people will over-run the Siberian empty spaces, that Khrushchev was therefore afraid of Communist China and willing to come to terms with the West is clearly mistaken for this reason alone.

The Communists themselves have always maintained the unity of the doctrine. The very fact that the combatants directly or by proxy call each other "deviationists," "dogmatists," "adventurists," "revisionists," or any of the other terms of Communist ideological abuse, shows their mutual accession to the principle of one Communist doctrinal line. The intention is to challenge the interpretation and application of the doctrinal system, not to break out of it. And when one examines the ideological argument itself, one finds that it is recent in origin, and thus not a matter of any long-standing convictions; that both sides have shifted their points of view at different times; that the most serious arguments are matters of emphasis of different aspects of a general policy on which there is no quarrel; that much of this argument is more concerned with abstract formulation than with practical policy; and that some of the polemics is purely demagogic.

Much of the conflict is not concerned with matters of immediate concern to the Chinese Communist government, such as the issue of Taiwan or the offshore islands, Southeast Asia where, in this writer's view, the Soviets and Chinese Communists have closely cooperated, or India, where an interpretation of divided roles can be as easily argued as one of conflicting policies. Rather, Mao's accusations against Khrushchev concerned the overall issues of how tough the policy should be toward the West, and what line to take on summit meetings, *détente,* Albania, Yugoslavia, and the support of Cuba.

In judging Mao's stand on these issues, it must not be forgotten that he is in opposition and not, as was Khrushchev, in a position of responsibility. It is always the advantage of opposition that it can demand more radical measures than the authority responsible for action can take, and thus discredit the opponent. Where Mao himself has had the responsibility for action, he has not been known as a reckless leader. His record in the civil war in China, his own writings on guerrilla warfare, his action toward the offshore islands and Taiwan have not indicated a willingness to take grave military risks; and his recent venture in India against an unprepared opponent does not contradict this record. Rather, the radical line expressed in Chinese statements has appeared only since the conflict with the Soviet leadership began. It is therefore more logical to regard the conflict as the cause of the radical line than to regard the radical line as the cause of the conflict.

Mao's rise to power within the Chinese Communist organization and the conquest by the Chinese Communists of the Chinese mainland occurred during Stalin's time. The Communist victory in China in 1949 differed from that of the Communist parties of Eastern Europe in that it was accomplished without direct Soviet help and even came as a surprise to Stalin and the Soviet leaders, who may have underestimated the Communist opportunity in China at that time. Though political and personal slights by Stalin may have rankled his mind, Mao still accepted Stalin's leadership without any sign of opposition. But after Stalin's death Mao had become the most senior among the leading figures in the Communist world.

At first Mao followed the line set by Khrushchev. The loosening of control that came with the "thaw," and the shift from Stalin's method of police control and terror, was taken up in Communist China by the policy of "The Hundred Flowers" and by more active Chinese participation in bloc policy. The Chinese leaders attempted to assist the Soviet leader in overcoming his difficulties with the East European satellites. They even followed Khrushchev's de-Stalinization policy, though with obvious reluctance and in a much more limited form. But already at that time—1956—there may have been doubts about the wisdom of Khrushchev's risky policy of attacking the former leader, and dissatisfaction with his practice of formulating policy without consulting the senior Chinese leader.

The change in the Chinese Communist line began in the years between 1956 and 1959, when Mao's expectations that he would play a major role as senior statesman of the Communist bloc and movement were rudely disappointed, and when he did not even receive from the Soviet leaders the economic support he so badly needed.

An indication that Mao now favored a more aggressive line in the continuing diplomatic battle with the West was his speech at Moscow University in November 1957, in which he stressed the superior strength of the Communist bloc gained by the sputnik and the development of intercontinental missiles. This was expressed also in the Chinese symbolism used by Mao: "The East Wind is now prevailing over the West Wind," a slogan to be repeated many times and used to press for a tougher Communist policy on the basis of a new interpretation of the "epoch." The same point had been used by Khrushchev to support the argument that war was no longer inevitable, since the new strength of the Communist bloc deterred the capitalist warmongers. The question of the exploitation of this changed situation became a matter of emphasis rather than of principle.

In the summer of 1958 the Chinese Communists still ostensibly supported Khrushchev's summit policy which aimed at the inclusion of India in a five-power meeting to handle the Near East crisis. Khrushchev's visit to Peking of July 31-August 3 was apparently the last real effort at consultation on major policy decisions.

During 1957 and 1958, this problem of consultation and participation in bloc policy-making became aggravated by an internal Chinese crisis that must have increased Chinese Communist impatience with Soviet strategy. The Hundred Flowers movement in China led to an explosion almost as serious as the uprising in Hungary. The loosening of the reins in China showed the bitterness against Communist policy not only among the population at large but especially among the students and intellectuals, including a large section of the party members themselves. The shift back to a reassertion of party control took the form of the "Anti-Rightist Movement," and, as in Eastern Europe, the thaw ended in China with the suppression of the opposition. At the same time, the economic problems caused by the unrest in Eastern Europe had endangered the economic program of the bloc and the availability of Soviet economic aid on which Communist China depended for its ambitious plans of industrialization.

This was all the more serious because the enforced collectivization of the last years had created difficulties in agricultural production that could be overcome only by permitting a greater freedom to the farming population, or possibly, by a system of greater control. These inner difficulties, in combination with decreased outside support, forced upon the Chinese Communists the alternative of a slow-down in economic development or a drastic shift in policy. If the missing capital that could not be secured from the Soviet Union had to be provided from within China, it seemed necessary to establish an iron control over the faltering agriculture that alone could produce the needed surplus.

It was at this moment that Mao Tse-tung decided to take the radical course of pressing ahead—and of "going it alone"—with a program which went far beyond the accomplishments that could be achieved with decreased Soviet aid. The "Big Leap Forward" and the commune policy, accompanied by so much fanfare, were the result of this decision. To justify this policy of autonomy in terms of the overall Communist line, Mao Tse-tung stressed now the necessity of applying the general Marxist-Leninist theory to the "concrete conditions" of China. . . .

The commune system was not only an attempted *tour de force* in the Chinese economic and social transformation; it was a direct challenge to Soviet leadership. The mess halls, community living, work teams, combination of agricultural and industrial work, and abolition of private property—none of these characteristics of the commune system was a deviation from Communist teachings. The Chinese Communists purported to introduce a more advanced stage of development in which the transition from socialism ("to each according to his work") to the more advanced stage of Communism ("to each according to his need") was already taking place; a stage which, according to Communist doctrine, could be reached only when production had advanced far enough to provide the affluence with which to satisfy needs. Thus with the commune system, Mao attempted to bypass the Soviet Union on the road toward the Communist millennium and to become the vanguard of the vanguard. In that he failed.

Khrushchev reacted strongly to the commune policy. The reorganization of Chinese agriculture was favorably reported in the Soviet papers until the Chinese claim of being ahead of the Soviet Union became known. Then there was silence, followed by a hostile reaction.

The commune policy was initiated in the Summer of 1958. At the end of the year the retreat began. In its resolution of December 10, 1958, the Central Committee of the Chinese Communist Party greatly modified the commune. It restored some private property to the farmers, the principle of payment according to work, and family living—all the items that would have put Communist China ahead on the way to Communism. At the same time, Mao resigned from the chairmanship of the republic, retaining only his position as Chairman of the Central Committee.

It can well be argued that this retreat was caused by the resistance of the Chinese peasantry. But the doctrinal importance of the retreat in Communist terms and the personal resignation of Mao Tse-tung are difficult to explain on that basis alone. The conjecture that behind this policy change was Khrushchev's pressure gains support from the events that followed. In January 1959, Chou En-lai went to Moscow to negotiate a new economic agreement for additional Soviet support for Chinese industrialization. It seems plausible that Mao's resignation was the price for Soviet economic aid in 1959. But Khrushchev went further. In June 1959, for the first time he openly attacked the principle behind the Chinese communes, stressing that such a stage in Communist development had to be preceded by vast progress in economic production. At the same time an attempt was made at the meeting of the Chinese Communist Central Committee at Lushan, in July 1959, to remove Mao from his leading position in the party. This attack, led by P'eng Teh-huai, the Chinese Minister of Defense, was, as we know today, made with the previous knowledge of Khrushchev. The attack failed and ended in the purge of P'eng and his group. But Khrushchev's attempt to defeat his potential rival initiated the acute phase of the Sino-Soviet conflict.

From that time on, Mao again built up his power as the leader of the Chinese Communist Party and government. When at the end of August 1959, Liu Shao-chi, Mao's successor as Chairman of the Republic—a reluctant dragon rather than a rival—called the Supreme State Conference to decide on important political matters, Mao did not appear. But in mid-September, Mao called an *ad hoc* conference, with the same participants and a few additions, to pass on the same agenda plus an amnesty as an obvious demonstration of his own authority.

Since that time the hero cult of Mao has risen to new heights in Communist China; the adulation of Mao today at least equals that of the Stalinist cult at its height. Not only is Mao *the* leader of Communist China, venerated in word and image in his role of guiding light, but he is also celebrated as the leading star in the

Communist world. Some eyebrows in Moscow must have been raised when statements appeared in the Chinese press such as that of January 1960: "Comrade Mao Tse-tung is the most outstanding representative of the proletariat in our country, and the greatest revolutionary leader, statesman, and theoretician of Marxism-Leninism in the present era."

Since then the conflict has been fought by mutual recrimination on a number of what have been called "ideological" issues. The most celebrated of these has been the disagreement over the inevitability of war and the possibility of peaceful coexistence, linked to the doctrinal interpretation of the "character of the epoch." Whether the growth of the "world socialist system" had advanced enough to secure peace or how much "imperialism" still threatened war became an issue used to attack or defend the methods of Communist strategy.

How little the Chinese Communists' more aggressive attitude has to do with any special Chinese ideological tradition can be seen if the present view is compared with the one expressed a few years back. In 1955, Communist China was known for its great success at the Bandung Conference as the propagator of peaceful coexistence, of Panchsheel. According to Chou En-lai, his country was quite willing to talk peace with the United States—the past and present arch-villain of Chinese Communist story. In 1956 Communist China accepted the theory that war can be avoided, advanced at the 20th Soviet Party Congress, and subscribed to it at the interparty meeting in Moscow in 1957.

The seeming shift in the Chinese position on this question was only an abstract argument to be used in the power struggle. The Chinese Communists did not return to the view that war was inevitable nor did they call for war. They challenged the more cautious Soviet policy of negotiation and demanded, in their role of the opposition, a more aggressive one. The argument shifted soon to different types of wars. Besides world war there were local wars which might or might not turn into world war, and there were revolutionary wars and wars of liberation which were "just" wars. In an argument that was shifting and demagogic on both sides, the Chinese Communists attacked the Soviet coexistence policy as shirking the support of revolutionary and just wars.

Related to the argument on wars was the one on the possibility of carrying out a revolution through peaceful parliamentary methods, as employed by European Communist parties. This brought upon the Soviets the Chinese Communist accusation of abandoning the revolution for the "peaceful road" of "revisionism."

The last major forum in which the Sino-Soviet battle was fought was the interparty meeting of all the parties of the Communist movement, after the personal conflict between Khrushchev and Mao reached its climax. According to a Soviet statement circulated among the delegates of other parties before the meeting opened, the meeting had been called by the Soviet leadership earlier than originally planned because the Chinese had violated the declaration of the 1957 meeting and had introduced a disruptive campaign within "certain foreign parties" and had even attempted to "denigrate and unseat Khrushchev personally, by incorrectly denouncing his travels in the West and his 'peace' policies."

In a comment at pre-meeting briefings, M. A. Suslov, member of the Presidium of the CPSU, pointed to the contradiction within the Chinese ideological statements and indicated that the other parties had to choose between the Soviet or the Chinese views. The four issues that were mentioned by the French Communist leader, Maurice Thorèz, as the basis of the debate, "the character of our epoch, problems of war and peace, paths of transition to Socialism, and the unity of the international Communist movement and rules which regulate the relations among fraternal parties," are the obvious doctrinal and organizational issues at stake in a power battle for leadership of the movement. The first two concern themselves with the general problems of coexistence, the toughness of the stand to be taken in negotiations with the "imperialists," and the question of either supporting national liberation movements à la Bandung or the promotion of armed uprising. The other two issues, those of transition to socialism and of the unity and rules of relations within the movement, are more directly concerned with the power struggle. The problem of transition to socialism concerns the question of who is ahead on the way to the final Communist goal and who, therefore, has the claim to lead the movement.

In the Statement of the Moscow meeting the Chinese Communists are given special mention after the Soviet party, but ahead of the other parties that have succeeded in conquering power in their countries. The people's revolution in China is mentioned for its contribution to shifting the balance of world forces in favor of socialism and for the impetus it has given to the national liberation movements, especially to those in Asia, Africa and Latin America. Next come the other People's Democratic Republics, which have shown "remarkable progress in Socialist construction" and together with the great Soviet Union "form the mighty Socialist camp."

The leading position of the Soviet Union is expressly declared at the end of the statement: "The Communist and worker's parties unanimously declare that the Communist Party of the Soviet Union has been, and remains, the universally recognized vanguard of the world Communist movement. . . ." The "experience" and the "example" of the Soviet party are stressed, and it is expressly stated that the decisions of the 20th Soviet Party Congress are not only of great importance for the Soviet party and the Soviet Union, "but have initiated a new stage in the world Communist movement, and have promoted its development on the basis of Marxism-Leninism." The Soviet vanguard role was thus firmly reasserted. It was on this role alone that Khrushchev's leadership was to be based.

Soviet leadership depends on remaining in overall development ahead of the other camp countries, especially Communist China. Soviet economic aid to members of the bloc, especially to China, will narrow the gap between Soviet and Chinese development and strengthen the Chinese leaders' rival claims. Chinese anger over the limitation of Soviet economic support to China and Soviet reluctance to give such support is therefore understandable also from the point of view of the power struggle for leadership. Will the Soviet Union maintain its leadership to the end and enter the millennium first? Or will she assist her fellow socialist countries to draw even so that all may move into the stage of Communism together?

In the 1960 Moscow Statement, this question is neatly avoided by a formulation that promises "extended cooperation and fraternal mutual assistance; gradual elimination, along these lines, of historical differences in the level of economic development, and the provision of a material basis for a *more or less simultaneous transition* of all the Socialist peoples to Communism."

The connection between this sudden preoccupation in the Soviet

Union with the future road to Communism and the Chinese experiment can be easily inferred. It was not enough for Khrushchev to refute the Chinese experiment; as leader of the vanguard he had to point out the true road. The greater experience, the more advanced stage, and the role as the vanguard on the road to Communism were his only claims to leadership which were not dependent on institutional methods of control that could be used against the Soviet Union. This explains the Soviet resistance against all Chinese attempts to continue to anchor the Soviet leadership in an institutional form that would permit a challenge.

If the Communist movement as a whole is to follow its vanguard, all that is meant by this equality of the fraternal parties is the freedom to apply the principles or policies worked out by the vanguard to the conditions of their own countries. This does not mean that each party, or "center," can go its own way. The Moscow Statement speaks of the camp as a "social, economic, and political community of free and sovereign peoples united by the close bonds of international socialist solidarity." They have "common interests and objectives" and follow the "path of socialism and Communism," adhering to the "principles of Marxism-Leninism and socialist internationalism." They are completely equal, but there exist no objective causes for conflict with national interests, since such conflict is possible only under the system of "national egoism typical of capitalism."

The Chinese, on the other hand, attempted to institutionalize the "leading role of the Soviet party" and thus submit it to criticism by the interparty meeting. Leadership in this case would not be based on the vanguard role of the Soviet party and its leader but would have to be maintained through the correctness of decisions. Since such decisions could be challenged, it would be possible in interparty meetings to express an opposing position which would be a "minority position"—a minority position which could remain on the record. According to the speech made by the Chinese representative, Teng Hsiao-ping, "the minority is not bound to adopt the general political line adopted by the majority." . . . That this was an open challenge to the Soviet leadership in the form of an organizational attack was clear to the other party representatives, and as the Belgians stated, "if the leading party can be ideologically and politically wrong, you begin to wonder who can take its place."

This also raises the question of a split. If it were to occur, it would not be the result of conflicting national interests or ideological convictions, but rather an open and violent means of power struggle. It would not be based on a geographic polycentrism but would nevertheless rend apart the movement as a whole. It would be fought in each party of the bloc and the movement, and would lead to factions within the parties siding with the ruling leadership or the opposition. It would lead to savage infighting in each party and government that would certainly weaken the Communist power.

It is obvious, then, that the enforcement of the political line has become a very complex problem for the leader of the center Communist power, the Soviet party. Behind the problematic organizational framework of the interparty conference are, of course, other means of enforcing the political authority of Moscow. There is still the authority of Soviet tanks, which worked in Poland, East Germany and Hungary, but will not work in China, Albania, or even Yugoslavia. But there is another weapon, a more important one, that the Soviet leaders can and will apply. This is the economic measures that the Soviet Union, as a powerful industrial country and the economic center of the bloc, can use to bring the obstinate into line.

But there is still, behind the power struggle, the unity of purpose and the common goal most important to all concerned. While Mao, in defending his position, may disregard the famine in large areas of Communist China, the weakening of Communist power which results from economic decline cannot long be ignored, and the weakening of the whole bloc that would result from Chinese Communist decline must be of grave concern to the Soviet Union as well. So there may well be a limit past which the battle will not be carried. . . .

The Sino-Soviet conflict is a battle for leadership fought in Communist terms. This kind of conflict, inherent in the Communist system, has been given a new organizational framework by the emergence within the movement of a bloc of Communist-controlled states. In the past, power struggles in the Communist system have often led to the political and physical oblivion of the loser. Total victory is still the purpose of the present struggle. To win, all doctrinal and institutional methods are used by the opponents; but in the amorphous institutional structure of the Communist bloc and movement it has become more difficult to fight a struggle for leadership to its necessary conclusion. Although the personal power struggle between Khrushchev and Mao Tse-tung ended with the removal of Khrushchev in October 1964, the leadership problems of the movement and the bloc have not been resolved.

This structural problem may be to our advantage. Yet the battle has not affected the character of the Communist movement, its purpose, and the interrelation between doctrine and strategy, which indeed has only been underlined by the conflict. The internal rivalries of the Communist movement must not be permitted to conceal the doctrinal and political entirety of the Communist system which poses a constant threat to the Western world.

SUGGESTED READING

Books:

Burch, Betty B., *Dictatorship and Totalitarianism,* Princeton: Van Nostrand, 1964.

Dux, Dieter, *Ideology in Conflict: Communist Political Theory,* Princeton: Van Nostrand, 1963.

Hudson, G. F., Richard Lowenthal and Roderick MacFarquhar, *The Sino-Soviet Dispute,* New York: Praeger, 1961.

Laqueur, Walter Z., and Leopold Labedz, *Polycentrism,* New York: Praeger, 1962.

London, Kurt, *Unity and Contradiction,* New York: Praeger, 1962.

Mehnert, Klaus, *Peking and Moscow,* New York: G. P. Putnam's Sons, 1963.

Zagoria, Donald S., *The Sino-Soviet Conflict: 1956-1961,* Princeton: Princeton University Press, 1962.

Articles:

Lowenthal, Richard, "China," in *Africa and the Communist World,* edited by Zbigniew K. Brzezinski, Stanford University Press, 1963, pp. 142-203.

Scalapino, Robert A., "Moscow, Peking, and the Communist Parties of Asia," *Foreign Affairs,* January 1963, pp. 323-343.

Zagoria, Donald S., ed., "Communist China and the Soviet Bloc," *Annals,* September 1963, pp. 1-162.

National Variations on
a World Communist Theme

Introduction to Part II

PART II OFFERS RECENT LOCAL AND NATIONAL VARIATIONS ON THE once harmonious theme of international Communism. In an age of multiple variants and deviants in the increasingly polycentric world of Communist parties and countries, only the most dramatically relevant case studies could be selected. Poland, Hungary, Yugoslavia, Albania, Czechoslovakia, and Rumania seem to be the timeliest and ideologically the most significant illustrations of the fluctuations and uncertainties currently gripping the Communist camp. Four interrelated essays examine here the pattern of change and the obvious disagreement in the interpretation and application of Marxism-Leninism.

Each of these studies is devoted to the discussion of a single issue or conflict-area. The central theme of Richard Staar's study is the impact of de-Stalinization on the leadership elite of contemporary Poland, with special emphasis on the controversial role of Communist Party boss Gomulka. Ferenc Váli's case examines in detail the acrobatic political maneuverings of the Kádár regime in postrevolutionary Hungary. The central issue here is whether the Party's frantic attempts to gain popular support by granting new economic and political concessions will succeed in the long run. The impact of de-Stalinization is also explored in connection with more liberal trends in the press, theater, literature, arts, and media of communication.

Gordon Skilling presents a broad comparison among the several baffling paradoxes of the contemporary Communist world while focusing his attention primarily on Albania, Yugoslavia, and Czechoslovakia. All three countries have shown "national Communist" tendencies and varying degrees of unwillingness to buckle under Communist great-power pressures. For entirely different reasons, they are currently playing prominent roles in the Sino-Soviet dispute. Indeed, at present the Yugoslavs' sharp disagreement with Maoism and, in turn, the hostility expressed toward Titoism by Communist China is interestingly matched by the Albanians' determined anti-Soviet stand. Stephen Fischer-Galati's case study of Rumania illustrates yet another form of dissension in the pattern of an *intra-bloc* objection to Soviet economic and political domination in the Balkans. He explores the Rumanians' economic polycentrism, always stressing that, for a number of compelling reasons, Communist Rumania must remain a loyal member of the Socialist camp and a "devoted friend and ally" of the Soviet Union.

The four studies of this part help to explain the intricacies of struggle which are currently raging among the forces of world Communism. This struggle proceeds along two levels simultaneously: one is the ideological conflict, the other is competitive power. The ideological dispute essentially revolves around a strict, or loose, interpretation of the major doctrines of Marxism-Leninism. The Soviet position holds the middle ground, neither overly violent, nor ready to compromise. Yugoslavia, Hungary, and Poland, although for different reasons, seem to pull Soviet policies toward moderation on the one hand, while on the other hand Communist China, East Germany, and Albania are exerting pressures toward the extreme of tough and uncompromising attitudes. The battle of ideas is persistent, and its winner may be the next single-leader of the Communist bloc. In the meantime, we have the sudden emergence of not one, but actually three divergent patterns within the over-all system of Marxism-Leninism, depending on who interprets it, and to what type of audience it is directed.

The second level of the struggle produces similar results of division and disagreement. This "power conflict" involves a search for solving one of the central questions in our world, namely: to what extent does national power and national interest motivate a Communist country's behavior toward other countries? What power-factors determine its over-all foreign policy? The concept of "national interest" can easily be illustrated in some of the subsequent studies. Russian, Hungarian, Polish, and Yugoslav foreign policies all reflect the permanent manifestation of this significant and basic world Communist theme. In the Soviet Union's case the "national interest" policies are the long-term, historic considerations which appeared long before the Russian Revolution and played an important role throughout the Tsarist period, and have asserted themselves independently of Communism or indeed of any other "ism." These policies have invariably been produced by "power-" and "security-drives" and not as a result of ideological forces.

However, for the past several decades Soviet and satellite political actions have been deeply influenced by the potent factor of

Marxism-Leninism. Often the "ism" of Communism has tended to obscure and camouflage the more obvious operation of nationalism. The current struggle within the Communist bloc continues to reflect the complicated interplay between the two alternative determinants: the pursuit of national interest and the belief in world Communism.

The four essays prove that these conflicts of interest are bound to weaken substantially the cohesion and understanding among members of the once-unified family of Communism. As the interpretation of Marxist theory and national practice moves along increasingly differing lines, the organizational bonds of the Communist countries can be expected to loosen even further. The manifold "roads to Socialism," as expressions of disunity, are gradually replacing the previously central theme of unity which had dominated the Communist world for so long.

4. De-Stalinization in Eastern Europe: The Polish Model

by Richard F. Staar

Because it is extremely difficult to assess the general impact of de-Stalinization upon the entire Eastern European bloc of nations, Richard Staar's model-building, analyzing the Polish variant of the theme, is particularly significant. Clearly, Khrushchev's secret speech of February 1956 set in motion tremendous political forces which ultimately led to the Polish and Hungarian revolts of October 1956. Although the author refuses to apply the term "revolution" to the developments in Poland and suggests instead that "what occurred in Warsaw during October 1956 merely comprised the temporary victory of one faction over another," these events still produced a major qualitative transformation in the domestic political life of Poland.

The Polish "model" is relevant as a case study of world Communism for several compelling reasons. In this essay the author presents strong evidence that a steady economic and political "retrogression" (a deterioration of the entire domestic atmosphere) has been taking place in Poland ever since the events of October 1956. The measures and policies by which party boss Wladyslaw Gomulka has presided over this "tightening" process are described in some detail. The Polish "model" also raises another dilemma: the difficulty for the Western observer of reconciling the mild and relatively "liberal" foreign policies pursued by the Gomulka regime abroad with the increasingly hard and tough line taken at home. Such are the challenging diversities that have marked the "Polish road to Socialism" ever since the 1956 change-over.

THE PHENOMENON KNOWN AS "DE-STALINIZATION" WAS LAUNCHED by Nikita S. Khrushchev, when he began moving in 1955 toward his first *rapprochement* with Yugoslavia. The formula including "different roads to Socialism," enunciated at the 20th Communist Party Congress in Moscow the following year, represented a logical continuation of this process and was aimed at facilitating it. After reconciliation with Josip Broz-Tito, subsequent moves appeared to be aimed at transforming the image of Soviet satraps in Eastern Europe from agents of Moscow into respectable proponents of "National Communism." This process is still under way.

It was Khrushchev's secret speech in February 1956, which formally initiated a reassessment of Stalin within the East European bloc. Extending beyond this limited sphere, the repercussions today confront most Communists throughout the world, with the notable exception of the Chinese and Albanians. The main problem they face is to disassociate themselves from crimes, finally being acknowledged, but only from those which were perpetrated against Communist party members during the period of the so-called "personality cult." Reactions to this period have included the following:

1. Stalin's mistakes in theory and practice, as well as those of his viceroys in Eastern Europe, represented merely an aberration without adversely affecting or vitiating the system;

2. The errors were mainly of a practical nature, and Stalin's contributions outweighed the adverse consequences of his negative qualities;

3. Crimes and betrayals comprised an integral part of U.S.S.R. history and, hence, Communism must rethink its tactics and even principles.

The first reaction, adopted by the Communist leaders in Moscow, is based on the claim that the Communist Party of the Soviet Union (CPSU) was unaware of Stalin's plans and subsequently remained powerless to prevent their implementation. The people and the Party, however, allegedly maintained their Leninist principles during the mass purges. Furthermore, an assassination of the tyrant would have been misunderstood and not supported by the people. Meanwhile, Khrushchev has stated that Stalin made vital contributions by industrializing and collectivizing the U.S.S.R. He is blamed only for having imposed a personal dictatorship over the Party, megalomania, military unpreparedness and the mismanagement of strategy in World War II.

The Chinese appear to be the main proponents of the second line. In addition to crediting Stalin with the industrialization and collectivization of the Soviet Union, they refrain from condemning his "personality cult" or his thesis regarding intensification of the class struggle. They state that he was a faithful guardian of Marxism-Leninism and associate his name with the theory of revolution in the underdeveloped countries, the general crisis of capitalism, and building Communism in the U.S.S.R. Stalin's works are being recommended for study in China even today.

A third view has been adopted by many Communists outside of the Soviet and Chinese territorial empires. Launched by the late Palmiro Togliatti, it was aimed clearly at foreign Communist parties. As early as the summer of 1956, Togliatti suggested that there must have been something radically wrong with the Soviet system itself to have made possible "such degeneration." The conclusion drawn by the Italian Communist Party was that the Soviet model should not be followed blindly by other parties. Togliatti propounded the necessity of full autonomy for individual Communist movements which should decide for themselves the pattern to be adopted in their own states.

What then is the truth of the matter? Khrushchev had failed to produce any meaningful analysis. His description of Stalin as a schizophrenic personality suggested one answer. In part, the crimes related to the "personality cult" represented an aberrational phenomenon, but in part also appear to have been the logical continuation of what preceded them. In the absence of revolution elsewhere and given the isolation of the U.S.S.R., forced industrialization followed by collectivization of agriculture could not have been attained voluntarily. These actions followed and continued Lenin's policies. The policies *per se* did not require the ruthlessness or violence involved in their implementation, and it is here that the element of aberration comes into the picture.

The personal dictatorship established by Stalin also included two elements. It involved a legacy of the revolution but in certain aspects developed along lines characteristic of his personality. To the outside observer, there appears to be a connection between a Communist-type revolution and Stalinism. Rule by one party, centralization of leadership, and other elements still are regarded as part of Communist orthodoxy. They contributed to the development of the "personality cult" in the U.S.S.R. and in Eastern Europe, where little Stalins emulated their mentor in the Kremlin.

CASE STUDY: POLAND

De-Stalinization in one of these satellites, namely Poland, actually should have commenced with emasculation of the secret police following the December 1953 defection of Lt. Col. Jozef Swiatlo. This man fled to the West via Berlin, while on an official mission to East Germany. He had served until that time as deputy director of the 10th department at the Ministry of Public Security, in charge of investigating Communist Party members. His revelations, transmitted as interviews by *Radio Free Europe* and the *Voice of America* as well as Free Europe Committee pamphlets dropped into Poland from balloons, contributed directly to the dismissal of the secret police chief in 1954 and of other ranking security officers subsequently.

It was not until two years later, however, that Khrushchev's metamorphosis planned for Eastern Europe received shock treatment in Poland and even more so in Hungary.[1] Despite the basically erroneous, and in certain cases even inspired, version of developments at Warsaw during October of that year, there is reason to believe that Wladyslaw Gomulka's return to power was welcomed by Khrushchev as part of his grand design. In order to understand what occurred within the leadership of the PZPR or Polish United Workers' Party, it is essential to begin with March 1956 and the sixth plenum of its Central Committee.

Khrushchev arrived in Warsaw at that time, officially to attend the funeral of Boleslaw Bierut, the veteran ex-Comintern agent and Stalinist who had ruled with an iron hand as Warsaw's viceroy since the end of the Second World War. In fact, however, Khrushchev really came to see that no follower of Stalin would become the new First Secretary. It is known that Roman Zambrowski otherwise would have been elected to this office. Zenon Nowak was reportedly Khrushchev's personal candidate. A man once allegedly described by Stalin as a "Bolshevik with sharp teeth," Edward Ochab, succeeded to Bierut's mantle as the compromise candidate.

---

[1] Admitted by Khrushchev himself in his speech to the Hungarian Communist Party congress. *Radio Moscow* (December 1, 1959).

TABLE 1

PZPR Political Bureau* (as of October, 1964)

No.	Names	Year Born	Soc. Class	Mbr. C.P.	Spent W. War	Mbr. P/Buro	Current Position
Full Members;							
1.	Gomulka, Wladyslaw	1905	prol.	1926	Poland	Nov. 42- Sep. 48; Oct. 56-	First Secretary, PZPR
2.	Spychalski, Marian	1906	midl.	1926	Poland	Aug. 44- Nov. 49; Mar. 59-	Defense Minister
3.	Ochab, Edward	1906	midl.	1929	USSR	Nov. 48-	Chmn., State Council
4.	Cyrankiewicz, Jozef	1911	midl.	1948	Pol/Ger	Dec. 48-	Prime Minister
5.	Rapacki, Adam	1909	midl.	1948	Pol/Ger	Dec. 48-	Foreign Minister
6.	Jedrychowski, Stefan	1910	midl.	1932	USSR	Jly. 56-	Chmn., Econ. Plan. Comm.
7.	Gierek, Edward	1913	prol.	1931	Belg.	Jly. 56- Oct. 56; Mar. 59-	I Secr. Katowice, PZPR
8.	Loga-Sowinski, Ignacy	1914	prol.	1932	Poland	Oct. 56-	Chmn., Trade Union Council
9.	Kliszko, Zenon	1908	prol.	1933	Poland	Mar. 59-	Secretary, PZPR
10.	Szyr, Eugeniusz	1915	prol.	1934	USSR	Jne. 64-	Deputy Premier
11.	Waniolka, Franciszek	1912	prol.	1942	Poland	Jne. 64-	Deputy Premier
Candidates;							
1.	Strzelecki, Ryszard	1907	midl.	1937	Poland	Jne. 64-	Secretary, PZPR
2.	Jaroszewicz, Piotr	1909	midl.	1944	USSR	Jne. 64-	Deputy Premier
3.	Jagielski, Mieczyslaw	1924	farm.	1945	Poland	Jne. 64-	Agriculture Minister

* Sources: Biographic data from *Trybuna Ludu* [People's Tribune], Warsaw, for December 21, 1956; March 13, 1959; December 22, 1956; January 15, 1957; December 29, 1956; July 29, 1956; February 27, 1957; and February 21, 1957; in numerical order; and June 21, 1964, for (10), (11), and the three candidates. Current identification is from the Communist press in Poland and *Radio Warsaw.*

Other identifications are from: Department of State, *Directory of Polish Officials* (Washington, D.C.: November, 1960), pp. 623; Marian Malinowski (ed.), *PPR: Kronika* [Polish Workers' Party: Chronicle], Warsaw, 1962, p. 23; and Czeslaw Madejczyk, *Zeszyty Naukowe Uniwersytetu Jagiellonskiego* [Scientific Notes of Jagiellonian University], XLII, No. 10 (Krakow, 1963), p. 22.

Following this intervention by the Kremlin, a group of younger Central Committee members, known as Natolinists, attempted to wrest control over the PZPR and the government from the thoroughly discredited Pulawska (Stalinist) faction.[2] The latter engaged in an intra-Party struggle to maintain their positions and began sacrificing certain of their more notorious and universally

[2] The names of the two groups are derived from villas at Natolin, a suburb of Warsaw, and fashionable Pulawska Street at the capital, where these factions held their strategy meetings.

hated members. The first to go was *éminence grise* Jakub Berman, ousted from the Political Bureau on May 6, 1956, on which he had served continuously since July 1944, and his return from the Soviet Union.[3]

The explosive events at Poznan during the following month must have hastened the subsequent agreement by both factions within the PZPR that, in order to avoid complete chaos, a change of top Party leadership had become a necessity. The city of Poznan in northeastern Poland experienced an orderly march of workers from the Cegielski Locomotive Plant, demanding bread and more freedom, which transformed itself into two days of bloody riots on June 28-29, 1956, after security police had fired on the demonstrators. According to official figures, a total of 38 persons were killed and 270 wounded.

Under the influence of events at Poznan, the seventh plenum met during the following month. It heard a Natolin spokesman demand that Gomulka be co-opted into the Central Committee, which suggestion was refused by the still dominant Pulawska group. Immediately after this plenum, rumors began to spread both inside and outside of Poland concerning the alleged anti-intellectual attitude, Stalinism, and contacts with the Soviet embassy in Warsaw of the Natolinists. Certainly, the Stalinist label could have been attached with more appropriate justification to the Pulawska faction, because it had ruled and still in fact controlled the country at this time.

Although there exists no documentary evidence as to what occurred exactly prior to the important eighth plenary session of the PZPR Central Committee, it is obvious that Gomulka had to decide from which group to accept his power. The process of decision making could not have been very difficult, since the Natolinists had been responsible for his 1951-1954 arrest and imprisonment.

It was the Pulawska group, therefore, completely mislabeled in the West as "liberal," which finally obtained Gomulka's support and arranged for the peaceful resignation of Ochab from the First Secretaryship. The initial step involved restoring Party member-

[3] The first formal Politburo was constituted in July and August 1944, when the 8,000 Polish Communists in the U.S.S.R. joined the 12,000 inside of Poland.

ship to Gomulka, and this was done on August 4, 1956, by action of the Central Committee.[4] Next, the chief economic planner and one of Gomulka's principal enemies, Hilary Minc, "resigned" from the Politburo. Gomulka himself was present when that body made preparations for the plenary session of the Central Committee which would return him to power. Who then was this man, agreed upon by both of the factions to occupy again the leadership of the Communist Party in Poland?

From his earliest days as a professional revolutionary, Wladyslaw Gomulka displayed the traits of an apparatus worker with talents that were primarily organizational. Born in the southeastern province of Rzeszow, he became a skilled locksmith and was connected with leftist groups already at the age of seventeen. For subversive activities against the Polish state, while an official in the chemical workers' trade union, he was first placed under arrest in 1926, but only briefly.

As a Communist, Gomulka spent the years 1932-1934 and again 1936-1939 in prison. The latter sentence paradoxically enough probably saved his life, because most of the Polish Communists in the U.S.S.R. were physically liquidated during the great purges and their Party dissolved in 1938 by action of the Comintern. In between jail sentences, Gomulka lived in Moscow two years and attended the International "Lenin" School of Political Warfare. This fact remains generally not known either inside of Poland or in the West. After two years in Soviet-occupied Lwow in the southeast, Gomulka returned to his native province and began organizing an anti-German Communist group following the *Wehrmacht* invasion of the U.S.S.R.

He next moved to Communist underground headquarters in Warsaw, becoming secretary of the Polish Workers' Party for that city, a member of the seven-man Central Committee, as well as one of the "directing troika" or embryonic Political Bureau toward the end of 1942, and finally was elected secretary-general or Party leader a year later. Gomulka additionally served as a first deputy premier and Minister for Recovered (formerly German) Territo-

---

[4] That same day, two other important persons were rehabilitated: Marian Spychalski (made Defense Minister four months later) and Zenon Kliszko (today, unofficial deputy to Gomulka).

ries after the war, until his removal on September 3, 1948, by a plenum of the Central Committee for the crime of "right-wing nationalist deviation." His parliamentary immunity was removed three years later, although it is now known that he had already been under arrest for several months.

THE OCTOBER "REVOLUTION"

The well-publicized Soviet intervention in October 1956, and its implications, have been interpreted to a great extent on the basis of conjecture and wishful thinking. What are the facts? The three-day plenum had hardly opened, when the arrival of Soviet leaders (Khrushchev, Molotov, Kaganovich, and Mikoyan) was announced and deliberations of the Central Committee postponed. Ochab admitted that developments in Poland "had aroused alarm among the Soviet comrades." It was revealed also at this plenum that simultaneous Russian troop movements had taken place in the direction of Warsaw as well as along the East German border and around Wroclaw in Polish Silesia.

The comrades from the U.S.S.R. apparently had good reason for being disturbed by events in Poland, because they had not been informed ahead of time about the proposed change in PZPR leadership. This matter was "discussed from the beginning to end as an internal [Polish Communist] Party matter." On the other hand, a few hours of conversation did accomplish at Warsaw what was attained only after the use of Soviet tanks in Budapest. It, therefore, represented on balance a net political victory for the Soviet Union. (In this light, the sensational reports that Gomulka threatened to arrest Khrushchev and his party probably stem from gossip.)

Gomulka, having made the basic decision to accept support from the Pulawska group, initially was able to bring into the reconstituted Politburo only one of his former adherents. It took him another 29 months before he could add two others who had been purged with him after 1948 for "right-wing nationalist deviation." In the meanwhile, Gomulka was forced to accept certain limitations on his freedom of action, not only due to the necessity for maintaining a balance between the two factions but also because of the revolt in Hungary which easily could have spread to Poland.

Rather than a "revolution," what occurred in Warsaw during October 1956 merely comprised the temporary victory of one faction over another.

Despite pressure reportedly exerted by the Pulawska group, Gomulka kept and still retains Aleksander Zawadzki as chairman in the Council of State and on the Politburo, Zenon Nowak as a deputy premier, and several other Natolinists in lesser posts. To this day, for example, members of the Natolin faction are well entrenched in the lower echelons of the Party apparatus throughout the country. Vis-à-vis the population, in his bid for support and pretending to be a "liberal," Gomulka released the Roman Catholic primate (Stefan Cardinal Wyszynski) who had been held incommunicado for three years by the Stalinist regime. A new Church-State agreement removed many of the former governmental restrictions on religious activities. Persecution of the clergy also ceased temporarily.

Accompanied by premier Jozef Cyrankiewicz, titular chief of state Zawadzki, and economic planner Stefan Jedrychowski, Gomulka next visited Moscow where negotiations culminated in a communiqué with the following points:

(1) Revision of the previous agreement on the status of U.S.S.R. forces stationed in Poland, with Warsaw control henceforth over movements, and the Soviet Union to pay the future upkeep of its two divisions on Polish soil;

(2) cancellation of debts owed to the U.S.S.R. [nominally, the equivalent of two billion rubles] in return for Warsaw claims based on coal deliveries to the Soviet Union [1946-1953] below cost of production;

(3) new credits of 700 million rubles from Moscow; and

(4) the promise to deliver during 1957 some 1.4 million tons of Soviet grain.

The mere fact that Gomulka had gained these concessions from the Russians, excluding the matter of continued stationing of U.S.S.R. troops inside of the country (which was justified as a defense against West German revisionism of the border along the Oder and Western Neisse Rivers), must have increased his popularity with many Poles.

He capitalized on these sentiments by calling for an election and attempting to obtain endorsement for his policies which, in

TABLE 2

Soviet and U.S. Credits to Poland, 1947-1964*
(in millions of dollars)

| Soviet Union | | United States | |
Dates	Amounts	Dates	Amounts
March 5, 1947	$ 28.0	June 7 and August 14,	
January 26, 1948	450.0	1957	$ 95.0
July 2, 1950	100.0	February 15, 1958	98.0
September 24, 1956	25.0	June 10 and November	
November 18, 1956	175.0	10, 1959; February	
same (grain only)	100.0	11, 1960	103.3
		July 21, 1960	130.0
Total	$878.0	December 15, 1961	44.6
		April 19, 1962	15.8
		February 1, 1963	51.6
		February 3, 1964	90.9
		Total	$629.2

* Sources: U.S. Department of Commerce, as cited in the *Congressional Record,* CIII (August 27, 1957), p. 14617; *Radio Warsaw* (September 20, 1960); *New York Times* (December 16, 1961); U.S. Department of State, *Press Release No. 260* (April 19, 1962); *Zycie Warszawy* [Warsaw Life], Warsaw (February 5, 1963 and February 4, 1964).

turn if attained, would project an image in the West of public support and perhaps enable the Warsaw regime to obtain credits from the United States. No opposition party was allowed, with all nominations carefully screened by the PZPR. One seemingly important innovation, and highly publicized as part of the fake democratization process, was the decision to allow a larger number of candidates than the total seats allocated to each electoral district. However, Communists represented 50%, the fellow-traveling Peasant party 25%, the stooge Democratic party 10%, and the remaining 15% the so-called non-party candidates.

The night preceding the election, Gomulka broadcast a special message to voters. With what seemed to be overwhelming conviction, he stated that "deletion of our [Communist] Party's candidates . . . is synonymous with obliterating Poland from the map of Europe." [5] This thinly veiled threat of Soviet intervention, together with the realization that the Poles had just barely missed the fate of the Hungarians, gave the PZPR some 51.7% of the ballots cast and 237 of the 459 seats in the unicameral parliament.

Yet another reason for this electoral victory appeared to be the widespread belief that Gomulka would implement the promises he had made in his November 29, 1956 speech. In brief, these included stopping the use of force in collectivization of agriculture, a slow-down in the rapid rate of development in heavy industry, and restoration of the principles of intra-Party democracy as well as "socialist legality" in general. Gomulka also promised a rise in living standards, greater personal freedom, and the prospects of more independence from the Soviet Union.

RETROGRESSION BEGINS

A good illustration of how false these blandishments would become can be found in Gomulka's attitude toward the excesses committed by the secret police. In the past, this organization had functioned as a direct tool of Stalin and his NKVD/MGB to intimidate the Polish Communist leadership. One technique for assuring that the PZPR, henceforth, would exercise control over the police was to reduce it in numbers. This was not accomplished, however, without complications. A certain Captain Makolagwa headed up a strike committee, claiming that the secret police had only implemented the orders of such "liberals" as Roman Zambrowski and Ochab. Although an investigation of police activities had been resolved by the PZPR Central Committee, it is interesting to note that no report has been mentioned over the past eight years.

Another promise that was fulfilled only grudgingly dealt with the field of agriculture. During the spring of 1956, collective farms had reached their peak of 10,600 units with about 220,000 members and covered an area of approximately two million hectares. Gomulka admitted in his speech to the eighth plenum, and gave figures in substantiation, that private entrepreneurs were more productive than either collective or state farms. He indicated that those collectives operating at a loss "should decide the matter of dissolving" their enterprises.

[5] *Radio Warsaw* (January 19, 1957).

The reaction to this speech probably far surpassed anything the regime had anticipated. By the summer of 1957 a total of 8,535 collective farms voted to disband, covering an area of about 1½ million hectares. A substitute, known as the "agricultural circle," is now being fostered to inculcate a collectivist mentality among the peasantry. The ninth plenum already in May 1957 indicated that the PZPR would provide "appropriate direction for all such activity." The resolution went on record in support of the poor peasants and promised to "surround with special care the production cooperatives [a euphemism for collective farms] by securing adequate state assistance and services from the state machine [tractor] centers." The Communists in Poland never have given up their long-term goal of collectivization.

It was during 1957 also that Gomulka's promises of greater personal freedom were shown to be fraudulent. The event which marked this retrogression revolved around the closing down by the authorities of the student weekly paper *Po Prostu* (Straight from the Shoulder), followed by four days of rioting in Warsaw. The disturbances commenced with quiet demonstrations at the university, transforming themselves on the third day into a widely based reaction against police brutality. The last two days of riots were characterized by heavy participation of working class youth who replaced the initial preponderance of students. It is noteworthy also in this connection that no looting took place in the course of these disorders, which were of a political nature.

Since the Pulawska faction had supported the demonstrations and may have even instigated them, Gomulka apparently began to look toward the Natolinists for backing. Although certain members of this faction had been expelled at the above-mentioned ninth plenum, the moderates among them soon began an attempt to adapt themselves to the new situation. An added impetus to this shift probably came as a result of the defection to the West in 1959 of Colonel Monat, who had directed espionage activities of Polish armed forces attachés abroad for U.S.S.R. intelligence. Changes in key personnel affected not only military security but also economic planning, at this time.

The two newly appointed deputy premiers, Eugeniusz Szyr and Julian Tokarski, prior to October 1956 had been in charge of economic planning and heavy industry. In addition to them, an-

other former deputy premier (Tadeusz Gede) was brought back
from the Polish embassy in Moscow to become vice chairman of
the Economic Planning Commission. The most shocking appointment, however, was that of Lt. Gen. Kazimierz Witaszewski as
deputy chief of the General Staff in charge of military intelligence.
He returned from Czechoslovakia, where he had been sent into
political exile as armed forces attaché.

It should be remembered that this same man once had threatened intellectuals in an early 1956 speech with a gas pipe beating
(hence, the nickname *general gaz rurka*), if they would not con-
form to the Party line. He also participated with U.S.S.R. Marshal

TABLE 3

*Composition of PZPR Central Committees**

(as elected at 3rd and 4th Congresses)

| No. | Faction | Strength | | Change |
		1959	1964	
1.	Gomulkaites	25	57	+32
2.	Pulawska Group	25	5	−20
3.	Former Socialists	11	8	− 3
4.	Natolin Faction	10	0	−10
5.	Partisans	0	14	+14
6.	Revisionists	6	2	− 4
	Totals	77	86	

* Sources: *East Europe*, VIII, No. 5 (May, 1959), p. 13; and R. F. Staar
"Gomulka haelt die Stellung," *Hinter dem Eisernen Vorhang*, X, No. 9
(September, 1964), p. 12.

Konstantin K. Rokossovsky, at the time "on loan" to Poland as
defense minister, and Natolin chief Franciszek Mazur, in drawing
up the names of some 700 Gomulka supporters to be executed in
a planned October 1956 counter *coup d'état*. Witaszewski soon
after his recall from Prague moved into the central PZPR apparatus
as chief of its section for administration (cadres), controlling all

important appointments of key personnel in the Party and government, which position he still holds as of this writing.

THE 3RD AND 22ND CONGRESSES

Gomulka showed himself to be in full control of the PZPR at its 3rd congress, originally scheduled for the end of 1957 but postponed several times and finally held on March 10-19, 1959. Jerzy Morawski, a member of the Pulawska faction who has since lost his position on the Politburo, stated in a speech to the congress that "on the basis of the historical achievement which we have attained, we can say today that there never had been any right-wing nationalist deviation in our Party." A resolution, passed unanimously by the delegates, erased the 1948 decision which had condemned Gomulka.

The newly elected Central Committee of 77 members only carried over 57 persons from the previous body. An analysis of this elite group indicates that Gomulka was able to increase his personal following to 25, that the Pulawska group also obtained the same number of supporters, the ex-Socialists dropped from 15 down to 11, and that the Natolin faction received the smallest allocation of 10 seats on this body. The number of names proposed for Central Committee membership was identical with the total seats, and no possibility of altering the list of candidates existed even though the actual balloting was secret.

After the congress, Gomulka began relieving many members of the Pulawska faction and replacing them with proponents of a harder line. Examples include education minister Wladyslaw Bienkowski as well as Morawski mentioned above, both dismissed in October 1959; deputy defense minister Janusz Zarzycki ousted in May 1960; and Secretariat member Jerzy Albrecht, who "resigned" in November of that year. All have been succeeded by much tougher individuals.

Paradoxically, the signal for a second stage in the orbit-wide de-Stalinization process and one that was out of step with developments in Poland came in October 1961 at the 22nd CPSU Congress in Moscow. The reasons for giving this fresh impetus are not clear, but they certainly included Khrushchev's desire to project an image of a more attractive Soviet empire. One important long-range result involved the new accommodation with Yugoslavia in August 1963 during the U.S.S.R. premier's "working holiday" in that country.

In Warsaw, the 22nd Congress unfortunately has not led to any significant relaxation. As a matter of fact, Gomulka most probably felt unwilling once again to rake over the crimes of the past and to arouse an apathetic public opinion, at the very time that he was preparing to introduce a reactionary new penal code. His first response thus came out on the defensive, with the claim that the PZPR had long before eliminated the "cult of the individual," defeated dogmatists within its ranks, and corrected all other deviations and errors.

At the Central Committee plenum, to which Gomulka gave his report on the CPSU Congress, it is probable (on the basis of his dismissal from the national Secretariat on November 30, 1963) that Wladyslaw Matwin objected to the consciously adopted trend toward elimination of all differences between Poland and the other satellites. This may have touched off the open conflict between the Pulawska faction and Gomulka, most dramatically illustrated when several hundred of the PZPR elite, including six former or current Central Committee members, attended the funeral of Henryk Holland.

Accused of having passed on some kind of gossip about Khrushchev's version concerning the liquidation of the former Soviet secret police chief Lavrenty P. Beria to the Warsaw correspondent of *Le Monde,* Jean Wetz, Holland underwent forty hours of continuous interrogation by the Polish secret police. He was then brought back to his fifth-floor apartment for a search of the premises and either jumped or deliberately was pushed from a window. There seems to be some basis for the latter conjecture, in view of the fact that Holland had attacked Gomulka very bitterly in the Communist press during the "right-wing nationalist deviation" period. If it were really suicide, then this experienced member of the Pulawska faction did so in protest against the secret police being above the Party, since intercession on his behalf by friends on the Central Committee had proven unsuccessful in obtaining his release.

At any rate, the PZPR Central Control Commission began to interrogate each Party member who had attended the funeral.

Gomulka personally undertook the questioning of the six most important individuals.[6] This in turn led to a new blow against the Pulawska group, with the dismissal of Colonel Antoni Alster from his position as deputy internal affairs (secret police) minister, which he had held since December 8, 1956, when Gomulka appointed him to this most sensitive of posts. His replacement is a Natolinist who also belongs to the so-called Partisan faction.

RISE OF THE PARTISANS

A considerable number of these "partisans" had joined the old Communist Party of Poland, prior to its dissolution by the Comintern the year before World War II broke out. They also stayed in the country during the Nazi occupation, and some of them joined the few Communist guerrilla units operating behind the German lines on Polish soil. The leadership of this group has been reported as being exercised by Zenon Kliszko, a member of the Politburo and unofficial Second Secretary, as well as by two generals (Grzegorz Korczynski, in charge of military intelligence, and Mieczyslaw Moczar, a deputy internal affairs minister in charge of secret police "investigations"), who are both on the Central Committee.

The main target of the group seemed to be Zambrowski, who had served on the Political Bureau continuously since August 1944, when he returned from the Soviet Union. Almost exactly twenty years later, he "resigned" from both the Politburo and the Secretariat. His appointment to the obscure post of deputy chair-

---

[6] These six included (1) Jerzy Morawski, a former member of both the Politburo and Secretariat, who has been relieved also as deputy chairman in the Supreme Control Chamber [an insignificant government post held by Gomulka, 1948-1949, after his purge], according to *Trybuna Ludu* (September 14, 1963); (2) Janusz Zarzycki, ousted in 1960 from control over armed forces political indoctrination and since then Mayor of Warsaw [the post he held in 1945, at the outset of his career], according to *Directory of Polish Officials*, p. 205; (3) Helena Jaworska, Communist youth union chairman until it collapsed in 1957, was demoted to candidate on the Central Committee and is currently in the Culture Department of the PZPR apparatus, according to *ibid.*, p. 244; (4) Romana Granas, also a candidate Central Committee member and formerly apparatus worker; (5) Oscar Lange, ex-lecturer at Chicago, now economics professor in Warsaw and deputy chairman in the Council of State; and (6) Leon Finkelsztajn, formerly on the 12-man editorial board of *Cominform Journal* [long defunct], who is not on the Central Committee at the present time.

man of the Supreme Control Chamber (an auditing agency similar to the General Accounting Office in the U.S. government) came on September 13, 1963. Zambrowski was replaced on the Political Bureau at the 4th PZPR Congress which was held in June 1964.[7]

A likely candidate for Zambrowski's position is Ryszard Strzelecki, who may even possibly succeed Gomulka as First Secretary and hence Party leader at some date in the future. Graduated from the Wawelberg Institute of Technology in Warsaw, he taught mechanics (1936-1939) at one of the capital city's technical schools. Although a member of the clandestine prewar Communist Party, there is no record of his arrest. During the German occupation, he remained in Poland and supervised the underground printing operations of the Polish Workers' [Communist] Party in the city of Warsaw, having close contacts with Gomulka who was then Secretary-General. After a postwar apprenticeship in province-level Party organizations, Strzelecki moved to the central apparatus, later becoming the minister of railroads/communications (1951-1960) on the governmental side of the interlocking system of directorates. He has been one of the six national Secretaries since early 1960 in charge of the military, security, and police matters.

In view of his position within the central apparatus of the PZPR, it is probable that Strzelecki played a vital part in the policy decision which led to the closing in 1962 of the last free discussion group in Warsaw. Although it numbered only 292 members at that time, the Crooked Circle Club (KKK) had been sending out approximately 2,000 invitations to its meetings. Guests included writers, lawyers, artists, newspapermen, PZPR functionaries, and government officials.

The *coup de grâce* was administered to the KKK by Adam Schaff, reputedly advisor to Gomulka on ideology. His lecture to the Crooked Circle Club on February 1, 1962, was met with criticism and extensive opposition. To this, Schaff responded with personal insults against his critics. Following this discussion, one of the men who had supported Schaff was assaulted physically in a café by a group of hoodlums. Even though he had not witnessed

---

[7] Another change occurred in Politburo membership with the death on August 7, 1964, of Aleksander Zawadzki, the titular chief of state. This latter position was filled five days later by Edward Ochab.

the attack, Schaff accused the KKK of having had an interest in this beating. The incident was used by the Communist regime as a pretext to close the Club.

All documents and files of this discussion group were confiscated by the International Affairs Ministry, and its department for investigations under General Moczar prepared an exhaustive report which allegedly was based on about 2,000 personal opinions (presumably of KKK guests) for transmission to the PZPR Central Committee apparatus. This report passed through the hands of Wincenty Kraske, director of the Culture Department.

Kraske has been quoted as stating openly at a meeting of the Journalists' Association primary PZPR organization that "we had to close down the Crooked Circle Club, because such was the freedom of speech there that its administration organized beatings of discussants who represented the Party viewpoint." [8] It is possible, therefore, that the entire chain of events really had been staged by the police, with the use of trained *agents-provocateur*.

In addition to the foregoing reason, the Communist regime in Warsaw also leveled a bill of particulars against the KKK which included charges of "right-wing nationalism" (the accusation against Gomulka in 1948), discrimination by the Club vis-à-vis Party speakers, seeking publicity in the West, soliciting contacts with foreigners, luring students and "unsuitable" elements to meetings, subverting the authority of PZPR academicians (Schaff). A news release distributed by the government to foreign correspondents in Poland falsely stated that the Crooked Circle Club had dissolved itself of its own accord.

The increasing influence of former Stalinists upon many decisions being made at the highest level could also be seen in the closing down in 1963 of the last two liberal weeklies of a literary nature. *Nowa Kultura* (New Culture) and *Przeglad Kulturalny* (Cultural Review) were replaced by a single periodical entitled *Kultura*. Less than a month after its first issue appeared, editor-in-chief Janusz Wilhelmi assumed the defensive against charges of neo-Stalinism. The most eminent among contemporary writers refused any contributions to this journal.

At the 13th plenum of the Central Committee, Gomulka himself

[8] Witold Jedlicki, *Klub Krzywego Kola* (Paris, Instytut Literacki, 1963), p. 161.

devoted the session to ideological questions. He stated that the PZPR bore "special responsibility for putting up a resolute and successful resistance to bourgeois ideology." Gomulka also announced that an Ideological Commission would be established within the Central Committee, directed by a Politburo member. "For years," Poland allegedly "has been a particular object of concentrated attack by imperialist propaganda."

It would appear that the political apathy and cynicism of the intellectuals, rather than the bogey of Western imperialism, represent the greatest source of weakness to the regime in Warsaw. This is especially true of the younger generation. Even it knows that Gomulka lied, when twice referring to the NKVD execution of thousands of Polish prisoners of war as that "Goebbels' Katyn provocation," in his speech at the 20th anniversary of the resurrected Communist Party.

This trend of dissatisfaction should become reinforced, as de-Stalinization in Poland is restricted to the removal of physical traces alone. Renaming of streets (Aleja Stalina in Warsaw back to Aleje Ujazdowskie) and even of towns (Stalinograd reverted back to traditional Katowice, Silesia) can only provoke derision. There is, of course, no mausoleum from which to remove Bierut's corpse nor any statue to be demolished, although the atrocious "Stalin" Palace of Culture and Art still dominates the skyline of Warsaw.

The current Soviet dispute with Albania probably has a similar effect. Prior to the 22nd CPSU Congress, the population of Poland had never realized that the people's "democratic" regime in Tirana differed from their own. Khrushchev himself announced in 1959 that the "remarkable victories" of the Albanian people were attained under the direction of their experienced leadership—the Albanian Workers' (Communist) Party and its Central Committee —headed by Comrade Enver Hoxha, "A glorious son of the Albanian people."

The sudden *volte-face* before some 5,000 delegates at the 22nd CPSU Congress, who were told to believe Khrushchev's words that "the Albanian leaders maintain their power by resorting to force and arbitrary repression" was not calculated to increase respect for authority on the part of the man in the street throughout Poland. He knows only too well that the essentials of the political system which Stalin imposed on his country will continue to be defended, regardless of the so-called de-Stalinization campaign and despite the particular Communist faction which happened to be in power.

SUGGESTED READING

Books:

Barnett, Clifford R., *et al.* (eds.), *Poland: Its People, Its Society, Its Culture,* New Haven: Human Resources Area Files Press, 1958, p. 471.

Dziewanowski, Marian K., *The Communist Party of Poland, An Outline of History,* Cambridge: Harvard University Press, 1959, p. 369.

Halecki, Oscar (ed.), *East Central Europe Under the Communists: Poland,* New York: Praeger, 1957, p. 601.

Staar, Richard F., *Poland, 1944-1962: The Sovietization of a Captive People,* Baton Rouge: Louisiana State University Press, 1962, pp. xviii-300.

Zurawski, Joseph W., *Poland, the Captive Satellite: A Study in National Psychology,* Detroit: Endurance Press, 1962, p. 194.

Articles:

Halacki, Oscar, "Poland," in Kertesz, Stephen D. (ed.), *East Central Europe and the World,* Notre Dame: University of Notre Dame Press, 1962, pp. 45-63.

Ptakowski, Jerzy, "Politics in Poland," *East Europe,* XI, No. 12, December, 1962, pp. 18-25; and *Ibid.,* XIII, No. 4, April, 1964, pp. 9-14.

Skilling, H. Gordon, "Two Unorthodox Satellites," *International Journal,* Winter, 1962-1963, pp. 29-42.

Staar, Richard F., "New Course in Communist Poland," in John H. Hallowell (ed.), *Soviet Satellite Nations: A Study of the New Imperialism,* Gainesville: Kallman Publishers, 1958, pp. 64-88.

———, "Profile of Poland," *Current History,* May, 1963, pp. 257-264; and "How Strong Is the Soviet Bloc?," *Ibid.,* October 1963, pp. 209-215.

———, "Warsaw's Quiet Congress," *East Europe,* XIII, No. 8, August 1964, pp. 2-6.

5. Hungary Since 1956: The Hungarian Road to Communism

by Ferenc A. Váli

In the following essay Ferenc Váli draws a careful profile of the political and social aspects of Kádár's regime which began in October 1956 and ended officially in July 1965. The most interesting comparative aspect between Polish and Hungarian forms of Communism is the feverish attempt of the latter to popularize and "liberalize" a regime which had its inception in an aura of total popular rejection. The author raises and perceptively discusses the key question in connection with Hungary's peculiar "road to socialism": has the present Communist party leadership succeeded in making itself acceptable to Hungarian public opinion? Has it been able to accomplish a measure of popularity and acceptance on the home front?

Váli cites some chilling facts as obvious barriers limiting the extent of Kádár's drive toward internal "relaxation." These are the "silent camps" of writers and intellectuals who have not written a word since the Revolution; the Soviet occupation forces and the Hungarian People's Army jointly exercising military control over the country; and the determined antireligious struggle of the regime, focusing on the hierarchy of the Roman Catholic Church. Nevertheless, by comparison with Gomulka's "retrogression" in Poland, Kádár's Hungary has undeniably succeeded in considerably improving its image, in terms of public opinion support and a minimum amount of respectability, both at home and abroad.

IN 1955 AN EMINENT HUNGARIAN WROTE: "THERE WERE AND ARE difficult times in the life of a nation when those in power . . . accept dependence, subordination, humiliating slavery—betraying the cause of national independence. . . . However, according to the lessons of history, these betrayals do not end with the destruction of the nation but with that of the traitors. . . ." [1] Although these words may sound as if they were written by some conservative nationalist, they were actually the words of the Communist Imre Nagy, one of the prime ministers during the 1956 Revolution, who was executed in 1958. One wonders whether these words still have significance for Hungary. In many respects they probably do.

Although there has been the passage of several years since the Revolution, the memory of the fateful events of 1956 is very much alive in the minds of the Hungarian people whether they support or criticize the present government. Both internal and external policies are still, consciously or unconsciously, influenced by these events. It does appear somewhat unusual that the events of 1956 are not often spoken about in public. Neither do the writers devote much attention to them. It is obvious that the year 1956 remains a touchy subject which, if handled at all, must be treated with care. The year 1956 has thus become conspicuous by the absence of practically all information, except for a few "official" statements. This would seem to indicate that the events of the year have not been simply forgotten, and indeed the present regime finds itself compelled to keep those memories alive by insisting on its own version of the events.

One of the various and often contradictory versions offered by the regime of Party leader and former Prime Minister János Kádár[2] is that the Western imperialists fostered the revolt by exploiting the discontent created by the "cult of the personality" under the Hungarian Stalinist Mátyás Rákosi. The regime claims that the workers, with Soviet assistance, then put down this "counter-revolution." Another version—for the students of the Party Academy—is that the Revolution happened as a result of a "premature adaptation of Soviet experiences in a different situation and in a different period." The moral which is drawn is that the lessons of the prerevolutionary period must be learned.

These explanations, however, are not accepted by the Hungarian people. In spite of what the present regime claims, the people know that the revolt was spontaneous, was fought by students and

[1] *Imre Nagy On Communism*, New York, F. A. Praeger, 1957, p. 24.
[2] In July 1965 Kádár yielded the office of Prime Minister to his long-time associate, Gyulá Kállay.

workers, and eventually was suppressed singlehandedly by the Soviet Army. This Army then reinstated a Soviet-controlled Communist regime under the leadership of the former Prime Minister, János Kádár. Whatever the success of Kádár's attempts to normalize the internal and external relations of his regime since 1956, the government's greatest political and psychological obstacle remains the stigma of the origin of the present regime.

THE AFTERMATH: 1956-1958

The Soviet Army having intervened successfully to reinstate a Soviet-controlled Communist regime, Kádár, as new head of the government, began to explain in Communist terms the reason for the Revolution. He blamed the Rákosi government for having created unjust conditions which resulted in discontent among the people and which ultimately prepared the way for the Revolution. He agreed to maintain the achievements of the Revolution and although he denounced Nagy, he declared that Nagy had helped the counter-revolution unknowingly. He even implied that Nagy's participation in the new government might be a possibility. Kádár requested that Nagy leave the Yugoslav Embassy where he had sought refuge, and promised him a safe-conduct pledge which was indeed agreed upon within a short time by the Hungarian and Yugoslav governments. Kádár's promise was broken, however, for as soon as Nagy left the embassy he was arrested by Soviet forces and removed from the country. This is only one of the many promises which Kádár made in the weeks immediately following the Soviet intervention. It was also one he ignored as he began to stabilize his control.

Kádár's principal problem was to gain the confidence and active support of the Hungarian people. For several weeks after the revolt had been crushed there were public anti-Soviet demonstrations, masses of people continued to flee the country, the workers' councils showed open defiance, and there were general and regional strikes accompanied by work slowdowns. Women, mourning their sons and husbands who had been killed in the Soviet interventions, dressed in black and marched through the streets and past Russian troops in a silent gesture of defiance. The workers' councils organized a paralyzing general strike early in December in protest of the deportation of Hungarians to Russia. In the face of such continued opposition Kádár was compelled to offer some sweeping concessions. He promised an early release and forgiveness for all who had taken part in the revolt, the institution of free elections, and the abolition of the secret police.

For a brief period Kádár appeared to be quite sincere in his liberal promises, and the wrath of the people began to subside. In order to improve the floundering economy of Hungary and at the same time gain the support of the people, Kádár relaxed economic policies, hoping to win over the peasants and the industrial workers. Compulsory deliveries of agricultural products were abolished, and the peasants were allowed to bargain with the purchasing agencies of the state as well as to sell their produce to private citizens. In addition, the peasants were allowed to leave the established collectives if they desired to do so. As a result production did increase and for a while the peasants received a considerably larger share of the national income. In order to help placate the workers wages were increased, but on the whole the corresponding increase in labor productivity which was hoped for did not materialize.

For a while Kádár permitted limited private enterprise and occasional criticism of the Communist Party not only by those who were members of the Party but also by those outside the Party. At the same time he began to reconstruct the Communist control apparatus. But this tolerant spirit did not exist for long. As soon as Kádár had consolidated his regime it became evident that his promises to form a coalition government and to permit free elections had been only empty phrases designed to appeal to the people who accepted them as being sincere. Once he felt himself in the position to do so, he turned his wrath against the workers, the intellectuals, and the students whom the Soviet government blamed for the Revolution.

In November 1957, after having been gradually suppressed throughout the year, the workers' councils which had been of great influence during the Revolution were definitely dissolved. Even earlier, in January 1957, the Hungarian Writers' Union was abolished. This suppression of the writers was to be answered by a long period of silent protest during which time few works of substantial literary quality were produced. The promise of forgiveness for all those who had taken part in the Revolution was conveniently forgotten, and political trials, deportations, arrests, and secret executions, reminiscent of the Stalinist Rákosi regime, once again became the order of the day.

The reason for this ambivalence on the part of Kádár's regime now seems to be rather obvious, and yet it created somewhat of a dilemma within the Party and the government. The regime found it difficult to permit toleration only within certain areas, and even though the government had attempted to placate the Hungarian people by offering certain concessions, passive resistance and unrest continued to exist. Perhaps a policy of terror was inevitable in such a situation where the only reliable support for the Kádár government was in the form of Soviet armored divisions which, as Kádár had stated in March 1957, would remain in Hungary "as long as necessary." But in any case, Kádár found himself in the embarrassing and ambivalent position of denouncing Stalinism and promising more freedom while returning to Stalin's methods and to the use of force.

In June 1958 the condemnation and execution of Imre Nagy, General Maléter, who had been arrested while representing the Hungarian government in negotiations initiated by the Soviet Union for withdrawal of Soviet troops from Hungary, and a number of their associates was announced both in Budapest and in Moscow. These acts, again reminiscent of Stalin's terroristic purges, constituted a severe breach of faith with those Hungarian people which had negotiated with Kádár and the U.S.S.R. and had believed their promises.

THE NEW LOOK: SINCE 1959

With the year 1959 Kádár, his regime having consolidated itself rather firmly through its suppressive measures, began to effect a radical shift in policy. Once again he decided to permit a degree of latitude. Since 1961 the government of Hungary has sought to narrow the yawning gap between the regime and the people by attempting to gain popular support through granting new concessions. In a speech before the People's Patriotic Front in December 1961, Kádár stated that "who is not against us, is with us" which in fact was the exact reversal of Rákosi's idea that "who is not with us, is against us." In March 1962, Kádár announced that while there were many different viewpoints in Hungary, there should be nothing to prevent people from living peacefully and working honestly. He claimed that most of the people realized that the regime was better for them than earlier governments had been and the only enemies of people were those who were trying to undermine the workers' power. Also, he suggested that the Communists' mistakes were more harmful than the acts of the class enemy. In this pronouncement Kádár in effect announced a new policy of coexistence with the "non-Marxist" majority of the Hungarian people. Later he announced that the policy of the government would be liberalized even more to allow the most capable people available, whether they were Communists or non-Communists, to fill the various government posts.

Among the manifold reasons that induced Kádár to attempt once again to placate public sentiment was the belief held both by the ruling Party elite in Hungary and the Soviet leadership that with the apparent consolidation of control the regime could afford the relaxation of the most stringent dictatorial methods without further endangering the stability of the government. It is also likely that former Soviet Premier Nikita Khrushchev urged Kádár and the other Hungarian leaders to "popularize" their rule in order to forestall the necessity of another bolstering of Communism in Hungary. The secret police no longer appear to be as important as they once were, russification has lost much of its impetus, non-Party experts are being allowed to hold positions of some economic importance, the cessation of discrimination against class enemies is promoted, writers are given greater elbow-room, and the living conditions of the people are being improved somewhat. At least in part these concessions are designed to gain popular support for Kádár's regime. They might also pave the way for a normalization of those international relations which have suffered under the impact of Soviet military intervention. The regime, having violently antagonized the intellectuals, the workers, and more recently, the peasantry, has begun to make attempts to regain the confidence of at least some segments of the two former groups.

It is questionable, however, that such attempts at "popularization" have had the success which was hoped for by the Hungarian government. Unless sweeping concessions are made to national sentiment, concessions apparently incompatible with Soviet interest and prestige, it appears unlikely that the Kádár regime will be able to effect a genuine *rapprochement* with large segments of the people.

The unsavory origins of the present regime have not been forgotten and Kádár himself still is hated and held in contempt by the masses, although perhaps not so much as formerly.

This degree of controlled liberalization is being accepted with satisfaction by all those who hope to gain by it. Such a reaction is only natural, since people on the whole want to live and, as far as possible, want to enjoy living. The relaxation of dictatorial control tends to increase the number of cautious opportunists; at the same time it tends to induce the people to think less badly of the ruling regime and to express some limited degree of appreciation for their relatively better conditions. Even though such a tendency exists, it does not necessarily follow that the people on the whole have given up their mental reservations or that they endorse or approve of the regime. It is significant that all these concessions—limited though they be—are not ascribed by the people to the magnanimity of Kádár's regime, but rather to the Revolution itself. It is likewise worthy of note that many of these concessions which the regime has deemed to be necessary are being criticized heavily by some leftist elements within the ruling Communist Party.

THE PARTY

The Hungarian Workers Party, which was the party of Rákosi and Gerö, was disbanded during the Revolution. A short time later the Party was reorganized under the leadership of Kádár, and was given a new name, the Hungarian Socialist Workers Party. Although the Party agreed to enroll individually all members of the old Rákosi Party who presented themselves voluntarily and agreed to accept the official line, a sizeable majority chose not to rejoin. The official explanation for the lack of enthusiasm of the people to associate themselves with Kádár's Party is that before the Revolution the old Party was packed with unreliables who felt no loss in deserting their Party. No doubt this explanation is partly true, for in Hungary, which had a population of approximately ten million in 1956, few of the nearly one million party members were convinced Communists.

The membership of the present Hungarian Socialist Workers Party is of a different nature. The characteristic feature of the Party today is that it is a party of functionaries. The rank-and-file member is practically non-existent. In a way this condition has tended to strengthen the Party, for now it can be relatively certain of the loyalty of its members. Also, they are bound together as participants in the suppression of the Revolution and in the execution of its leaders. "Party members today are even more a 'sect', and live at an even greater distance from the people than the looser and broader Party membership before the Revolution. There was no glory then in being a Party member, but neither was there shame." [3]

The seventh Congress of the Hungarian Communist Party, which met during November and December 1959 and at which Khrushchev was present, marked the consolidation of Kádár's power within his own Party. Although earlier in the same year Ferenc Münnich had succeeded him as Prime Minister, Kádár retained his position as First Secretary of the Communist Party and enhanced his position by the maintenance of a strong personal friendship with the Soviet Premier.

Although the history of the Hungarian Communist Party is one filled with intraparty conflicts and sweeping changes in the leadership, these conflicts within the Party have been increased by the Sino-Soviet rift. Prior to the Twenty-Second Soviet Party Congress in 1961, Party condemnations and purges were directed primarily against revisionists even though the Party had stated its opposition against both revisionism and dogmatism. Since 1961, however, the emphasis of the Party has been on de-Stalinization, a policy which serves as good accompaniment for the "popularization" campaign. Statues of Stalin had been destroyed as early as 1956 by the people during the Revolution. Kádár commented, however, in a speech made before the workers of Csepel that those who had destroyed the large statue of Stalin in Budapest were not to be praised or even forgiven for their action, for they had acted not because they hated Stalin, but rather because they hated Communism.

The first de-Stalinization acts of the Party involved the renaming of the one town and of the various streets in the country which had been named after Stalin.

The major purge of former Stalinists from their positions and even from the Party came in 1962 and ended before the eighth

[3] Tibor Méray, "Genealogical Troubles," *Survey*, No. 40, January 1962, p. 88.

Party Congress in November 1962. In March, Kádár announced that twenty "old-line" Party officials had been removed from key administrative and managerial posts and that they had been replaced by young technicians. In keeping with the new "popularization" campaign, he announced at the same time a policy of coexistence with the "non-Marxist" majority. In August, Kádár purged the Party still further by expelling 25 Stalinist leaders—amongst whom were two former Party chiefs, Mátyás Rákosi, who lived in exile in the Soviet Union until his death in 1963, and his successor, Ernö Gerö, who had first asked for Soviet military intervention in October 1956. Another prominent figure who was purged was Judge Olti. He had presided over many rigged trials, including that of Cardinal Mindszenty. A number of security police were purged, and others accused of organizing "factions" were expelled.

In addition, several high Party dignitaries were replaced or given positions of lesser importance. Dögei, a former Minister of Agriculture and Ambassador to Peking, was ousted from the Party; and Marosán, who was famous for his vulgar speeches and coarse attacks against the intellectuals, was removed from his position as a Party secretary. Károly Kiss, a former Hungarian Party secretary, vice premier, and foreign minister, was dropped from the Politburo of the Party, but he was not expelled from the Central Committee. The official report which Kádár submitted on behalf of the Party leadership to the Eighth Congress condemned Stalinism and strongly censured those Party members who were held responsible for past illegalities and abuses, committed mainly against fellow Party members. In a way this report sought to condemn the entire Stalinist era in Hungary, during which "Rákosi and his clique" seized and misused the power of the Party and of the state. By its implications this report also sought to promote the regime's efforts to gain the acceptance and support of the majority of the Hungarian people.

The method of deciding just who is a Stalinist and who is not, appears to be quite arbitrary. Both Khrushchev and Kádár were beneficiaries of the Stalinist era and both shared in Stalinist excesses. Before his imprisonment, Kádár himself was the Minister of Interior in 1949-1950, during the worst period of Stalinist leadership. By virtue of their positions, however, both Khrushchev and Kádár have been in a position to decide who happens to be a Stalinist.

Kádár maintained a strong friendship with Khrushchev. Since the origin of Kádár's regime was dependent on Soviet support and the continued existence of his regime in power depended primarily on the aid given by Khrushchev, it was only logical to expect Kádár's role to be closely linked to the current Soviet leadership. In the entire Soviet bloc there was no leader more loyal than him. When the split began to occur between the Soviet Union and Albania, and between the Soviet Union and Communist China, Kádár enthusiastically joined Khrushchev's bandwagon. Some of the purged Party members countered by forming a pro-Chinese faction of sorts. In January 1962 the theoretical Party journal reprinted a speech by a member of the Politburo which included the following high-level interpretation of the Sino-Soviet conflict:

The Soviet doctrine of Communism is a mature one whereas the Chinese is still immature, replete with ideas which might directly endanger the victory of the doctrine itself. The Chinese opinions must be weeded out from the consciousness of the Hungarian Communists.[4]

In September 1961 Kádár replaced Münnich as Prime Minister, a position which Kádár had relinquished in January 1959. As a result, Kádár for a few years shared with Khrushchev the distinction of being the only Soviet bloc leader who combined the post of First Party Secretary with that of Premier. Kádár's leading associates were Béla Biszku, Minister of the Interior until 1961 and now one of the leading Party secretaries, and Gyula Kállay, who succeeded Kádár as Premier in July 1965.

As is generally true in all of the countries of the Communist bloc, the real locus of power in Hungary rests in the Party. While the National Assembly is not the most important center of control, neither is the Party Congress nor the Central Committee. The real ruling body is the leading Party clique known as the Politburo which is composed on the whole by friends and creatures of Kádár. In recent years the Party leadership has undergone a drastic change. An attempt has been made to reorganize the economic, political, educational, and administrative machinery. While there have been no additional purges of note since 1962, a deliberate rejuvenating process appears to be going on. The older generation of leaders,

---

[4] From the speech by Politburo member Nemes given at the Party Academy, as reported in *Társadalmi Szemle*, February 1962.

including such Party leaders as former Premier Ferenc Münnich and former Foreign Minister Endre Sik, are gradually being replaced in the top government posts by people of a comparatively younger age group. Ultimately, however, the control of Hungarian affairs rests with the Kremlin, although its degree of control is less obvious today than during the years following 1956.

THE MILITARY

Since the end of 1957 little change has taken place in the total number of Soviet armed forces in Hungary. The troops remaining in Hungary have been reduced from the large occupation force, which crushed the Revolution and brought Kádár to power, to four divisions and some anti-aircraft personnel and ancillary units. Shortly after Kádár assumed leadership he promised that all Soviet troops would be withdrawn. But this proved to be just one of his empty promises, made to settle the continuing unrest in the country. Later he declared that the troops would remain only as long as he deemed it necessary, hinting at the possibility of withdrawal in the not too distant future. In recent years all rumors of withdrawal have ceased, and it begins to appear that the presence of Soviet troops on Hungarian soil must be considered a permanent feature of Hungarian life. Lately there has not been a great deal of expressed opposition to the maintenance of the Soviet troops in Hungary. The leaders are careful to prevent situations which might possibly create violent and widespread opposition. There is little contact between the Hungarian people and the Soviet forces. The soldiers are warned not to cause trouble among the people, and they are urged to remain primarily within the Soviet camps. These directions on the whole are heeded extremely well.

The Hungarian People's Army (HPA) has been organized by the Hungarian government in 1948 from the limited defense forces of Hungary under Soviet pressure. By 1952 the HPA had grown from an army of four poorly equipped divisions to a totally equipped force of 165,000 men and over 300 tanks. As a result of the Revolution of 1956 the HPA was almost totally disbanded. Only a small auxiliary force was maintained and a limited number of politically dependable officers, noncommissioned officers, and specialists were granted the opportunity to continue their study and training in military matters.

The Hungarian People's Army continued as a limited auxiliary force until 1960 when the HPA was reorganized as the Workers' Guards, a paramilitary force of 35,000 men who were equipped with automatic weapons. Another reorganization occurred the following year, and in 1962 the Hungarian military budget reached a record high of 7.4 billion forint (about $740 million) compared with the low budgets of 1957 and 1958 of only 2 billion forint (about $200 million). The morale of the reorganized and strengthened Hungarian People's Army is being boosted by Kádár's regime, and the Hungarian youth are strongly urged to participate in this new national defense program. But many of the young Hungarians appear unconvinced as of yet and voice objections to what appears to be a contradiction between the Party's slogans of peace and its policy of rearmament.

In addition to the combat forces of the Hungarian People's Army, there are several armed detachments at the disposal of the government. They are maintained to deal with internal disturbances, and include the Police, the Workers' Militia, and the Domestic Security Forces, which is the military arm of the Security Police. What was formerly the secret police, AVO or AVH, is now known as the Security Police and is administered as part of the ordinary police, although its functions and powers have gone unchanged. It is, however, considerably more restrained and discreet in carrying out its activities than it was during the years when Rákosi was in control of the government or during the first years immediately following the Revolution. As in the case of the Soviet Union, the Party leadership now exercises full control over the Security Police and through the retribution which it has meted out against former AVH officers, the Party gives warning to those who are now in command.

POLITICAL PRISONERS

In April 1960 the government granted an amnesty to a limited number of political prisoners. This proved to be less broad than it was first anticipated, for it applied only to those prisoners whose sentences were less than six years. By 1963, even with two previous amnesties having been granted, it was estimated that there still remained in Hungary between 10 to 15 thousand political prisoners. On March 21, 1963, in a speech before the National Assembly, First Secretary János Kádár announced a new amnesty which clearly applied to those who were convicted of antistate crimes for participating in the Revolution or contributing to the unrest and continued opposition to the Kádár regime in the years that followed the fall of Imre Nagy from control of the government. In addition, the amnesty was to apply to war criminals, those convicted of abuses of power during the era of the personality cult, persons convicted of such offenses as inciting against collectives and attempting to cross the border without an exit permit, and various groups of people who had committed ordinary crimes. Among those specifically excluded from the amnesty were those who had committed certain anti-state crimes such as espionage and high treason, those who had been convicted of certain ordinary crimes such as arson and murder, and "habitual criminals." The decree of amnesty officially went into effect on April 4, 1963, on the eve of Hungary's liberation anniversary.

It is difficult to determine how many political prisoners in fact were granted amnesty. No complete list of those who were released or of those who were eligible for release was made public. Important, well-known figures often were delivered secretly to their homes by car. The most prominent and perhaps the most important victim of the Kádár regime to be released was István Bibó, leader of the National Peasant Party during the 1956 Revolution and Minister of State in the last government of Imre Nagy. He had received a life sentence in 1958 on undisclosed charges. Other rather prominent figures to be released included Sándor Rácz and Sándor Bali, leaders of the Greater Budapest Workers' Council who helped to organize resistance within the city during the 1956 Revolution; Father Egon Turcsányi, former private secretary to Cardinal Mindszenty; Sándor Kopácsi, the Budapest Police Chief during the revolt; György Ádám, an economist and the President of the Revolutionary Council of Hungarian Intellectuals; Sándor Fekete, former cultural editor of the Party newspaper; and László Kardos, a former director of the Budapest Museum who helped to smuggle Imre Nagy's political writings out of the country. Also, nearly all the Roman Catholic priests and laymen who had been sentenced for anti-state activities were given amnesty. The number of political prisoners and of people under special police surveillance has definitely been reduced, but there is wide disagreement of just how great the reduction is. Since none of the amnesties have applied to those convicted of treason or espionage, or to those freedom fighters sentenced for homicide and other common crimes, it is evident that a sizable number of political prisoners is still serving sentences.

Doubtlessly, these much heralded amnesties constitute another factor in the present dual attempts at de-Stalinization and "popularization." The amnesty, however, is of international significance as well, for it helps to remove one of the primary obstacles to the acceptance of the Kádár regime by the West on the same basis as other Communist countries. It appears in this respect that the amnesty coupled with other factors has been successful. Not only have the governments of the Western countries been attempting to normalize their relations with Hungary, but also shortly after the amnesty was granted in 1963, the United Nations decided to forego further examination of the Soviet suppression of the Hungarian revolt in 1956 and to accept the credentials of the Hungarian delegation to the General Assembly. From 1964 on, even the United States began to discuss normalizing relations between the two countries—an indication of the growing interest in economic expansion for both nations.

LITERATURE

The death of Stalin in 1953 came as a blessing to Hungary's Communist and non-Communist writers alike. The necessity of conforming to sterile "socialist-realism" began an immediate decline. The next three years saw evidence of growing literary protests. Nationalism, which previously had remained suppressed, suddenly revealed itself and created a bridge between the Communist intellectuals and the Hungarian people. Following the Twentieth Congress of the Communist Party of the Soviet Union in 1956, the determination of the writers to write according to the dictates of conscience rather than to the dictates of the Party found strong support not only in the readers but also in the non-reading public in Hungary. The writers served as the mouthpiece for a considerable number of people.

After the military defeat of the Revolution, Kádár, recognizing the important role the writers and intellectuals had played in the uprising and the following which they had among the people, hoped to win their co-operation and support. As a result there was at first little attempt made to exercise stricter control over the writers. Before the end of the year it began to appear obvious that the writers were not going to co-operate with Kádár, but instead they were going to resist and protest the Soviet instituted regime in their own peculiar way. While many of the writers fled to the West, several of those who stayed in Hungary fell strangely silent, refusing to write or submit anything for publication. To fill the literary void created by the silence-strike, Kádár promoted the efforts of third-rate writers including such unknowns as Lajos Mesterházi and Imre Dobozy. The works which were published by these writers sold poorly. In due time the regime began to realize that the publishing of books and periodicals which were read primarily by the authors themselves and some Party members was not a fruitful activity. Such a reality was disturbing to the Kádár regime, for it realized that in order to assure its survival, it had to find the means of overcoming the antagonism of the people in general and the hostility of the young people and the intellectuals in particular.

In order to counteract this influential position of the writers, Kádár embarked on a campaign to discredit them. He helped to decimate the ranks of the creative writers by arresting and imprisoning many of those accused of participating in the Revolution, including such personages as Tibor Déry, Gyula Háy, and Zoltán Zelk. He disbanded the Hungarian Writers Union, which had played an influential role in the build-up of intellectual ferment prior to the Revolution. In 1959 the regime permitted the Union to reorganize and directed that it should promote the publication of "socially useful" literary works and also that it encourage the "silent camps" of writers and intellectuals to begin publication once more. Most of the writers who had been imprisoned were released in the amnesty granted in March 1960 and others were given their freedom later in the year. On the whole, however, the silence strike continued. Kádár continued to threaten, and the Party launched bitter attacks against such leading writers as György Lukács and Tibor Déry for their lack of co-operation. In some cases the books of an author were withdrawn from publication throughout the Soviet bloc.

After 1961 there was a shift in the policies of the Kádár regime

toward writers and intellectuals. Connected with the de-Stalinization program, which received Khrushchev's blessing, and the new
attempts at "popularization," the regime has somewhat liberalized
its censorship of the theater, of periodicals, and of the press, which
has been in line with the change in over-all literary policy in the
Soviet Union. With the relaxation of the requirement for "party-
mindedness" in art, many publications have permitted writers
greater laxity for self-expression. Books which have been suppressed have reappeared in new publications. Many of the writers,
who since 1956 have refused to publish anything at all or to do no
more than to translate or to re-edit former works, have recently
broken their silence and have begun to publish again. Works from
non-Hungarian writers are also becoming more evident in the
country. Although the major portion of these works come from the
Soviet bloc, the greatest interest is in the increasing number coming from Western capitalist countries. In addition, a number of
Western dramas and American "musicals" are beginning to appear
in the theaters. Although there has been a definite relaxation of
control over literature, writers still do not dare to disapprove
openly of the regime.

While there exists more tolerance and generosity in Hungary today than existed during the Stalinist years, the people are careful
not to overestimate its significance. The present relaxation of controls is considered not as a right of the people, but as an act of
charity of the regime. Everyone is made to feel that freedom is
granted at the discretion of the government and if the Party should
so desire, it could take away all that has been given.

RELIGION

Following the 1956 Revolution, the Hungarian churches enjoyed
a brief period of non-interference by the new regime. Since mid-
1957, however, the churches have been subjected to increasingly
heavy pressure and have had to compete with anti-religious and
atheistic propaganda sponsored by the government. The Kádár
regime has appointed its own choices to key posts in the Protestant
churches and has used a variety of techniques to control the
Roman Catholic Church, continuing the Church policy of its
predecessors without major change. The Church leaders have been
allowed very little contact with the Vatican. In November and

December 1963, however, the five Hungarian bishops and one Apostolic Administrator were allowed to attend the Ecumenical Council meeting in Rome. Such a move may indicate a further attempt by Kádár's regime to improve its image abroad. Church appointments down to the nomination of parish priests are subject to government approval. The Archbishop of Kalocsa, József Grösz, deputizing for Cardinal Mindszenty as head of the Hungarian hierarchy until his death in October 1961, was pressed to join a group of excommunicated "peace priests" to make statements favorable to government policies, including the collectivization of agriculture. The Hungarian government has continued its financial support of the Church as promised in a 1950 agreement, but in recent years it has reduced the amount of aid and has instituted measures to achieve the abolition of the remaining religious educational institutions. The regime is even attempting to substitute "civil sacraments" and "socialist ceremonies" for the Church's sacraments and Christian ceremonies. Late in 1960 a new series of anti-Church moves was initiated and in June 1961 a number of secular priests along with some members of suppressed religious orders were arrested and sentenced to several years' imprisonment for having participated in "illegal" organizations engaged in anti-state activity. It is likely that they were released under terms of the 1963 amnesty.

Although the Church is tolerated by the present regime, it is hindered in every way in carrying out its mission. Peasants and elderly people who do not hold important positions have nothing to fear by attending services; but such participation is not without its dangers for students, intellectuals, school teachers, and other white-collar workers. Although most are not likely to lose their jobs or to be arrested, they are considered suspect and are often asked to relinquish their practice of religion. If they continue to attend Church services and to participate in religious ceremonies they may be handicapped in their careers and their children may have difficulty in being admitted to colleges. Churches on the whole are well attended, except for those which are under the leadership of excommunicated priests, who have become extremely co-operative with the regime. Many look to the Church as the last and legal channel of resistance to the Communist ideology and the Kádár regime. It may be that many people attend mass not for their love of God but for their dislike of Kádár. In a way the Church is regarded as a symbol of Hungarian independence and enduring national values, and continued church attendance may indicate an unwillingness to submit completely to the dictates of the government.

Despite the strong religious feelings in the country, the strict control over the Church by the government presages a bleak future for institutionalized religion in Hungary. The nominations of many of the leaders of the Roman Catholic Church which come from Rome have been declared unacceptable by the government, and the nominations made by the regime have been refused by the Vatican. By 1964 all the archdiocesal posts and half of the bishoprics were vacant. The Primate of the Hungarian Catholic Church, Cardinal Mindszenty, continues to live in the United States' Legation in Budapest since he first sought asylum there in 1956. It appears safe to say that Mindszenty's following is not as great as it once had been, especially among the intellectuals. Then memory of this Church leader is alive primarily among the peasantry.

THE ECONOMY

Because the Hungarian Revolution of 1956 proved to be costly not only to Hungary but also to the Soviet Union, the Hungarian economy still suffers from the aftermath of the Revolution. The general strike provoked by the intervention of Soviet troops in late 1956 practically paralyzed the Hungarian economy, and the continued unrest caused the stocks of existing goods to dwindle even more. Thus the task of rebuilding the economy began under rather unfavorable circumstances in 1957. The economic position was improved somewhat by allowing the peasants to leave the collectives and by suspending the compulsory deliveries of agricultural produce to the state, an act instituted by the revolutionary government and maintained by Kádár's regime. Further improvement resulted from small-scale private industries being allowed to enjoy a certain amount of elbow-room in the production of consumer goods. The credits which Hungary received from countries in the Soviet bloc helped to bolster the sagging economy. The Soviet Union contributed nearly $300 million worth of credits and goods in the first year of Kádár's regime. Finally, as a means to normalize the economy the rate of investment was lowered in favor of an increase in consumer income. However, the measures which promoted favorable economic conditions were not to be permanent. By 1959, when the government felt strong enough to begin to move away from the policy adopted in 1957, the rate of wage increase began to decline, the number employed in private enterprise began to be reduced, and a new wave of collectivization started.

At the time of the 1956 Revolution only about 10 per cent of the total arable land in Hungary was included in the collectives. By contrast, the government announced in 1961 that only 10 per cent of the country's arable land remained under private control, a complete reversal within a period of five years. The new program of collectivization of agriculture was pushed through with utmost ruthlessness as trained agitators were being sent into villages to "persuade" the peasants to sign up. These oppressive measures then had the effect of turning the peasants, normally a rather passive element, into an actively hostile segment of the population. They reacted by hoarding grain, by slaughtering animals illegally, and by participating in blackmarket practices. As a result there has been a general decline in production and agricultural export. Food shortages have become a problem in recent years, and Hungary, the former "granary of Europe," has recently been forced to import large quantities of grain products, upsetting the current Five Year Plan. In March 1962 the Minister of Agriculture dramatically admitted that the agricultural collectives had not achieved the expectations of the regime. He stated that in 1961, the year collectivization was completed, collectives and state farms produced only 37 per cent of crops whereas private plots produced 63 per cent of the total farm output.

The latest Five Year Plan, completed in 1965, was reported to have done well despite the fact that agriculture was lagging behind schedule. At the 1962 Party Congress, Kádár announced that industrial output overfulfilled the Plan in 1961, but consumer products were off by four per cent. In the 1960's Hungary proved to be more prosperous than any of its neighbors in the Communist bloc. Industrial production increased seven per cent and real income went up almost five per cent. More consumer products were made available to the public, and credit could be obtained rather easily through the state banking system. Besides agriculture, another area that has not reached the quota set up under the Five

Year Plan, is the industrial manufacture of machine tools and telecommunications equipment. Although Hungary's standard of living is one of the highest in the Communist bloc, many of the officials are becoming quite concerned with the lack of improvement in worker productivity, which has been especially poor in the building industry. This industry has consistently fallen short of its projected plans, and there has existed a critical housing shortage. To improve the workers' morale and stimulate greater interest in production, the factory councils, which were established by the government following the abolition of the workers' councils, have been reorganized to allow for greater worker participation.

With the obligation to repay credits to the Soviet Union, an increased military expenditure, and growing investments in industry, the leaders of Hungary have made it clear that there can be no significant rise in the living standard. No doubt Hungary's economy would become much sounder if its resources were to be utilized more rationally. Such actions as the importing of goods, to be resold at a loss, the paying of discriminatory prices imposed by the Soviet Union, and giving aid to underprivileged countries, are not wise economic moves. With the present economic policies Hungary's leaders will find it difficult to extort a higher output from the workers without increasing the amount of reward. To do so with a minimum of difficulty, it will be necessary for Hungary to produce more, export more, and to export in such a manner that it will be able to obtain the necessary raw materials for industry and, at the same time, reduce the foreign indebtedness.

FOREIGN RELATIONS

Hungary's position in international relations has improved gradually since the fateful Revolution of 1956. Kádár has gained some stature in the Soviet-Communist bloc. In the Soviet-Albanian split and the Soviet-Red China dispute, Kádár was quick to throw his support to the then Soviet party leader Khrushchev, and even published an article in *Pravda* on December 26, 1961. Previously, in 1960, Kádár accompanied the Soviet Premier to the United Nations in New York and gave a speech.

For reasons of prestige, Hungary's position in the United Nations was of substantial importance to Kádár's regime. Until 1963 the United Nations General Assembly yearly condemned both the

Soviet Union for the suppression of the Hungarian revolt and the Hungarian government for the violation of human rights and the reluctance to permit free elections. From 1958 to late 1962 a former General Assembly President, Sir Leslie Munro of New Zealand, served as the United Nations' representative on Hungary; but he never gained admittance to Hungary because neither the Soviet nor the Hungarian delegations recognized his mandate. In the years subsequent to 1957 the United Nations resolutions on Hungary received a gradually dwindling number of affirmative votes, and on December 18, 1962, the General Assembly requested Secretary General U Thant "to take any initiative that he deemed helpful in relation to the Hungarian question." But by mid-1963 the United Nations had decided to recognize fully the credentials of the Hungarian delegation and disregard the issue of the Hungarian Revolution. No doubt these decisions were influenced by the steps which Kádár had taken to improve the image of his regime abroad, including an amnesty for many political prisoners and a general easing of the conditions of life.

The Hungarian People's Republic has established around the world over 50 trade missions, legations, and embassies. In some instances they tend to serve primarily Soviet interests. Since the Communist take-over of power in Hungary after World War II, the United States has maintained only a *chargé d'affaires* in Budapest. Relations between the two countries have been strained, especially since 1956. It was not until the summer of 1960 that American passports were validated for travel to Hungary. The Kádár government has harassed the United States Legation rather frequently, expelling the United States assistant military attaché in April 1957 and limiting travel by United States diplomats to a zone of 25 miles from the center of Budapest. As to the latter restriction, the State Department retaliated by applying the same restriction to Hungarian diplomats in Washington and New York City. Both sides later lifted these travel restrictions. Since 1960 relations between the United States and Hungary have been much improved. For example, many travel restrictions no longer exist. In 1962 some 8,000 Americans, including some refugees of the 1956 Revolution, visited Hungary, and it is estimated that Hungarians now visit the United States at the rate of 400 a month. Elderly persons are permitted and even encouraged to emigrate at the rate of 80 per month to the United States alone. In doing so they give up low rent apartments and modest pensions which the government is able to put to good use. Because of the full acceptance of the Hungarian delegation to the United Nations by the General Assembly and its withdrawal of further consideration of the 1956 Revolution, both the United States and the Hungarian governments appear eager to restore diplomatic relations. Barring unforeseen events, the two countries may be expected to restore full political relations in the near future.

Yet, in spite of the "New Look" in Hungary, there remains at least one black mark against the present regime. The one event which people remember most is the Revolution of 1956, and it is the one about which the least is said. It continues to be *the* subject which must be avoided or misrepresented. Until the Hungarian government becomes convinced that the events of 1956 can be a topic of free and honest discussion, it will not be able to claim the full support and co-operation of the Hungarian people.

SUGGESTED READING

Books:

Fischer-Galati, Stephen, *Eastern Europe in the Sixties,* New York: Praeger, 1963.

Kertesz, Stephen D. (ed.), *East Central Europe and the World—Developments in the Post-Stalin Era,* Notre Dame: University of Notre Dame Press, 1962 (The contribution on "Hungary," pp. 120-155, was written by the editor).

Váli, Ferenc A., *Rift and Revolt in Hungary—Nationalism Versus Communism,* Cambridge: Harvard University Press, 1961.

Articles:

Barankovics, István, "The Position of Catholic Faith and Church in Hungary," *Hungarian Quarterly Publication II,* New York, 1963 (in Hungarian).

Király, Béla K., "The Tide Turns," *Military Review,* December 1962, pp. 80-84.

Urbán, George, "Hungary," *Survey,* No. 42 June 1962, pp. 72-80.

Tikos, Laszlo M., "Hungary: Literary Renascence," *Problems of Communism,* May-June 1964, pp. 24-34.

Váli, Ferenc A., "Hungary Faces the Future," *Current History,* May 1963, pp. 288-293.

6.   National Communism
in Eastern Europe*

by H. Gordon Skilling

This essay presents a comparison of several Eastern European countries that have displayed various patterns of national Communism with a startling degree of impunity. Interestingly, Albania and Yugoslavia, two of the nations examined here, withdrew from the European Communist bloc at a time when the Soviet Union was unable and unwilling to exert force to keep them within the once-monolithic Soviet camp. Probably neither could have succeeded in its flagrantly deviationist attempt if it had been situated geographically closer to the Soviet Union, nor if it had "made its break" toward the establishment of national autonomy at another period in Soviet and world history.

Gordon Skilling stresses the inevitable fragmentation of the Communist system into separate and competing blocs, embracing various degrees of national Communism and conflicting with each other on ideological and power-political terms.

Essentially, the two key countries of Albania and Yugoslavia defected from the U.S.S.R.'s iron control because they wanted to maintain their national identity and independence. Although both have suffered from a severe "encirclement complex," Albania's fanatic intransigence was such that it cut itself off almost completely from the assistance of outside sources. This factor explains to a large extent why it became Communist China's relatively pliable bridge-head in Southeastern Europe. As long as the Sino-Soviet dispute progresses with unabated vigor, both of these Communist

* Reprinted, with editorial changes, from *The Canadian Journal of Economics and Political Science*, Vol. XXX, No. 3, August 1964, pp. 313-327. Permission granted by the author and the editors of the *Journal*, Toronto, Canada.

mavericks, Albania and Yugoslavia, along with the somewhat more orthodox nations of Czechoslovakia and Rumania, are bound to profit from the confusion and diversity in the camp of international Communism. However, if the Chinese Communists and the Soviets were to reach a new agreement, such a big-power reconciliation could fatefully affect at least the ideological, if not the political and economic, evolution of all national Communist regimes in Eastern Europe. Thus, for the cautious observer, their current and proudly nationalistic ex-satellite status might appear to be both provisional and totally dependent on the vagaries of world Communist tactics.

SEVERAL YEARS HAVE ELAPSED SINCE THE HISTORIC 22ND Congress of the Communist Party of the Soviet Union. In contrast to the dramatic repercussions in Eastern Europe of the 20th Congress five years earlier, the impact of the 1961 meeting was at first much less striking. The renewed assault on Stalin, this time open and unrestrained, did not generate a comparable intellectual ferment or unleash political forces capable of producing a crisis of the dimensions of 1956. No doubt Khrushchev and the other Eastern European leaders were anxious to avoid the disastrous consequences of that year, when the stability, and indeed the very existence, of Communism hung in the balance, at least in Hungary and Poland. This time, certainly, their efforts carefully to control the direction and tempo of change were more successful, and the modest thaw did not produce a flood. Nonetheless, there *were* serious consequences, often slow in manifesting themselves and differing substantially in each country, but having a long-run potential for modifying profoundly the shape and content of Communism in Eastern Europe.

An entirely unforeseen result of 1956 had been the emergence of China as an influential force in world Communism, challenging the hitherto predominant position of the Soviet Union. Her extraordinary intervention in the affairs of Eastern Europe during and after the Hungarian revolt had greatly contributed to the stabilizing of the situation, but had marked the emergence of a balance of power within the Communist system and the beginning of a serious conflict of policy and doctrine between the two great Communist states. Although the full effect of this Chinese challenge was at first somewhat obscured from view, it became increasingly clear that it would have an even more profound impact than earlier defiance by smaller states such as Yugoslavia, Poland, and Hungary. At the 22nd Congress only the tip of the iceberg of Sino-Soviet differences protruded in the form of the Chinese protest at Khrushchev's public denunciation of Albania. The full measure of the divergence was revealed in the subsequent two years, reaching a climax in the confrontation of mid-1963. The expulsion of Albania from the inner Soviet bloc was no doubt designed to warn the Chinese and, indirectly, the other East European leaders, of the penalty of resisting Soviet directives. This action did not, however, have serious disintegrating results in Eastern Europe, since the other Communist states, including even Yugoslavia, rallied closer to the Soviet Union. Nonetheless, the event, and the mounting controversy with China, marked a further stage in the evolution of a Communist system, polycentric in form, and national in substance.

National Communism is not a recent phenomenon in Eastern Europe. Present to some extent even in 1944-1945, it assumed greater significance after the Soviet-Yugoslav break in 1948 and became increasingly marked immediately prior to the 1956 events in Poland and Hungary. Somewhat quiescent after the crushing of the Hungarian revolt, except for its continuing manifestation in Yugoslavia and Poland, it received a new fillip from the 22nd Congress, and in particular from the condemnation of Albania and the Sino-Soviet conflict.

National Communism may take one or both of two closely related forms: (1) some degree of freedom from Soviet control of the individual Communist countries; (2) some degree of distinctiveness of their political systems, their policies, and their ideologies.

This is not to deny, of course, that these national elements coexist with some degree of continuing Soviet influence or control [1] and with the persistence of certain features common to all Communist

[1] Control is taken to mean the ability of the Soviet Union to compel other states to take action desired by it. "Influence" is taken to mean the ability of the Soviet Union to affect the action taken by other states. Broadly speaking, the difference between "control" or "influence" corresponds to the difference between "coercion" and "persuasion." There are five main types of Soviet control or influence: (1) diplomatic, (2) political, (3) military, (4) economic, and (5) ideological, exercised either directly on the individual state or through the medium of the organizations of the Soviet bloc.

states. The term "national Communism" is a relative concept, its significance varying with the country, the period, and the problem under consideration. In our preoccupation with the fact of the uniformity and dependence of the smaller Communist states, we have however tended to ignore, or to minimize, the fact of differentiation and independence—so much more pronounced since the Moscow congress in 1961.

I

The expulsion of Albania from the Soviet bloc, one of two spectacular events at the 22nd Congress, had a significance which was seen only later in its full dimensions. The beginning of the rift between the USSR and Albania may be traced back to Khrushchev's *rapprochement* with Yugoslavia in 1955 and his attack on Stalin in early 1956, and assumed serious proportions at the Bucharest and Moscow conferences in 1960. It was in October 1961, at the 22nd Congress, that Khrushchev's brief but savage condemnation of the Albanian leadership publicly bared the full gravity of the controversy to the Communist movement and to the world at large. As in all historic events, the issues were many and complicated. No doubt, from the Albanian viewpoint, one of the decisive factors was the traditional fear of outside control, and in particular of Yugoslav influence, and the distrust aroused by the Soviet reconciliation with Yugoslavia. No doubt, too, the Stalinist character of Albanian Communism was distasteful to Khrushchev in his campaign of de-Stalinization. Albania's cardinal sin, however, was her involvement in the Sino-Soviet dispute on China's side, and her challenge, implicit and explicit, to the authority of the U.S.S.R. in the world Communist camp. On the most sensitive issues of bloc leadership, foreign policy, the strategy of revolution, and even domestic affairs, the Albanians identified themselves with the "leftist" or "dogmatist" position of the Chinese and repudiated what they considered the "rightist" or "revisionist" views of the Russians.

As a result of her defiance of the U.S.S.R., Albania found herself, like Yugoslavia in 1948, excommunicated from the community of the faithful, and against her own will, and by the unilateral action of Khrushchev, compelled to tread the path of national Communism. She thus joined the category of East European states—no less than four of the eight "satellites"—which have, in the short period of less than two decades since the establishment of Communism, frontally challenged the Soviet Union on fundamental issues of policy and doctrine. Albania's "success" was complete and, like Yugoslavia, she achieved a status of full independence which she had neither sought nor expected. In a somewhat different manner, Poland and Hungary, in their turn, had defied Soviet leadership, but with contrasting results. In the one case, that of Poland, a compromise settlement permitted her a considerable margin of autonomy in the conduct of policy at home in return for her voluntary acceptance of the Soviet position in world affairs and bloc relations. In Hungary, the effort to stake out an independent course failed, and a new leadership was imposed by force of arms, leaving only a limited room for maneuver in a common effort to avoid a repetition of the 1956 catastrophe.

From 1962 through 1965 the chasm between Albania and the Soviet Union remained wide and apparently unbridgeable. From the outset the U.S.S.R. terminated all commercial relations with Albania and, going further than in the Yugoslav case in 1948, withdrew her entire diplomatic representation from Tirana. After June 1962, Albanian delegates were not invited to attend meetings of the Warsaw military alliance or of Comecon and its committees, so that to all intents and purposes Albania has been expelled from the inner Soviet bloc. Both sides professed a willingness to engage in bilateral discussions, but only on conditions unacceptable to the other side. Except for an occasional lull, mutual recrimination on matters of ideology and policy has persisted. The Albanians have centered their attacks on Khrushchev personally, as the chief architect of an anti-Albanian policy and as a traitor to Marxism-Leninism. The *rappochement* between the U.S.S.R. and Yugoslavia, from the late spring of 1962, has been denounced as a "process of fusion" of Khrushchev's and Tito's "revisionism." Like the Chinese, the Albanians have bitterly attacked American imperialism and decried Khrushchev's efforts to reach agreements with the USA through negotiations, including the treaty on nuclear tests. As the gap between the Soviet Union and China widened, the Albanians and Chinese have given each other mutual support on all major issues in dispute.

Albania found no support for her position among her fellow

Communist states of Eastern Europe. Even in those countries which had shared a common experience at the hands of the Soviet Union, namely, Yugoslavia, Hungary, and Poland, Communists, while sometimes admitting privately in conversations, that Khrushchev had used methods hardly distinguishable from those of Stalin in 1948, treated this as a regrettable but necessary means of seeking to force Albania to toe the line. No one joined in the attack against the Albanians more vigorously than the Hungarian, Kádár, who in an article in *Pravda* called them Trotskyist in their outlook. The Hoxha regime represented for him the threat from the Stalinist or dogmatist wing of world Communism which he was seeking to destroy in Hungary. In particular, he resented the Albanian view of the Hungarian crisis of 1956 and their effort to shift the blame for it from Rákosi's Stalinist policy to the more liberal course initiated by the 20th Congress.[2] Not surprisingly, the more subservient satellite leaders, in East Germany, Czechoslovakia, Rumania, and Bulgaria, who had shown no will to resist the Soviet Union in 1956 or at any other time, were at one with the others in condemning Albania and in supporting the Soviet Union. Whatever understanding they might have felt for Albania's reluctance to de-Stalinize, they evinced no sympathy for its "leftist" course, and still less for its determination to resist Soviet pressure. There were no more vociferous supporters of Khrushchev's line than Novotný in Czechoslovakia, or Zhivkov in Bulgaria, the latter manifesting his devotion by paying an official visit to Belgrade in January, 1963. More recently, both Kádár and the late Gheorghiu-Dej visited also. Rumania, although less clamorous in denouncing Albania and China, developed intimate economic relations with Yugoslavia, with the joint launching of the Iron Gate power project on the Danube. Even East Germany, which because of unfinished business in East Berlin, might have been tempted by the radical views of Tirana and Peking, felt compelled to adopt the more moderate tactics of Moscow on Berlin and other international issues.

All seven Communist countries of Eastern Europe, whether Stalinist or anti-Stalinist in their own internal course, whether independent or subservient in relation to the U.S.S.R., thus found

[2] Dec. 26, 1961. Cf. *Népszabadság*, Jan. 20, 1962 (transl.) which wrote: "The Hungarian counterrevolution is a warning example showing where international dogmatism could lead. . . ."

themselves brought together by their common allegiance to the Soviet Union and their support of Khrushchev's "rightist" position. Any individual sympathizers that Albania might have had within some parties such as the East German, Hungarian, or Bulgarian were submerged by the campaign of denunciation launched by the leaders. All seven parties severed their associations with the Albanian Workers' Party, and treated it as an outcast from the world Communist movement. Unlike the Soviet Union, however, the governments maintained slender diplomatic links, withdrawing only their ambassadors, and all renewed their trade treaties with Albania.

The 22nd Congress had at first little noticeable impact on Yugoslavia's position. The general tenor of its proceedings was welcomed in Belgrade, but the persistent criticism of Yugoslav socialism and her alleged revisionism was deplored. No secret was made of the doctrinal differences between the Yugoslav party and the Soviet, and especially of the undesirability of a single center for world Communism and the possibility of the construction of socialism outside the Soviet bloc. As the Sino-Soviet conflict intensified, signs of change appeared, beginning with the visit to Yugoslavia in the spring of 1962 of Foreign Minister Gromyko, followed by that of the Soviet president, Brezhnev, and culminating in Tito's triumphal return to the U.S.S.R. at the end of the year. Tito's trip was paralleled, it should be noted, by the simultaneous Asian tour of Kardelj and succeeded the participation of Yugoslavia in the Cairo conference of developing countries. President Tito, after his return declared that Yugoslavia "could not change its foreign policy," and that the "closest cooperation with socialist countries" did not "encroach on our independent policy" or involve the abandonment of friendship with all, including Western countries.

Was this the end of the policy of nonalignment, and the return of Yugoslavia to the Soviet bloc? Nonalignment had not in the past excluded support of the Soviet goal of "peaceful coexistence" and of the major foreign policy objectives designed to achieve that end. The decisive factor in the shift of attitude toward Moscow was the deepening controversy between China and the Soviet Union, and the Yugoslav belief that the main danger in international Communism, and in world affairs generally, was "the Genghis Khan policy" of China, as Tito termed it. Consequently, in spite of divergences in doctrine and in domestic policy, it was in the interest of Yugoslavia to develop more and more friendly relations with the Soviet Union and its allies, and to support them in their struggle against Chinese "dogmatism." In a speech to the Central Committee on May 18, 1963, Tito, referring to the "international revolutionary working class movement," even went so far as to say: "We must be aware that we are a part of that movement and not something outside it." Even this statement, and the presence of a Yugoslav delegate at the Congress of the SED (Socialist Unity Party) in Berlin at the end of 1962, did not indicate the return of Yugoslavia to the Soviet bloc. She remained outside both the Warsaw alliance and Comecon, and was not committed to obey the leading member, the U.S.S.R., still less to take military or economic actions resulting from bloc decisions, except by her own free choice. The return visit of Khrushchev in the fall of 1963, while contributing to the more friendly relationship, does not seem to have led to any profound change in the situation.

Indeed the events described have profoundly affected the nature of the Soviet "commonwealth" and the role of its members. Although the Albanians and Chinese had been proponents of a unified bloc and the necessity of a single center of leadership, their own actions have done much to undermine these features and to bring about the very system of polycentrism which both had deplored. The views of Yugoslavia were thus vindicated, although paradoxically she was not willing to apply her doctrine of polycentrism to the Chinese case and to recognize the right of powerful China to share the direction of world Communism. Although the immediate result of the Sino-Soviet split and the Albanian defection has been to bring the European members of the bloc closer to the Soviet Union and has led them once again to emphasize the idea of a single leading center, and a total break between Peking and Moscow might strengthen these centripetal forces, the ultimate effect of these events is more likely to be to stimulate the centrifugal forces and promote the freedom of action of the individual members. This has been demonstrated in striking fashion by a country long regarded as totally servile to Soviet will and lacking all the prerequisites of an independent policy, namely Rumania. During the past three years she has resisted full integration in the international division of labor proclaimed by Khrushchev and implemented by Comecon and its organs, and has shown a determination to maintain her own program of full and rounded industrial development, based on an independent evaluation of her national interest.

In terms of national Communism, as expressed in degree of freedom from Soviet control or influence, we may then classify the Communist states of Eastern Europe as follows:

a. *Independent states, entirely free of Soviet control:* Yugoslavia and Albania. Neither is a member of the Soviet camp, and neither is therefore subject to the diplomatic, political, military, or economic controls exercised through the camp's organizational system. Each has exercised its right to formulate its own fully independent foreign policy and to interpret Marxist-Leninist doctrine in its own manner. Neither can be forced, against its will, to obey the commands of Moscow in its external or internal affairs. Both may, however, be subject to Soviet influences resulting from certain ideological sympathies, or from diplomatic consensus, or from the threat of military action or economic pressure. Except for the first factor, such influence of the USSR differs not so much in kind, as in degree and in form, from that which it exerts on other nearby states such as Finland or Austria, or indeed from that which any large power exerts on a smaller neighbor.

b. *Semi-independent states,* not entirely free of control, and subject to substantial Soviet influence, but *exercising considerable autonomy of action in domestic affairs:* at present, only Poland. Membership in the camp and its organizations, and the presence of Soviet troops, limit freedom of action, but as her experience in 1956 shows, are not guarantees of absolute control. The most important source of autonomy lies in the nature of the leadership, which owes its existence and much of its domestic support to its resistance to Soviet pressure in 1956, is not totally subservient to the CPSU (Communist Party of the Soviet Union) and displays a marked independence of spirit. The leaders, however, feel much sympathy for the policies of the Soviet regime, and they recognize the necessity of associating closely with the U.S.S.R. and of accepting its direction. To this extent Soviet influence is voluntarily accepted, and an entirely independent role is not demanded. Autonomy permits marked divergencies in domestic policy, and some degree of ideological independence, in some cases going beyond the limit of what the Soviet Union regards as desirable.

c. *Dependent states,* subject to a high degree of Soviet control and influence, and *exercising a much lesser degree of autonomy:* Bulgaria, Czechoslovakia, East Germany, Hungary, and Rumania. All are subject to control through the Warsaw military alliance, bloc economic coordination, and strict ideological and political conformity. Although only East Germany and Hungary are under direct military restraint through the presence of Soviet troops on their territory, the others are open to the possibility of military action from Soviet forces in adjacent countries. In none of these respects is their position different in kind to that of Poland. The decisive factor, explaining their status of dependence, has been the submissive character of their leaderships. Each owed its position initially to Soviet intervention, and has regarded the closest solidarity with the bloc and acceptance of Soviet primacy as essential guarantees of the maintenance of its regime. Nonetheless all possess a certain autonomy of action, manifesting itself in all except Hungary and to some extent Bulgaria in a reluctance to introduce serious changes in the Stalinist system; in Hungary, in a somewhat freer and more flexible course of domestic policy; and in Rumania, in sturdy resistance to the economic integration pressed by the Soviet Union.

It should be noted that the lines between these several categories are not always sharp nor are they rigid and unchanging, as countries may shift from one to another group. Even where Soviet control persists in the fullest degree, it is not absolute in all situations, and as the Albanian case shows, may amount to no more than an "influence" that can, if desired, be rejected. Soviet power is also subject to some limitations resulting from actual or potential lack of sympathy with Soviet policies at home and abroad on the part of certain satellite leaders, or of certain factions, in Poland, Hungary, and Bulgaria, who, although traditionally favorable to a more compliant attitude toward the U.S.S.R., are paradoxically not favorably inclined toward certain present Soviet policies. As we have seen, the balancing of China and the Soviet Union within the bloc, and the influences of Yugoslavia exerted from outside give all members, no matter how dependent and weak, some leeway from freedom of action.

II

The other salient feature of the 22nd Congress was the broadening and deepening of the campaign against Stalin and his legacy of ideas and practices. As in 1956, this assault on Stalinism was closely connected with Soviet domestic affairs, and represented an effort to discredit traditions and persons standing in the way of the measures favored by Khrushchev in his refashioning of Soviet society. It was also a useful instrument for tarnishing the reputation of the Chinese and the Albanians by linking them with the bane of Stalinism. As for the other Eastern European states Khrushchev was no doubt anxious to see them press ahead with a gradual revision of continuing Stalinist features, not merely in symbolic terms, through the removal of statues and the changes of street names, but also in real terms in the lessening of terror, the broadening of freedom, and a more rational economic policy, all within carefully defined limits which would exclude the danger of a qualitative transformation of the system as a whole. Above all, certain shifts in leadership were desirable, both to exclude from office, or to bar from a return to power, those continuing to think in Stalinist terms or resisting the policies sponsored by Khrushchev and his supporters. Nonetheless Khrushchev was ready to tolerate considerable diversity of action, including the maintenance of much of the Stalinist legacy intact in East Germany, Czechoslovakia, and Rumania, provided these states acknowledged, as they did, Soviet leadership on the major issues of foreign policy, and, in particular, threw their support to Moscow in its battle with Peking.

In view of the explosive implication of the assault on Stalinism and the inflammable nature of the materials at hand, it is remarkable how slight were the changes in the social and political order in the year after the 22nd Congress. In the states sometimes referred to as "orthodox," in a Stalinist sense, namely Albania, East Germany, Czechoslovakia, Rumania, and Bulgaria, the process of de-Stalinization had been minimal ever since the death of Stalin. Even the events of 1956 left them largely unscathed. Only in Bulgaria were there significant changes in leadership, with the elimination of Chervenkov from the main seat of power, but this was not accompanied by far-reaching alteration of institutions or policies. In the same way, after the 22nd Congress, again apart from Bulgaria, the *status quo* was in large part maintained. At the other extreme, in the states normally thought of as "unorthodox," Yugoslavia, Poland and, to a lesser extent, Hungary, modifications in the wake of the 22nd Congress were also minor, and the *status quo* was maintained, although for the opposite reasons. In these countries, the worst aspects of Stalinism had been destroyed earlier, in the years after 1950 in the case of Yugoslavia, in 1955 and 1956 in Poland and Hungary, and again more recently in Hungary. For all of them, the 22nd Congress represented a vindication of the line already being pursued, and a safeguarding of its continuance.

The initial reaction of the 22nd Congress in Czechoslovakia was not unlike that in Rumania, with an assault on Stalinism that was largely verbal, and the assigment of responsibility for past evils to Slánský, executed in 1962, and to a limited extent to the dead former leader, Gottwald himself. Even the symbolic measures announced in November 1961, such as the destruction of the Stalin statue on the Letná height, and the transfer of the embalmed body of Gottwald from the Zizkov mausoleum, were carried out only after great delay, almost a year later, and the changing of street and place names, and the removal of lesser monuments, proceeded at a snail's pace. Even more significant was the slowness of the rehabilitation of those who had suffered at the hands of the terror, many of whom had been released from prison, but without formal revision of their sentences or public exoneration. The report of the commission charged with the re-examination of the trials of the Stalin period was never published and its chairman, Rudolf Barák, Minister of the Interior after 1952, was arrested and imprisoned on charges of embezzlement in early 1962. It was impossible to tell whether the question of rehabilitation was involved, and whether Barák had stood for more vigorous de-Stalinization, as some assumed and had had political aspirations to overthrow Novotný, as the latter insinuated. Certainly the elimination from the Presidium of a man of relative youth and intelligence, not so closely associated with the worst of the Stalinist period as his colleagues, removed the only serious alternative leader capable of carrying through a somewhat more liberal program.

The Twelfth Congress of the Communist Party of Czechoslovakia, held in December 1962, after two months' postponement, and following the Bulgarian and Hungarian party congresses, aroused expectations that were not fulfilled. Once again, no changes of leadership or policy were announced. There was a renewed and somewhat more vigorous attack on Gottwald, although not comparable to the total denigration of Chervenkov or Yugov, and there was no rehabilitation of Slánský. Potentially significant, as events were soon to show, was the statement that the rehabilitation commission had revised the cases of thirty persons (unnamed) and would be asked to continue its investigation of political trials between 1949 and 1954 and to report within four months. Somewhat ominously Novotný accused Barák of having used his position as chairman in his own interest, suggesting that the final report might further blacken his reputation. It soon became clear that many were dissatisfied with the failure since 1956 to come to a reckoning with Stalinism and its aftermath, and that the party leadership had been compelled at last to remedy some of the injustice of the Stalin period.

Events which one Slovak writer called "revolutionary" came in April and May of 1963, with the dismissal from the Party Presidium of two Gottwald veterans, Karol Bačilek, Slovak party chief, and Bruno Köhler, secretariat member, as a result of a decision of the Central Committee taken in April but announced only six weeks later. This was coupled with an announcement that the rehabilitation committee had turned its report over to the Supreme Court and the General Prosecutor for action. Although this was published in abbreviated form only months later, it soon became known that the trials of the fifties had been completely repudiated, and many of the leading victims, including Slánský and his closest associates, and Slovak leaders, such as V. Clementis, Laco Novomesky, and others, had been at least legally rehabilitated. Slánský, and some of the others were, however, not fully acquitted of serious political failings nor were those still alive restored to party membership.

The preliminary announcements opened up the floodgates of wrath and censure, expressed in particular at conferences of Slovak Writers, Slovak Journalists, and Czechoslovak Writers in April and May, 1963. Frank and bitter speeches denounced in unqualified terms the crimes of the Stalin period, the "terror and hysteria," the "fear," the "cowardice," the "literary stagnation" of those times and openly lamented the failure to take meaningful corrective measures after the 20th Congress in 1956. The wave of criticism reached not only to the dead in the persons of Kopecký and Bašťovánský, but also the living, including Štoll, for many years cultural dictator, and Viliam Široký, then prime minister. There were voices declaring that "the fight between new and old" had just begun, that much had to be done to make up for the time lost since 1956, and that there was grave danger of a relapse. Whether the writers had entered, as Novotný put it in a speech on June 12, "on a dangerous road" or whether the Czechoslovak regime, and the Novotný leadership itself, would be shaken by the further course of events, is not yet known.[3]

Nowhere in Eastern Europe was the 22nd Congress welcomed with greater enthusiasm than in Poland, where it was regarded as a continuance of the process of eliminating Stalinism inaugurated by the 20th Congress and as a victory over reactionary forces in the Soviet party. The party's theoretical journal *Nowe Drogi*, described the cult of personality as a system of rule that had "warped and distorted almost all fields of life" and had "done incalculable harm," affecting "everyday human relations and the relations between the public and authority, and the methods of administering the economy," causing "the bureaucratization of social life and above all of party life," and "hampering the development of creative Marxist thought." "The breaking of these fetters became an historic necessity."

Paradoxically, the Congress produced few spectacular results in Poland itself. It was treated as a corroboration of the line which had been followed since 1956, strengthening the hand of Gomulka and requiring no significant changes of leadership or policy. There was no departure from two of the great gains of 1956, namely the end of collectivization, and the *modus vivendi* with the Church. In agriculture, indeed, the proportion of collectives dwindled substantially, and although complete collectivization was still proclaimed as the ultimate goal, there was no sign of an impending drive to achieve it by other than voluntary means. Relations with the Church were marred by mutual attacks and new restrictions on its activities, but no fundamental change in its position occurred. Nor, on the other hand, were there any basic alterations in the system of rule, with the smaller parties continuing to play a minor role and the supremacy of the Polish United Workers' party remaining undiminished. A spirited debate on the meaning of freedom in science and scholarship during the winter of 1961-62 suggested the high

[3] Most recently, a reorganization of the Government has eliminated not only Široký, but other veteran associates of Gottwald, including Dolánský, D'uriš, and Krosnář.

value put upon liberty of thought by Polish intellectuals, but did not fundamentally alter the actual situation. Although Poland continued to be intellectually the freest country in the Communist world, there was no broadening of this freedom, as some might have wished, and indeed a certain narrowing of the limits of discussion was observable. This became particularly noticeable a year later, at the Central Committee meeting in July 1963, when Gomulka and others waged a vigorous campaign against ideological weaknesses and called for a return to orthodoxy.

Few states had done more than Yugoslavia in dismantling, long before the 22nd Congress, the ideas and institutions inherited from the Stalinist past. Agriculture had been largely decollectivized; industrial administration substantially decentralized; workers' control, and local and republican autonomy had also modified earlier centralism; Marxist doctrine had been revised distinctively, although by official action rather than individual freedom of interpretation; greater cultural freedom and international interchange lessened the party's control of the arts and scholarship; the continuing cult of Tito's personality was combined with a genuine collective leadership and broader public participation. As we have noted above, the initial reaction to the Congress, although positive, was circumspect, and for some time Belgrade held a watching brief on the progress of de-Stalinization, particularly in the neighboring Communist states.

Paradoxically, the *rapprochement* with the Soviet Union in the spring of 1962 coincided with a substantial tightening up of the Yugoslav system. After Tito's speech at Split in May, there ensued an enhancement of the role of the League of Yugoslav Communists as the directing force of Yugoslav society, as well as an intensification of its own unity and discipline; a reversion to stricter centralist control of the economy; a re-assertion of the need for a single national economy and rejection of "localism" or "republican narrow-mindedness"; and an emphasis on a common Yugoslav national feeling as opposed to the more restricted nationalism associated with the individual republics and their dominant nationalities. Simultaneous with this trend toward greater centralism and unity were the trial and re-imprisonment of Djilas, for the publication of his book *Conversations with Stalin,* ostensibly for revealing official data and, as the verdict put it, "warming up the campaign of slander against Yugoslavia." These measures were interpreted by some western observers as closely associated with the *rapprochement* with the U.S.S.R. and were indeed cited by Khrushchev as corrections of previous errors, which justified his own policy of accord with Yugoslavia. It is more likely that these actions were taken largely to meet the economic crisis and did not mean an abandonment of the specifically Yugoslav "path to socialism." Even the imprisonment of Djilas seems to have represented not so much a "sacrifice" to Moscow as a reaction to what was regarded as his provocative behavior that was causing embarrassment and resentment among his former colleagues in the leadership. Nonetheless, these departures from the distinctive Yugoslav pattern of Communism certainly created a climate more favorable for the *rapprochement* with the U.S.S.R. which was dictated in any case by considerations of foreign policy.

The process of de-Stalinization in Eastern Europe has been uneven and spasmodic, and has probably not run its full course. The attack on Stalinism was bound to generate hopes and demands for greater freedom among all the Eastern European peoples, and where these ambitions were not satisfied, to produce renewed frustration and discontent. The purges in Bulgaria and Hungary and still more, the ferment in Czechoslovakia, coming as that did almost two years later and in a country long notorious for its passivity, suggests the long-term implications of the Congress for the whole of Eastern Europe. There is no reason to be surprised if continuing factional struggles and group pressures produce further delayed reactions elsewhere. Although the effect of a complete break between China and the Soviet Union on the course of de-Stalinization is difficult to predict, it seems likely to weaken the position of those Communists who have looked to Peking for support in their resistance to de-Stalinization and to encourage others to respond to deep-seated popular desires for a more radical elimination of the worst features of Stalinism.

The analysis of de-Stalinization is a complicated matter which has not been fully explored in the above comments. Stalinism is itself a complex phenomenon, embracing not only the despotic rule of one man, the cult of his personality, and the terror and police methods associated with his rule and the regime of his prototypes in Eastern Europe, but also certain key features of Communism as developed by Stalin and imitated in the satellites, including for instance, centralized planning and industrial management, collectivized agriculture, party control of culture, and the bureaucratization of the party. Correspondingly, the negation of Stalinism, or de-Stalinization, is not something easily measured. Certainly the mere removal of statues or pictures, or even verbal denigration of Stalin and his counterparts elsewhere, do not provide an accurate index of progress. The U.S.S.R. itself has carried through only partial de-Stalinization, and retains in greater or less degree certain essential traits of the old system. In the same way, in Eastern Europe some countries have moved faster and further than others, and have changed more in certain respects than in others. For each of the major aspects of Stalinism there is a spectrum of change in Eastern Europe, the individual country, including the U.S.S.R., occupying a different point on each scale. Nor is the position fixed, as official policies move in one or other direction from time to time.

Discussion of de-Stalinization does not exhaust the problem of analyzing the heterogeneity of Communism. A more precise measure of the national distinctiveness of the Eastern European states, including the U.S.S.R., might be better attained by comparing and contrasting them, not with Stalinism, but with each other in respect to individual features of the Communist model. Such features include continuity of leadership, degree of personal absolutism, cult of personality, extent of terror, and of party and governmental democracy, the degree of intellectual freedom, of ideological distinctiveness, of centralization of the economy, and of collectivization of agriculture. For each of these items, an individual country may be placed at some point on a continuum, the position occupied varying on each scale, and fluctuating with changing circumstances. For instance, in intellectual freedom, the gamut would run from Poland (greatest) at one extreme to Albania (least) at the other; in continuity of leadership from Albania, East Germany, and Rumania (greatest) to the U.S.S.R., Poland, and Hungary (least); in collectivization of agriculture, from the U.S.S.R. (greatest) to Poland and Yugoslavia (least); in terror, from Albania or Czechoslovakia (greatest) to Poland (least); in ideological distinctiveness, from Albania (most Stalinist or dogmatist) to Yugoslavia (most revisionist). None of these scales of variation would be easy to construct or exact in definition, but such an attempt would afford a more realistic image of the mosaic of national Communism than our present impressionistic sketches.

Finally, it should be noted that the categories of national differentiation do not coincide at all with the classification according to degree of freedom from Soviet control. The struggle for external autonomy was, for instance, not necessarily correlated with internal thaw. Albania and Yugoslavia, although both independent, stand at opposite extremes according to most of the above criteria of differentiation. Departure from the bloc does not necessarily involve (*vide* Albania) fundamental and immediate changes in domestic policies and institutions, nor does it exclude (*vide* Yugoslavia) later shifts toward closer association with, and greater approximation to, the U.S.S.R. Nor does continued membership in the bloc rule out considerable experimentation in the ways of Communism or significant striving for autonomy. Poland, which is less free of Soviet influence than Yugoslavia, has shown in certain respects greater diversity from the Soviet pattern than the latter. Czechoslovakia and Hungary, although both extremely dependent on the Soviet Union, differ greatly from each other and from her, the former being more, and the latter less Stalinist in spirit. Rumania, Stalinist to the core, has shown marked evidence of independence of action, while East Germany, equally Stalinist, remains devoid of such tendency. None of the generalizations made above has been maintained without modifications over the past few years, and none will remain unchanged in the future. The theme of national Communism will continue to be answered by the counter-themes of Soviet influence, and of Communist uniformity, in an ever modulating counterpoint, defying any rigid or schematic analysis. The aftermath of the 22nd Congress clearly suggests that national Communism in its various forms is likely to intensify rather than to decline in the future, and that it remains a complex and kaleidoscopic force that must be reckoned with in the Communist systems of Eastern Europe and the world.

SUGGESTED READING

Books:

Fischer-Galati, Stephen, *Eastern Europe in the Sixties,* New York: Praeger, 1963.

Griffith, William E., *Albania and the Sino-Soviet Rift,* Cambridge: MIT Press, 1963.

Hamm, Harry, *Albania: China's Beachhead in Europe,* New York: Praeger, 1963.

Hoffman, George W., *Yugoslavia and the New Communism,* New York: Twentieth Century Fund, 1962.

Tomasic, Dinko, *National Communism and Soviet Strategy,* Washington: Public Affairs Press, 1957.

Articles:

Freidin, Seymour, and Harry Hammι, "Albania: Where Stalin Still Rules," *The Saturday Evening Post,* March 17, 1962, pp. 17-23.

Schlesinger, Arthur, Jr., "Kremlin's Unruly Little Brothers," *Harpers' Magazine,* February 1960, pp. 7-8.

Skilling, H. Gordon, "Communism in Eastern Europe: Personal Impressions, 1961-1962," *Canadian Slavonic Papers,* Vol. VI, Toronto, 1964, pp. 18-37.

Taborsky, Edward, "Czechoslovakia: Out of Stalinism?" *Problems of Communism,* Vol. XIII, No. 3, May-June 1964, pp. 5-14.

Vucinich, Wayne S., "Albanian-Soviet Rift," *Current History,* May 1963, pp. 299-304 *et seq.*

7. Rumania: A Dissenting Voice in the Balkans

by Stephen Fischer-Galati

Rumania presents a fascinating case of a Balkan Communist country in which the internal political and economic "relaxation of tensions" of the past decade has produced far-reaching concrete results. One of the more interesting by-products of this trend toward a "New Course" has been the ability of the Rumanian Communist leadership to pursue a distinctly nationalist *economic orientation, while still being forced to toe a fairly strict political line determined by the Soviet Union. The most significant aspect of Rumania's wavering line has been the shrewdness of its native, homegrown leadership which continued to pay lip service to the principle of Soviet supremacy and intrabloc loyalty even while pursuing with determination its own national goals of "socialist construction" on the home front. In recent years these goals have implied a clearly pro-Western and discreetly anti-Soviet orientation in terms of both political* rapprochement *and foreign trade relations with such arch-capitalist nations as the United States, France, and West Germany.*

As Stephen Fischer-Galati's essay indicates, whenever the Rumanian Party leadership stresses the principle of "socialist patriotism," it is in reality expressing a small-nation claim to the primacy as well as the right to determine the lines of its own internal development.

In retrospect, the firm stand taken by the late Gheorghiu-Dej may have been one of several major factors contributing to Nikita Khrushchev's downfall in October 1964. The Rumanian Communists' open refusal throughout the 1961-1965 period to have their economic and political plans altered by dictates from Moscow sup-

plied further conclusive proof to Khrushchev's colleagues that East-
ern European affairs were being mishandled and polycentrism was
rampant in the Communist bloc.

PERHAPS THE MOST NOTABLE DEVELOPMENT IN RECENT SOVIET
bloc politics has been the growing independence of Rumania from
Russian tutelage. Some experts would have us believe that the
current Rumanian regime is overtly defying Moscow and that this
modification in the traditional Rumanian position of subservience
is the immediate consequence of the growing Sino-Soviet conflict.
Others, minimizing the significance of the Peking-Moscow feud,
regard the new Rumanian policies as a nationalist reaction to Russian domination, as an inevitable consequence of peaceful coexistence. Yet, however divergent the interpretation of the "New
Course," it is generally believed to be directly connected with
Rumanian plans for industrialization, which came into conflict
with the Russian views on the balanced economic development of
the member-nations of the Council for Mutual Economic Assistance
(COMECON).

After the formulation of the Rumanian position of dissent in
March 1963, such actions as the exclusive publication in the Russian bloc of the Chinese "25 Points" in June, Gheorghiu-Dej's
conspicuous absence from the summit meeting in East Berlin in
July, the closing of Russian cultural institutions in Bucharest, the
"re-romanization" of the alphabet in the fall have been considered,
if not as outright anti-Russian moves, at least as expressions of
Rumanian Communist nationalism inspired by the COMECON
dispute. To what extent are the assumptions, theories, and explanations valid?

The inevitability of the development of friction between Russia
and Rumania has been debated for a long time. The conventional
arguments would point to the historic antagonism between the
two nations, originating in the late eighteenth century, intensified
after the annexation of southern Bessarabia in 1878 and rein-
flamed by the outright seizure of all of that province as well as of
Bukovina in 1940, and reaching its zenith in the years immediately
following World War II. But this "historic view" is rather mean-
ingless, for it is based on the premise that territorial quarrels and
anti-Communist sentiments are at the very root of Russo-Ruma-

nian difficulties. Revisionism was not a mass movement in pre-Communist Rumania, nor is the existence of a genuine popular anti-Russian tradition borne out by historic evidence. The postwar mass opposition to Communism cannot be characterized as an overtly anti-Russian phenomenon. It was anti-Russian only by identification of Russia with Communism, but the immediate "enemy" was the Rumanian Communist Party. Therefore, any analysis of the current "nationalist" trends should revolve around the historic relations between the Rumanian and Russian Parties and the reasons for which the Rumanian Party is pursuing policies at variance with those of the Soviet Union.

The existence of an anti-Russian trend among the present leadership, commonly identified as the "national" or "Rumanian" group, was suggested as early as 1952. This theory was based on the officially confirmed existence of two rival groups in the upper party echelons—one headed by Gheorghiu-Dej and the other by Ana Pauker. The struggle for control was resolved in favor of the former in that year.

Gheorghiu-Dej's group consisted primarily of native Rumanians who had no direct contact with Moscow prior to their liberation from prison in 1944, while Ana Pauker's group was primarily a clique of nonethnic Rumanian Communists who were trained and installed by Moscow. Consequently, the purging of the latter was conveniently interpreted as the victory of the Rumanian over the foreign, as an expression of Rumanian nationalism within the Party and a sop to the hostility of the masses toward the "Russian" group. This explanation cannot be accepted without qualification. In statements made at the time of the purge of the "anti-Party" group as well as later remarks Gheorghiu-Dej accused Ana Pauker and her cohorts of a variety of infractions: arbitrary personal rule, violation of Party discipline, admission of untrustworthy elements into the Party, encouragement of the kulaks' exploitation of the poorer peasantry—all covered by the master formula of anti-Leninism. But most significantly, Gheorghiu-Dej's denunciations also accused the anti-Party group of three cardinal heresies: separating the Party from the masses, opposing the plans for Rumania's economic development, and fomenting dissension among the various nationalities.

If the anti-Pauker actions were an expression of nationalism, that nationalism was profoundly different from the traditional one. It was definitely not an expression of dissatisfaction with Moscow policies *per se,* with which there was no possibility of disagreeing in 1952, as witnessed by Gheorghiu-Dej's abject adulation of Stalin. It is evident, however, that the Rumanian group had profoundly resented the high-handed methods of Ana Pauker, the protegée of Malenkov, Beria, and other members of the Russian "anti-Party" group of later years, and sought an opportunity to translate their theoretical power into actuality in the Rumanian Party. The Gheorghiu-Dej group also exploited the Korean crisis to settle accounts with the anti-Party group. The nature of the accusations leveled at Pauker, Luca, and Georgescu, and the promises that the results of their deviations would be corrected helped to forestall retaliation from the Kremlin and indeed appear to have been found acceptable by Stalin. Nor is there any evidence to substantiate the belief that the removal of the "foreign" group was designed either to appease or arouse popular anti-Russian sentiments or for that matter necessarily to ingratiate the "Rumanian" group with the masses.

In effect, Ana Pauker and Luca were not despised because of their Russian backing but because of their power in the Party and government. Their respective Jewish and Hungarian origins doubtlessly were an additional irritant, but the fact that Gheorghiu-Dej, Chivu Stoica, or Apostol were native Rumanians did not particularly endear them to the population. The new ruling group could hardly disassociate itself from its purged colleagues and did not even attempt to alter the unpopular policies with which the Party was associated. Nor did it try to "Romanize" the composition of the government. In fact, the victors promised rigid adherence to Stalinist precepts, a ruthless struggle for strengthening the purity and discipline of the Party, vigorous pursuit of the class struggle in town and country, and elimination of all other deviations "to the right" or "to the left." If any nationalistic hopes were entertained by those rejoicing in Pauker's and Luca's political demise, they were immediately frustrated by the promotion of pro-Gheorghiu-Dej Jews and Hungarians to positions of leadership and by the unequivocal denunciation of old-time, "bourgeois" nationalism by the new ruling clique. Party purity, promises of closer contacts between the Party and the masses, increased vigilance, and the likelihood of further purges did not serve to identify the "Rumanian"-led Party with the "nationalist" (that is, anti-Communist) positions and aspirations of the people.

On the whole, two fundamental concepts of a new "Communist nationalism" emerged at the time of the purges. The first was that the Rumanian Party was the democratic political organization of all Rumanians regardless of national origin; the second, that the democratic Party was dedicated to the construction of socialism in the Rumanian People's Republic through the industrialization of the country and the socialist transformation of agriculture. The sabotage of socialist construction, as broadly formulated at the National Conference of the Rumanian Communist Party in 1945, was the ostensible reason for the downfall of the anti-Party group; the attainment thereof was to be the *raison d'être* of the new leadership and of all loyal members of the Party. The attainment of socialism now became the *national* goal of a Party representing and acting for all inhabitants of Rumania.

It was to the credit of Gheorghiu-Dej that with dogged determination he and his close associates have devised and pursued policies designed to attain this goal. The Communist leadership has maintained that the blueprint for socialist construction in Rumania, including the electrification plan and the policies related to the socialist transformation of agriculture, were originated by Gheorghiu-Dej and have expressed the true desires of Rumanian Communists. If these aims could not be translated into practice earlier, it was because of the activities and interference of Ana Pauker and her group. The actions of 1952 thus stated, in effect, that no such interference would henceforth be tolerated in the Party. But what about *external* interference?

On this score, too, Gheorghiu-Dej appeared to have been consistent and realistic. Until Stalin's death and for that matter until mid-1955, Rumania's political and economic dependence on the Soviet Union was so vital to the attainment of the Party's goals that to follow a policy of total subservience was the only possible choice. The massive purges of followers of the anti-Party group, culminating in the trial and conviction of Luca in 1954, the concurrent removal of exponents of the "bourgeois-nationalist" philosophy of the formerly disgraced Party leader Pătrăşcanu, did not encourage political innovation. The realization of the aims of the

"New Course," adopted in 1953 to expedite the attainment of the Party's immediate political and long-term economic goals, could not be envisaged without continuous assistance from the U.S.S.R. The political and economic hostility of the West as well as the inadequacies of the economic and political structure at home both militated in favor of continuing a bona fide satellite relationship with Moscow. By 1955, however, alternatives were presenting themselves or, more accurately, were being sought by Gheorghiu-Dej.

In retrospect it is now evident that the recently heralded "independent" Rumanian policies were tentatively developed in 1955. They were spelled out in Gheorghiu-Dej's report on the activities of the Central Committee to the Second Party Congress in December of that year. The Rumanians wholeheartedly embraced the Khrushchevian views on peaceful coexistence and relations among members of the socialist camp, adapting them, however, to specific national interests and problems. In the case of Rumania the blueprint was first traced in 1945, subsequently implemented by various Party decisions, and redrawn in the program of the Second Congress in light of a realistically conceived progress. The socialist transformation of Rumania did not have to be subordinated to, but rather harmoniously blended with, the interests of the socialist camp headed by the Soviet Union. Although close collaboration with members of the camp was both desirable and necessary to attain the national and international socialist aims, the "de-satellization" principle was unequivocally contained in Gheorghiu-Dej's view. He stressed the Marxist-Leninist principle of interaction between socialist patriotism and proletarian internationalism as the basis of correct intercamp relations. His interpretation of these relations (defined as "relations of the new type") was that they were "based on mutual respect for state sovereignty and equal rights of all countries, on their national characteristics, on their contribution to human progress." The same basic interpretation was applied to coexistence with nonsocialist nations.

In concrete terms Gheorghiu-Dej sought the continuing protection and economic support of the Soviet Union while at the same time trying to mend his fences with the West. By increasing trade with the non-Communist world he would gain a modicum of economic independence from Moscow and advance the cause of socialist construction at home. The "spirit of Geneva" and the reestablishment of friendly relations of "the new type" between Moscow and Belgrade were evidently exploited by the Rumanian leadership. This, however, was not a Titoist position. Dependence on Russia for the execution of the program of the Congress and for the very survival of the unpopular regime precluded the adoption of Yugoslav Communist patterns, even if Gheorghiu-Dej had contemplated such steps.

The spectacular developments of 1956 permitted the refinement of the doctrines inherent in these "nationalist" plans. Khrushchev's views on the international Communist movement, as expressed at the Twentieth Congress in February, that ". . . all the Communist parties base themselves on the national peculiarities and conditions in every country, giving the fullest expression to the national interests of their peoples," were grist to Gheorghiu-Dej's mill. Nor could the Rumanian leader voice anything but satisfaction with the Soviet theories of coexistence and relations among members of the socialist camp; they coincided with his own. Indeed, every speech made by members of the top Rumanian Party echelons stressed the importance of national and historic conditions in socialist construction and cooperation among members of the socialist camp.

The dissolution of the Cominform in April 1956 and the Soviet "Declaration on the Principles of Development and Further Strengthening of Friendship and Cooperation between the Soviet Union and Other Socialist States," issued at the height of the Hungarian crisis in October, were regarded by Gheorghiu-Dej and his associates as a mandate for the execution of the Rumanian Party's goals. Even Khrushchev's denunciation of Stalin and the cult of personality at the Twentieth Congress was interpreted as an endorsement of Gheorghiu-Dej's correct Marxist-Leninist views and policies. Stalinism was identified with the activities of Ana Pauker and her cohorts who had practiced the cult of personality. The counterargument advanced by an apparently sizable segment of the Party (namely, that Stalinism could be equated with Gheorghiu-Dej's own policies) was ruthlessly silenced. The unequivocal condemnation of these "deviations" and the resultant 1956 purges in the Party were conclusive evidence of Gheorghiu-Dej's doctrinairism. Yet, any other interpretation of the lessons of the Twentieth Congress and subsequent Russian statements on coexistence or relations among members of the socialist camp would probably have led to a Rumanian October.

The national and international reactions to the Hungarian revolution temporarily arrested the polycentric tendencies that were becoming apparent throughout the bloc. Although the Rumanian leadership continued to pay lip service to the principle of equality of rights among socialist states, the deterioration of relations between the West and Russia necessitated an emphasis on the unity and vigilance of the socialist camp at the expense of the liberal interpretation of peaceful coexistence. At home, fears for the safety of the regime brought a clearer definition of the Party's policies and a firm restatement of their correctness. At the celebrated Plenary Session of the Central Committee, held on December 27-29, 1956, the leadership vowed to stamp out all manifestations of "bourgeois nationalism" and related foreign ideologies, and to redouble its efforts to insure harmonious relations among all nationalities in Rumania. It then reaffirmed its intention to attain the national goal of socialist construction. The specific economic measures designed to improve the Rumanian people's standard of living, announced at the time, were interpreted not as political concessions but as dividends of socialist progress distributed by a "democratic," but all-powerful Party.

These basic Rumanian positions were restated in Gheorghiu-Dej's interpretation of the Moscow Declaration of 1957. Rumania's principal contribution to the cause of peace and socialism was the execution of the tasks set by the Second Congress. These tasks were to be carried out under the direction of a Party dedicated to the pursuit of the class and ideological struggles against all opponents, foreign and domestic. The strengthening of the unity of the socialist camp and the blending of Rumania's national interests with those of the socialist nations were the cardinal principles in foreign affairs. "Peaceful coexistence" with all nations was nevertheless desired. For practical purposes, however, the proper functioning of COMECON, reactivated after the Moscow Conference, became the principal concern of the Rumanian Party.

It is evident that Gheorghiu-Dej was less than enthusiastic about putting all his eggs in one economic basket. His constant insistence on the maintenance of "relations of the new type" in all interbloc relations was clearly a reflection of his fears that coordination of economic activities under COMECON would necessarily be directed by Russia and could interfere with the fulfillment of Rumania's frequently restated goals of 1945. It was not accidental then that Gheorghiu-Dej cautiously explored the possibilities of concurrent, if not alternate, economic contacts with non-Communist nations within the limits of maneuverability afforded by the doctrine of peaceful coexistence.

Whether Gheorghiu-Dej's "nationalist" economic orientation was determined by the realization that integrated bloc planning would be detrimental to Rumania's interests, is a matter of conjecture. Rumanian official comments on the Moscow meeting of COMECON (May 1958) underlined that all common decisions for economic coordination, including interrelated planning, were reached by unanimous vote. But common planning for the attainment by all member nations of an equally high level of economic development—as envisaged at the meeting—could have imposed the principle of selectivity in the economic development of member nations and thus alter the Party's blueprint for Rumania's industrialization. By the same token, the doctrine of concurrent entrance into Communism could have been interpreted as a mandate for rapid industrialization to allow Rumania to assist the less industrialized nations of the socialist camp. These issues, so important in the mid-1960's were left in abeyance in 1958. But the specter of eventual implementation, under pressure from the "more advanced" nations, loomed large behind Gheorghiu-Dej's decision to accelerate the rhythm of national economic development. At the Plenary Session of the Party's Central Committee in December 1958, he recommended emulation of the Soviet Seven Year Plan as a prerequisite for strengthening the socialist camp. It is also significant that as early as February 1959, Gheorghiu-Dej and his closest associates emphasized the Rumanian Party's paramount role in postwar economic planning, in the historic struggle for national and social liberation, and in leading the country toward the national goal of socialist construction.

Increases in wages, price reductions, liberalization of the requirements for admission into the Party were all intended to demonstrate the rectitude of Gheorghiu-Dej's interpretation of socialist patriotism and proletarian internationalism. And indeed the report submitted by Gheorghiu-Dej to the Grand National Assembly on the "Fifteenth Anniversary of Rumania's Liberation from the Fascist Yoke" on August 23, 1959, attributed the country's marked economic progress to the constant interest of the leadership in the well-being of the Rumanian people, and a devotion to the cause of the socialist camp headed by the Soviet Union.

The Rumanian interpretations of the Bucharest (June 1960) and Moscow Declarations (December 1960) appear, at first sight, identical with those of the Soviet leadership. The common denunciation of American imperialism, revisionism, bourgeois ideologies, and dogmatism are emphasized by both, and indeed, the determined Gheorghiu-Dej regime could wholeheartedly subscribe to these sections of the two statements. Whatever differences existed between Rumania and Russia in 1960 were apparent only in the respective views on how best to insure the unity and victory of the socialist camp. Although in complete agreement on the need for such unity as a prerequisite for victory over capitalism, the Rumanian commentators, headed by Gheorghiu-Dej himself, emphasized the primacy of national development and strength of individual member nations as a *sine qua non* for the attainment of these common aims. "Insuring the bright future of our country is the primary aim of our domestic and foreign policies" stated Gheorghiu-Dej in August 1960, in commenting on the Bucharest Communiqué.

In December of the same year, following a lengthy endorsement of the principles of the Moscow Declaration, he laid particular stress on the fact that: ". . . the theses of the Declaration once again confirm the correctness of the political line of our Party, of the evaluation and decisions of the Party's Third Congress. Fighting under the Party's leadership for the continuous progress of our socialist economy and culture, the working people of our country will contribute, alongside the working people of the other socialist countries, to the continuous strengthening of the unity and power of the world socialist system." At the same time the Rumanian leader underlined the improvement of relations between Rumania and Western European countries in recent years and the country's desire to improve relations with the United States to allow closer economic relations in the spirit of peaceful coexistence and on the basis of relations "of the new type."

Khrushchev's displeasure with the constant Rumanian emphasis on the primacy of internal development may be deduced from the occasional professions of loyalty to COMECON appearing in the Rumanian press in 1961 and 1962. It is also brought out in the official communiqué issued on the eve of the Berlin Crisis in August 1961, following Gheorghiu-Dej's visit to Moscow. That document pointedly stressed Russia's approval of Rumania's economic progress and policies and assurances of support, through closer economic cooperation of the construction of socialism in Rumania. By the same token, Gheorghiu-Dej promised to work for closer economic coordination with COMECON member states in order to expedite the victory of socialism and strengthen the economic development of the camp. These apparent compromises did not necessarily resolve the differences that were developing between Russia and Rumania on the relative significance of tightly coordinated—and thus largely Soviet-directed—economic development.

It is apparent, however, that both the Russians and Rumanians regarded the understanding of August 1961 with mutual suspicion. Gheorghiu-Dej took special pains to slant Khrushchev's statements made at the Russian Party's Twenty-Second Congress in October to justify the correctness of the traditional Rumanian theories of "national" economic development. The building of socialism in Rumania, according to the latest directives of the Third Rumanian Congress, was the country's contribution to the strengthening of the socialist camp. To bolster the validity of this view the Rumanian leader revived his accusations against Ana Pauker and her purged colleagues stressing that this group had prevented the implementation of the correct "historic line" of national economic development first traced at the Party Conference in 1945. The Russians, however, appeared unimpressed by the Rumanian arguments and, holding the upper hand, pressed for positive economic cooperation among COMECON members in a manner detrimental to Rumania's "national" interests. The battle was formally enjoined at the COMECON meeting held in Moscow in June 1962.

The communiqué issued at the end of that meeting stressed the subordination of national to bloc interests. Cursory examination of the document would reveal no irreconcilable differences between the Rumanian views and those contained in the communiqué. The subordination of national interests to those of the bloc did not apparently preclude the development of strong national economies. The expansion of extra-bloc trade relations was also one of Rumania's long-standing desires. However, it is now clear that the extent of subordinating Rumania's national plans contemplated by Moscow was unacceptable to Gheorghiu-Dej. The Rumanian reaction, first expressed in a major editorial in the Party's organ *Scînteia,* was to emphasize the points of discord by underlining the Rumanian aims. Stress was placed on the "taking into account of specific national characteristics and possibilities" in the formulation of international policies, on the "full equality of rights" of all member nations and on COMECON's encouragement of international trade relations with all countries. The Rumanians, regarding themselves as an advanced socialist nation, *de facto* refused to have their plans altered by dictates from Moscow. Russia's aim was to prevent both the economic integration of the West and the development of polycentrism in the bloc. The dissatisfaction of the Rumanians was evident, but there was scant opportunity for maneuverability considering the status of international affairs in the summer of 1962. The solution envisaged at the time was to convince the Russians of the truly remarkable economic progress attained in Rumania by the Party's proven methods and thus to secure recognition and concessions from COMECON.

Gheorghiu-Dej's subsequent support of the COMECON decisions of June 1960 lacked sincerity. Greater autonomy within the limits imposed by international considerations was sought during the summer and early fall. The reiteration of the correctness of the Party's traditional policies was accompanied by measures designed to bring closer identification with the masses. The Party was depicted as the leader of the national liberation movement in 1944 in much clearer terms than previously when most of the kudos were bestowed on the "Glorious Soviet Armies." Thus the national goals and aspirations of the Rumanians—liberty and socialism—could be credited to the historic efforts and actions of the current leadership. Liberalization of admission requirements to the Party both in terms of the social background and previous political orientation of would-be members was declared possible as a consequence of wide mass recognition of the wisdom of the Party's leadership and its policies. The execution of the goals set by the Third Congress and of the Six Year Plan in particular became the constant theme of propagandists. Technological progress —the prerequisite for attainment of the national goal—had to be achieved at all cost including that of hiring experts from non-socialist countries. Intensification of trade with non-COMECON members was urged, particularly on the occasion of the visit of the French Minister of Industry, Maurice Bokanowski, in July of that year. The principle of "full equality of rights" in international relations was emphasized whenever the opportunity arose.

Between October 1962 and March 1963 the Rumanian regime reiterated the now standard themes of its historic role in the national liberation movement, the significance of the decisions of the Third Congress, and the great progress attained by the Rumanian people under the wise leadership of the Party. At the same time it consistently supported the Russian positions in international affairs, both in regard to relations with the West and with the Chinese-Albanian axis. On March 9, however, a communiqué was issued by the Party's Central Committee denouncing the decisions reached at the recently concluded COMECON meeting in Moscow. The communiqué in effect stated that the principles of economic cooperation established at the COMECON meeting of June 1962 as well as those inherent in the Moscow Declaration of 1960 had been violated. The Russian plans for the economic integration of the bloc, supported by Czechoslovakia and East Germany as the more advanced industrial nations, would have restricted the attainment of national economic goals and relegated Rumania to a position of relative inferiority among COMECON member-nations. This the Rumanians were unwilling to accept. The Rumanian views were repeated at the executive meeting of COMECON held in Moscow in April and resulted in the visit of a high-powered Russian delegation headed by N. V. Podgorny to Rumania in May 1963. That visit, reminiscent of Khrushchev's in 1962, did not bridge the existing differences. The Russians, while agreeing that enormous progress had been made in Rumania, pointedly emphasized that even greater progress had been made in the Soviet Union and, to add insult to injury, pointed out that the Rumanian achievements could never have been realized without Russian aid.

Gheorghiu-Dej, however, stuck to his guns. Cooperation had to be based on the principles of equality of rights, strict observance of national sovereignty and independence, comradely mutual aid and mutual benefit. Moreover, he was able to impress Podgorny with the existence of advantageous trade and technical cooperation agreements concluded with Italy, France, Belgium, England, West Germany, and other advanced nations in the 1962-1964 period. By implication it was understood that the Rumanians could expand the scope of these agreements, if necessary. The Rumanians, however, professed their eternal friendship with the USSR, emphasized their constant support of Soviet foreign policy and significantly underlined the greater-than-ever need for unity in the socialist camp. This was their strategy in the conflict with the USSR, hopefully based on policies that would insure the maximum benefit and minimum risk for their plans.

Then, as now, the Rumanian leaders have been most realistic about the extent of their area of maneuverability. They have exercised utmost care in their actions, protecting themselves against all possible contingencies. The initial movement in their self-assigned role of promoters of socialist unity was the returning to Tirana of the Rumanian ambassador. Others followed after Podgorny's departure. In June 1963 the Rumanians, alone in the bloc, published the celebrated Chinese Twenty-five Points of controversy with Moscow. Early in July Gheorghiu-Dej pointedly substituted a telegram for his presence at the bloc summit meeting in East Berlin summoned by the then Soviet Party leader Khrushchev to formulate a common policy toward the Chinese. Expanded cultural exchange and scientific cooperation agreements were signed concurrently between Rumania and Communist China in Peking. The press stressed the correctness of the Party's historic line, and its role in the nation's liberation and the subsequent construction of socialism. On July 28, the communiqué issued after the Communist summit meeting in Moscow dedicated to economic integration, recorded the apparent victory of the Rumanian views on COMECON. The validity of the principles of 1962, as formulated by the Rumanians in March 1963, was unequivocally restated. The desirability of strengthening the economic ties between COMECON members and other nations of the socialist camp and even the "underdeveloped" nations of Asia, Africa and Latin America was explicitly expressed. Thus Rumania's role as an economically advanced country was acknowledged and her justification for further economic development recognized.

It is a matter of speculation to what extent the Soviet recognition of Rumania's position was directly motivated by the seemingly pro-Chinese movements of the Gheorghiu-Dej regime. The entire course of the Rumanian-Russian dispute militated against Rumanian support of Peking's adamantly anti-Western orientation. The Chinese interpretation of "peaceful coexistence" was essentially opposed to that of the Rumanians' interpretation. Granted that the Chinese view on the unity of the socialist camp, with emphasis on the equality of all of its members, was in accord with Rumania's immediate aims, its execution could hardly be advanced by the economically underdeveloped Chinese bloc. The possibility of substitution of Western economic and technological assistance for Russian, which the Rumanians dangled before Moscow's eyes, could also be largely discounted by the Soviet leadership as an immediately feasible alternative. Nevertheless, the prospect, no matter how unreasonable, of Rumanian defection from the Russian bloc was hardly worth the price of intransigence in 1963 and 1964. Thus, Soviet "capitulation" and Rumanian "victory" were both more apparent than real. And it is in terms of the reality of the situation that Rumania's current policies must be appraised.

The Rumanian position on COMECON and its interpretation of the Moscow Declaration of 1960 are not *per se* incompatible with Russian aims and certainly not provocative enough to invite retaliatory measures from Moscow. Granted that the Russians would prefer to exercise control over matters related to economic integration and international relations in the bloc, they do recognize the realities of the "post-Cuban" period. A modicum of compromise has become necessary. The pursuit of a "national" course by Rumania may thus be tolerated as long as it does not assume an overtly anti-Russian orientation. And the Rumanians have been careful to avoid any such actions as being fraught with dangers, including even the possibility of direct or indirect Russian intervention in Rumanian affairs.

The Rumanian regime can ill afford true independence from Moscow. For reasons of domestic security it must limit its contacts with the West to technological and economic exchanges. Ideological contacts must be rigidly controlled lest they encourage bourgeois ideology, bourgeois liberalism and, most significantly, "bourgeois-nationalism" at home. Such developments would undermine not only the doctrine of "socialist patriotism" in all its implications, but could also jeopardize the very existence of the present Rumanian leadership. It is significant that the so-called "nationalist" and "anti-Russian" manifestations, including the romanization of the alphabet, abolition of the compulsory study of Russian in schools, and the closing of the Maxim Gorki institute were merely designed to emphasize the "nationalism" of a nonsatellite. Nevertheless, Communist Rumania remains a loyal member of the Socialist camp and a devoted friend and ally of the Soviet Union.

At the present time the Rumanian economy is insufficiently advanced to justify the risk of incurring the wrath of Moscow and the possible loss of economic contacts with the West. Ultimately the middle course of the late Gheorghiu-Dej was the safest for the execution of his modest plans. As long as Rumania is recognized as a respectable and important member of the socialist camp, adhering to the principles of peaceful coexistence and championing socialist unity, it can further strengthen its domestic economic structure, trade freely with all nations, control its population and, under the protective umbrella provided by the Soviet Union, continue to "build socialism." Within this framework of calculations, the Rumanian regime may voice dissent with Moscow-dictated solutions in a manner compatible with the realities of its relations with the Soviet Union.

SUGGESTED READING

Books:

Cretzianu, Alexandre (ed.), *Captive Rumania,* New York: Praeger, 1956.

Daicoviciu, Constantin, *et al., Rumania,* Foreign Language Publishing House, 1959.

Fischer-Galati, Stephen, *Romania,* New York: Praeger, 1957.

———, *Rumania: A Bibliographic Guide,* Washington: The Library of Congress, 1963.

Articles:

Braham, Randolph L., "Rumania: Onto the Separate Path," *Problems of Communism,* May-June, 1964, pp. 14-24.

Fischer-Galati, Stephen, "Rumania," in Stephen D. Kertesz, ed., *East Central Europe and the World: Developments in the Post-Stalin Era,* University of Notre Dame Press, Notre Dame, 1962, pp. 156-168.

Tomasic, D. A., "The Rumanian Communist Leadership," *The Slavic Review,* October 1961, pp. 477-494.

Wolff, Robert Lee, "Rumania," in Stephen D. Kertesz, ed., *The Fate of East-Central Europe,* Notre Dame: University of Notre Dame Press, 1956, pp. 249-273.

PART III

World Communist Areas of Strength

Introduction to Part III

IN PART III WE OBSERVE THE AREAS OF RELATIVE STRENGTH IN the broad and complex field of Communism. Our three studies reach the conclusion that the most obvious patterns of world Communist strength are essentially the following:

a) A flexible ideology combining long-term strategic considerations with swiftly changing short-term tactics;

b) A geopolitical equilibrium which offers tangible advantages in a global Cold War, provided that ideological disunity can be kept under control; and

c) Economic strength, the use of available resources, provided that these factors can be judiciously exploited through the proper "development strategies."

A FLEXIBLE IDEOLOGY

In order to develop a truly flexible strategy, the leaders of contemporary Communism have for their own purposes divided the nations of the world into several general classifications. Ranging from the heartland of the Soviet Union at one extreme to the opposing power node of the United States at the other, these categories include the nations allied with the Soviet Union, their counterparts in the Western military and economic alliances, and those in-between, neutral nations which for the most part have newly emerged from colonial domination. This has resulted in a new tactic: competition for the loyalties of the developing nations of the world. Apparently Communists are convinced that since the governments of the Western imperialist powers are too strong as yet to permit the triumph of a proletarian revolution within their own borders, their collapse must be brought about by other means, namely, by depriving them of their essential overseas markets. Since, in Communist theory, the primary need of Western imperialists for colonies is an outlet for surplus capital, this effort will only be effective if the underdeveloped areas can acquire industries of their own, and in the process become either economically independent or else dependent on the Communist bloc for investment and assistance.

This strategy is an outgrowth of a further modification of the Marxist view of the capitalist world: Lenin's never too clearly espoused "dialectic of backwardness." Lenin, in effect, took the theory of class struggle and expanded it to world-wide dimensions to meet the peculiar circumstances of the twentieth century. Instead of a few monopoly capitalists who dominated the economic systems of the several imperialist nations, he divided the world into capitalist and exploited *nations*. The major function of the former was the establishment of an economic hegemony over the underdeveloped nations of the world. Thus, where once there had been individual capitalists and workers, these roles were now assumed by the imperialist powers and their colonies. And where previously it had been the workers who were regarded as the explosive element in society, this role was now taken over by the oppressed, backward nations, for which the Soviet Union stood as the leading figure and example.

These nations were encouraged to imitate the industrial and productive capacity of the West so that they might eventually be in a position to declare their "economic independence," as distinguished from mere political independence. Consistently with this line of reasoning, Lenin had contended that it was in the interests of the Soviet Union and international Communism to make common cause with the underdeveloped areas, aiding them and exploiting any revolutionary situation which might prove detrimental to Western interests. However, this policy of the revolution occurring first in the underdeveloped areas was in almost direct contradiction to the order foreseen by Marx and Engels, in which the proletarian revolution would, of course, occur first in the most highly developed areas. In their view, the underdeveloped countries would first have to achieve independence, then undergo a bourgeois revolution, and finally a socialist revolution of the proletariat. It thus remained for Lenin to provide the guidelines for a revision of this strategy. Nor was it seen by him to be in any way a contradiction of true Marxism. He recognized the fact that both Marx and Engels were speaking of a particular world situation as they conceived it; but the tasks and peculiarities of a new epoch demanded the institution of a new strategy.

The opportunities for a revolution in the backward areas of the world were largely ignored by Stalin, who seemed to be more concerned with the possibilities of enlarging the frontiers of the Soviet Union than with accommodating Communist doctrine to the revolutionary aspirations of the non-Western world. Indeed, the appeal which Communism might have had in these areas was systematically thwarted by the subjection of the policies of the international movement to directives from Moscow, where, far removed from the colonial situation and having little understanding of it, the program set forth by the leaders was nothing more than an extension of general Soviet policy. In much of the non-Western world, nationalism had not yet become a dominant force, and Communist ideology tended to regard the national leaders, in the few countries where they had gained prominence, as pawns in the capitalist system. It remained for Khrushchev in the middle 1950's to recognize and begin to exploit the revolutionary possibilities in Asia, Africa and Latin America. The emergence at this time of several small, independent states of questionable viability provided the Soviet Union with an unparalleled opportunity.

The Bandung Conference in 1955 represents the turning point in Soviet policy toward the underdeveloped areas. The famous Five Principles (mutual respect for territorial integrity, non-aggression, non-interference in another country's internal affairs, equality and mutual benefit, and peaceful coexistence) provided an opportunity for the Communist bloc to assert its common cause with the newly independent states. The national-liberation movement, which had formerly been regarded as at best a bourgeois revolution, was now seen as a progressive anti-colonial force, though for a time it was felt that the national bourgeoisie and the intelligentsia were being forced by the working classes to assume a more radical position.

No doubt the Soviet Union was unduly optimistic in the years immediately following the Bandung Conference, as several policy statements would seem to indicate. For a brief period the October Socialist Revolution became the prototype for national-liberation movements throughout the world, and the progress of these struggles was regarded as moving the world closer to the inevitable goal of socialism. In the 1957 Moscow Declaration, for example, it was reported that "During the last 12 years . . . 700 million people have shaken off the colonial yoke and established national independent states. . . . The progress of socialism and of the national-liberation movement has greatly accelerated the disintegration of imperialism." [1] The proletarian revolution, though it

---

[1] G. F. Hudson, Richard Lowenthal, and Roderick MacFarquhar, *The Sino-Soviet Dispute*, New York: F. A. Praeger, 1961, p. 47.

could preferably be achieved by peaceful means, was still to be led by the working classes guided by the Communist Party in cooperation with peasants and the petty bourgeoisie—in Communist terms, a national democratic liberation front in which the Party had asserted, or was in a position readily to attain, a hegemony.

Meanwhile, Soviet policy-makers divided the underdeveloped countries of the world into four major categories, each of which, within certain broad limits, was subjected to a particular variation of Soviet tactics. In the first group, those countries which were already independent received the full support of the Soviet Union regardless of the attitude of the leaders toward Communism itself. The sole criterion was that they exhibit anti-Western tendencies to some as yet unspecified degree. In the second group were those countries which had attained nominal independence but were still victims of "neo-colonialism," that is, some form of economic imperialism. These countries must be assisted by the Communist bloc to achieve economic independence as well.

In a third group of countries, violence seemed inevitable. The object against which this violence was directed, seemed to vary according to special circumstances. Rebellion could and often did erupt in areas still ruled by a colonial power, but revolutions were also to be encouraged against national leaders who, having brought their country to independence, were consciously choosing an alliance with the West. Into this category, then, would fall not only such areas as the Portuguese colonies in Africa, but also countries like Senegal or the Philippines.

Finally, in a fourth category were countries where all other tactics were either inadvisable or impossible. Here Communists were instructed to spread chaos wherever and whenever possible. This tactic would apply primarily in those areas of the underdeveloped world which had been independent for a considerable period of time but which simply had not progressed under "bourgeois" leadership, such as several of the countries of Latin America, or even the Republic of South Africa, where a small elite rules tyrannically over a much larger indigenous population.

In several areas of the world the Communists were faced with the immediate problem of no organized Communist Party and no prospects for creating one in the near future. But in many ways this contributed to, rather than detracted from, the new Soviet strategy. Having once realized that the value of any national-liberation movement lay not in its being pro-Soviet but rather anti-Western, the famous time-factor was once again extended. Since the triumph of Socialism was inevitable, a really militant Communist Party was considered unnecessary in most situations. The new tactic became one of increasingly active support for the new national governments, while simultaneously efforts were made to dispel any local doubt regarding the eventual aims of Parties, or incipient Communist groups, where they were strong enough to represent a distinct element within the country. As for the Communists themselves, they were instructed, in the words of the 1960 Moscow Statement, to "go deeper among the masses," that is, to infiltrate, so that eventually they might dominate.

By 1960 a new ideological understanding had evolved, the so-called "non-capitalist path of development." Contained in this term was the theoretical justification for Soviet cooperation with nationalist leaders, for the lack of encouragement of militant Marxist-Leninist parties, and finally, for extensive economic aid. It was now felt that if sufficient socialist influence could be exerted in the early stages of independence, and the resources and production potential sufficiently developed to enable a state to obtain independence from the West, it could conceivably skip the bourgeois stage of development entirely and develop peacefully into a socialist state.

In examining ideological justifications, it is important to stress that one of the basic categories of Communist thought is a sharp distinction between strategy and tactics. This new approach is a tactical move to strengthen the Soviet position in world affairs; however much it may be explained and justified in ideological terms, it does not alter the basic strategy of the dialectic of backwardness. The emphasis is to isolate the United States in a sea of socialism, and thereby establish the Communist way of life as a definite and decisive trend of the future.

In further justifying this tactic, the Soviet leadership has often referred to Lenin's strategy of exploiting diversity wherever it may be found. This included both the reapplication of the "united front" technique (wherever the leaders of the underdeveloped countries would permit the legal operation of the Communist Party) and an extensive foreign aid program. Both of these efforts, however, met with strong objection from a new voice emerging within the Communist bloc itself—the People's Republic of China.

It has been correctly stated that the Chinese are thirty to forty years behind their Soviet comrades, and tend to view the world through the discarded spectacles with which the Russians looked at the 1920's. Thus, where the Soviet leaders once feared capitalist encirclement and tried to counter this threat by encouraging revolutions of the working masses, the Chinese now regard the revolutionary spirit stalking the underdeveloped countries as Communism's greatest opportunity. Their emphasis on aiding any rebellion against colonialism regardless of the consequences has often come into direct conflict with Moscow's attempts to split the Western alliance, which it regards as providing the greater threat—and opportunity.

The Chinese, on this basis, do not recoil from war with a weaker enemy out of the fear of destroying life and civilization. War, for them, is not only desirable but probably the only means by which Communism will eventually triumph. A delay in the utilization of this method only postpones the development of those states in which Communism is already implanted. Thus they tend to regard the Soviet leaders as ideological revisionists for their premature emphasis on peaceful coexistence.

The variety of tactics, the amazing flexibility of the ideology itself, the bewildering array of charges and countercharges, the inevitable contradictions and denials, can still best be summed up in the words which Lenin first contributed to Communist theory in 1904: "One step forward, two steps backward. . . . It happens in the lives of individuals, and it happens in the history of nations and in the development of parties. It would be criminal cowardice to doubt even for a minute the inevitable and complete triumph of the principles of Social-Democracy." [2]

Thus the underdeveloped countries, and indeed the non-Communist world at large, must be prepared to see themselves described and exploited in whatever manner best fulfills current Soviet and Chinese strategies. The range of Communist tactics is legion, and ideological justification can always be found to make these tactics appear as servants of a greater cause which is pictured as coinciding with the aspirations of a significant portion of the non-Communist world.

[2] Lenin, *Selected Works,* Vol. I, Moscow, 1947, p. 306.

8. Geopolitical Equilibrium and the Sino-Soviet World

by Saul B. Cohen

Saul Cohen's essay discusses the geopolitical consequences of the Soviet Union's historic landward-orientation or "continentality." It indicates that both Czarist Russian and Soviet Communist foreign policies have been deeply affected by long-term trends of geographic expansion directed essentially toward "landward areas."

One of Saul Cohen's major conclusions points up the permanent agricultural weakness of both the Soviet Union and Communist China. He views this problem not only as an "economic development-lag," but primarily as a continual social and political issue in the Communist world. Unless rural living standards can be substantially elevated, he foresees no quick and easy solution—the Communist countries will not be able to meet their long-range food deficits in a rapidly developing and over-crowded world.

The author is convinced that as a result of current geopolitical trends in Peking-Moscow relations, a reconciliation of present differences will occur between the two Communist giants, and a greater future interdependence will develop between them. In view of the bitterness of the current Sino-Soviet dispute, this surprising conclusion is reached here despite the "contradictory political forecasts." As an expert political geographer, the author stresses that a close Sino-Soviet interdependence may be achieved precisely because of the two major powers' condition of "mutual vulnerability."

OURS IS A POLITICALLY DIVIDED WORLD—DIVIDED BECAUSE MAN wills it and because nature reinforces this will. Whereas in the past the national state was the unchallenged framework for this division, today's meaningful global partitions are composed of broad, multi-functioning, diverse, and overlapping groups of states. These groups operate mainly, but not solely, through national governments, for the national state system cannot maintain itself by exclusive concern with the "closed political space" that national boundaries embrace.

The political forces that globally knit together man's natural environment are not isolated; they operate in a continuous interaction with major socio-cultural systems. Admittedly, the clash between "closed political space" and the economic, social, and technological forces that transcend national boundaries has been and remains a major problem of our time. That this clash will be resolved is no longer in serious doubt. Its eruption has triggered a series of supra-national political impulses, emanating from nations, groups, and individuals. These impulses have created new concepts of political regionality and internationalism, just as valid and strong as those related to national interests.

What prevents this divided world from becoming hopelessly fragmentized is a delicately balanced system comprised of man living in political interaction with the natural environment. The system needs continual adjustment to respond to these four interrelated processes: (1) changing patterns of population distribution and growth, (2) new uses of and adjustments to material resources, (3) technological advancement, (4) social and ideological change. In the interaction of these processes lies the basis for a dynamically balanced system which, because the forces concerned are spatially arranged and spatially interrelated, can be described as a *geopolitical* system. The role of politics in maintaining the global unity of the earth-man system is obviously pivotal. However, politics are so thoroughly interrelated with the economic, social, and technological fabric that the state of equilibrium which exists can only be defined as a *geopolitical*, not a *political* state.

GEOSTRATEGIC AND GEOPOLITICAL REGIONS

Geopolitical equilibrium is not based upon a world that is partitioned along hard and fixed boundaries, or that is composed of uniform components. Instead, this world is divided geopolitically into regions which operate at two levels: the one, *geostrategic,* is globe-embracing; the other, *geopolitical,* is framed by geographical regions.[1] The lines of influence which unify these sets of regions vary in intensity and value with changed conditions.

The geostrategic region must be large enough to possess certain globe-influencing characteristics and functions, because today's strategy can only be expressed in global terms. Location, movement, trade orientation and cultural or ideological bonds are the bases for the establishment of this region. The geopolitical region is a subdivision of the geostrategic unit. Because the geopolitical region is derived directly from geographic regions, it provides a framework for common political and economic actions. Contiguity of location and genuine complementarity of resources and economies are distinguishing marks or goals of such regions. Geopolitical regions are the basis for the emergence of multiple power centers within a geostrategic region. Thus, where a decade ago only single power cores existed (the United States and the Soviet Union), today multiple power cores have emerged around which the world is geostrategically organized.

The two major geostrategic regions which are set forth here are: (1) The Trade-Dependent Maritime World and the Eurasian Continental Power World. Their respective cores include: A) the Maritime United States—Maritime Europe, and B) the Soviet Industrial Triangle and North China.

Distinct from these two geostrategic regions are their geopolitical subdivisions. The Maritime World includes: (a) Anglo-America and the Caribbean, (b) Maritime Europe and the Maghreb, (c) Offshore Asia and Oceania, (d) South America, and (e) Africa, South of the Sahara. The first three have a high order of internal unity, the last two have not. The Eurasian Continental Power World, on the other hand, contains: (a) The Soviet Union and Eastern Europe, and (b) East Asia. Two Shatterbelts (Middle East and Southeast Asia) have replaced Europe's Rimland as the major power clash zone. South Asia maintains a separate geopolitical identity, with prospects for emerging as the core of a third, but lesser, Indian Ocean geostrategic region. Between West and East Europe and East and Offshore Asia, unprecedentedly sharp boundaries have emerged to separate the two geostrategic regions. The most significant geopolitical event of the 1960's has been the

[1] Saul B. Cohen, *Geography and Politics in a World Divided,* New York: Random House, 1963, pp. 56-90.

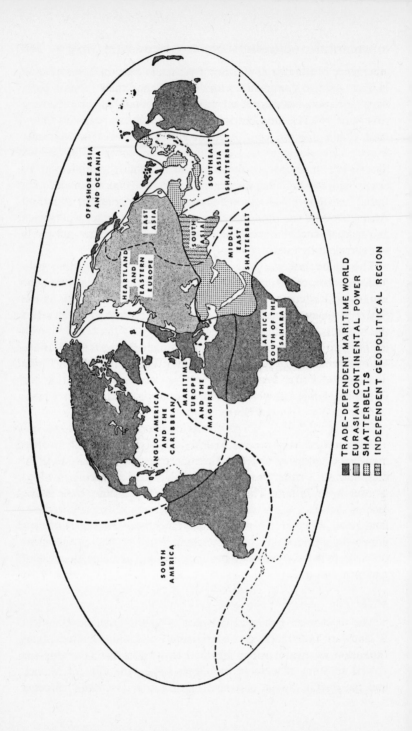

emergence of the two new cores of power in Maritime Europe and in East Asia to complement and to challenge their "senior partners." Friction between the United States and Maritime Europe over Suez, NATO, the Common Market, Southeast Asia and Mainland China may be considered evolutionary stages in Maritime Europe's development as a genuinely equal power core. So, for Sino-Soviet relations, is the ideological conflict, withdrawal of Soviet aid from China, Soviet reaction to China's attack upon India, and Sino-Soviet competition throughout much of Asia and Africa. Despite the bitterness of current disputes, interdependence and mutual vulnerability of the two sets of power centers are likely to override internal differences.

This study is concerned specifically with the interacting geopolitical character of the various elements that constitute the Eurasian Continental Power geostrategic region. The focus is the Soviet State, but treatment will be conducted on three levels: (1) the U.S.S.R. as a national Communist state, (2) the U.S.S.R. with its geopolitically unique and extraordinary interests in Eastern Europe—interests that differ in degree from the concern in China or from those of Communist Parties elsewhere in the world, and (3) the U.S.S.R. as a geostrategic partner of Communist China.

THE U.S.S.R. FROM A NATIONAL VANTAGE POINT

The increased tempo and scale of Soviet international involvement has a tendency to divert attention from the internal scene. In fact, however, within its borders the U.S.S.R. is as deeply involved as ever in its historic task of developing the resource base in the face of such barriers as distance, emptiness, and diversely rigorous landscape. While shifts of population and recast strategies of economic organization are major characteristics of this development process, reliance upon long-distance hauling remains a constant and fixed factor.

LANDWARD ORIENTATION

The most important spatial aspect of this internal development is landward-orientation or "continentality." Unlike United States expansion westward, which has had as its goal the favorably-endowed maritime reaches of the Great Lakes, the Gulf of Mexico and the Pacific, Soviet eastward expansion is essentially directed to landward areas. In contemporary terms, the meaning of such an orientation is two-fold: (1) trade contacts with the outside world are becoming increasingly penalized by distance, and (2) greater dependence upon landward forms of bulk-transportation, more costly and less flexible than sea carriers, adversely affects total transportation costs. Thus, the railroads of the Soviet Union take 81 per cent of all goods carried and roads another 5 per cent, as compared to 47 per cent for railroads and 20 per cent for roads in the United States. Despite substantial improvements in efficiency, Soviet railroads remain the most heavily loaded in the world, with attendant problems of wear, maintenance and delays. Moreover, absence of a first-class road network means absence of the flexible type of transportation service that a specialized national economy should have: a factor of time—cost as distinct from distance—cost.

While a new pipeline grid has recently been laid down from the Urals-Volga to the Baltic and through Eastern Europe, and another system is under construction eastward to Eastern Siberia, limitations of pipeline transportation in international oil trade cannot be minimized. Pipeline costs are not strictly competitive with waterborne movement. In the United States where 17 per cent of all tonnage is moved by pipeline, most of this movement is either of the feeder variety or of specialized products (refined) and natural gas. Bulk movement of crude oil goes by sea wherever possible—a significant contrast to the Soviet development posture which continually contends with the friction of long distance land transportation. In brief, then, the farther eastward the extension of Soviet development areas, the longer the average distances over which goods must be hauled and the higher the cost.

Current inland extension of the economic frontier is but a continuation of the historic Russian thrust from the forested lands around Muscovy into the drier, more marginal lands of the Eastern Ukraine and the Volga, and into the mountainous and desert reaches of Asia populated by Turkic and Mongol peoples. This thrust has always faced the challenge of serious natural environmental liabilities. Marxism-Leninism was not unaware of nature's limitations, but nonetheless took the position that Soviet man could and should reject the implications of environmental restrictions. For nearly half a century, the Communist Party has spearheaded wide-sweeping attempts to extend agriculture and to create industrial combines in areas of rigorous challenge to human use. Soviet man's goal has been to change, not to strike a balance, with nature. The goal has been fired by Communist Party policies of achieving self-sufficiency, rejecting most forms of dependence upon foreign raw materials. Complete utilization of domestic natural resources has had the further objective of opening up remote, backward areas populated by national minorities with the express purpose of giving to the latter a share in the nation's total productive capacity. Finally, to compensate for the liabilities of distance, Lenin formulated the policy of establishing the means of production close to the sources of raw materials, thus reducing transportation hauls. As a result of these processes, the U.S.S.R. was subdivided into small-scale economic regions, inefficient in factory output and in the use of local raw materials (including local wood, peat supplies, over-emphasis on coal and high cost grains and metals). The inefficiency and impracticality of such a policy prevented it from being carried to its logical conclusion, and long-distance movement remains a paramount feature of the Soviet landscape.

NATIONAL BOUNDARIES

Territorial expansion is an historic process that may not yet have run its course in the U.S.S.R. Since 1939, the Soviet state has acquired 265,000 square miles, and increased the size of the country to 8,606,300 square miles, or 50,000 square miles more than the territories held by the Czarist Empire at its 1904 zenith. Far more than additional land, these acquisitions on the Baltic, Black, Okhotsk and Barents Seas have specific strategic, economic, and cultural importance.

Historic claims seem to be important only as they relate to the above factors and play an insignificant role within the Soviet propaganda mechanism. The strategic objective is defensively motivated in seeking to assure command of interior and marginal seas and land gateways. It also serves an offensive function in increasing the vulnerability of neighboring states to Soviet pressures. Economic objectives play a major role in providing Russia with improved port facilities in the Baltic for foreign trade. They play a minor role with respect to the needs of specific localities. Thus,

Leningrad uses the hydroelectric stations of territory annexed from Finland, and Kiev takes natural gas and petroleum from Western Ukrainian lands formerly belonging to Poland. Nationality objectives relate not only to Pan-Slavic ambitions but also to the unity of minority peoples that operate within the Soviet nationality-administrative framework. Not only were Russian-inhabited parts of Latvia annexed to the R.S.F.S.R., and Ruthenian portions of Poland to the Ukraine, but much of the Karelian-inhabited portion of east central Finland was added to Soviet Karelia.

How to weigh the relative importance of these objectives in assessing the motives behind Soviet territorial annexations is difficult, and it is complicated by the fact that two or three of these objectives can be simultaneously served. If, however, we were to single out two overriding elements, one would be the World War II inspired strategic needs of some of the most important cities of the U.S.S.R. for defensive depth, and the second would be a fear of invasion from Germany.

It would be unwise to assume that territorial annexations along the periphery of the U.S.S.R. have run their course. The Soviet Union has shown itself quite capable of reviving territorial claims previously renounced. In the past, Russia's borders have included the upper Aras, upper Kura, and middle Coruk river basins. These are now in Turkey and claims to their major towns, Kars, Ardahan, and Artvin, as belonging to Soviet Armenia and to Georgia, were revived in 1945, at the time of Soviet demands for control of the Straits. Indeed, claims of Soviet Georgian professors for all of northeastern Turkey up to Samsun, on the grounds of its once having been Georgian, were given wide publicity at that time.[2]

Iran, too, is not free of Soviet land annexation pressures. For a brief period (1723-32) all of the southern shore of the Caspian Sea was held by Russia. Soviet interests have been somewhat more restricted, to date, encouraging separatist movements in Persian Azerbaijan and in Kurdish Iranian areas south and west of Lake Urmia. From such positions, Turkey would be hemmed in on two sides, and northern Iraq would be directly exposed to the Soviet Union. In Chinese Central Asia, the Dzungarian Gate—the grassy plain headwaters region of the River Ili that connects Chinese

[2] Royal Institute of International Affairs, *The Middle East—A Political and Economic Survey,* London, 1950, p. 46.

Turkestan and Russian Central Asia—was once briefly occupied by Russia (1871-81). While present circumstances hardly suggest the raising of a claim to this region, it might be reactivated in the event of Sino-Soviet friction or simply as part of a strategic-area "swapping" process.

Whatever the future territorial claims of the Soviet Union may be, their formal basis is likely to continue to be on nationality lines. Natural features and historic claims become objectives as they coincide with nationality frontiers. Demands based upon nationality can be an effective weapon for territorial expansion, for within the border reaches of the U.S.S.R. are many minorities with ethnic ties to peoples in neighboring states.

These include Armenians (with kinsmen in Turkey); Kurds (with fellow-Kurds in Turkey, Iraq, and Iran); Azerbaijanis (with counterparts in Iran); and Tadzhiks (with related tribesmen in Afghanistan). Soviet minorities also have kindred groups in Outer Mongolia (the Mongols) and in Chinese Turkestan (the Turko-Tatars). Sustaining exiled groups which have kinsmen within U.S.S.R. border areas is an advantage that the Soviet Union has never been loath to exploit, and the demographic pattern that finds minority groups overlapping borderlands fits in well with internal subversion within neighboring states. Only along the Manchurian border are significant border-overlapping minorities absent.

The region that is likely to remain the most persistent focus of Russian pressure is the Middle East. In addition to the specific land claims on Turkey and Iran already discussed, the broader problem of the Straits remains a major concern to the Soviet Union. Soviet support of renewed Bulgarian demands for Greek Thrace territory could be conceived of as one way to outflank the approaches to the Dardanelles. With the elimination of the Suez Canal as a Western base, and with various Soviet port activities along the Mediterranean (Latakia and Alexandria) and the Red Sea (Hodeida), Russian interests in the waterways to the Far East have taken on new vigor. Past emphasis upon the Black Sea and the Straits was essentially defensive, for Soviet fear of attack through the water routes was well-founded. Today's emphasis, however, is far more offensive, in the total political-economic-military sense. Never before has Russia had so large a potential stake in the Suez Canal-Indian Ocean-Far East sea route. If commercial and military traffic to China, U.A.R., Iraq, India, and Indonesia continues to increase, the U.S.S.R. may exert unprecedented pressures and take considerable risks to gain the virtual control of the Straits and Persian Gulf that have heretofore been considered desirable, but not strategically essential. Thus, we can describe the Black Sea-Mediterranean as the Soviet "offensive zone" in contrast to its Baltic "defensive zone."

AGRICULTURE

To recognize nature's limitations is not to succumb to them, but merely to take advantage of such knowledge. While Stalin showed little such recognition, Khrushchev has, albeit belatedly. Thus, limitations arising from climatic deficiencies (desert and permafrost), soil inadequacies (peat), and mountainous terrain can be overcome provided that adequate attention is placed upon irrigation, drainage, storage, and distribution. As long as investments remain inadequate, farming represents a major economic, social and political problem to the U.S.S.R. This cannot be otherwise in a country whose rural populace is still 50 per cent of total and whose agricultural workers are 42 per cent of all workers.

Agriculture suffers from an economic development-lag—not, to be sure, in a few favored areas such as the industrial croplands of Central Asia and Transcaucasia, and the grain lands of the Ukrainian steppe, but elsewhere—in the Baltic, in Byelorussia, in the old Muscovy Center, in Polesye (the northwestern, forested Ukraine) and in Western Siberia.

Agriculture is a social problem because of the social backwardness of most rural folk. It is well to remember that there are actually more rural people in the U.S.S.R. today (110 mil.), than there were in Czarist Russia of 1914 (100 mil.). While these rural folk now support a total population almost double the 1914 population, they can be said to have only doubled their agricultural productivity in the face of five- and six-fold productivity increases in the Western World during the comparable period. A nation with such a large number of lower-income farmers as the Soviet Union will face increasing social tensions as the living standards of urban dwellers improve, unless rural standards can also be substantially elevated.

Current agricultural problems focus on the hitherto unsuccessful gambles that have been made in the agricultural triangle, to grow wheat in semi-arid North Kazakhstan under dry farming conditions (the 150 million acres Virgin Lands Scheme) and the conversion of wheat to a mixed corn-livestock economy in the Ukraine. Lacking sufficient large-scale investment in chemical fertilizers and irrigation works, these plans have failed to produce anticipated results. Indeed, the failure of the Virgin Lands Scheme, which has occasioned the Soviet import of wheat and has triggered new debates and political tensions within the Soviet Union, may have long-term and serious psychological implications for the Soviet's public opinion.

The political problems of agriculture must be noted in their Cold War context as well as in domestic terms. Grains, especially, but also industrial crops will be needed in surplus if: (1) the Eastern European countries which have been encouraged in their desires to industrialize and to specialize are to have their foodstuff deficits met by the U.S.S.R., and (2) the U.S.S.R. is to compete effectively with the Western World in meeting the long-range deficit food needs of a rapidly developing world.

Foreign trade in food will become more important as the distributional and storage capacity of developing countries improves. The U.S.S.R., at present, lacks the capacity for competing with the Maritime World as a food exporter. This gap may well increase when the West introduces new packaging and distributional means to reach to what is today the highly underdeveloped consumer market of the tropical and sub-tropical world. The vicious circle in which the U.S.S.R. is caught is underscored by the fact that spectacular advances in agriculture depend upon investment in machines, chemicals and irrigation works. These investments will not create better employment opportunities for the bulk of the agricultural workers; instead, investments will displace workers—or, at best, simply widen the gap between the well-to-do scientifically-run farms and the older villages. The farm surplus labor problem that could be triggered off by a chemical-mechanical revolution will have to look to manufacturing for its resolution. This, then, is the dilemma. Agricultural investment will increase productivity, but will not solve the attendant surplus farm labor problem. This can be solved only by the process of simultaneous industrial investments.

MANUFACTURING ORIENTATION

The Leninist-Stalinist period was characterized by the policy of establishing self-contained and self-sufficient economic regions. These crystallized into rigidly isolated entities within which industrial complexes were developed without genuine regard for cost, including labor as well as capital equipment and transportation.

In 1957, Khrushchev promulgated a new form of economic regionalism based upon existing administrative regions on the oblast scale. 104 *Sovnarkhoz*-es were established, with emphasis upon specialization and inter-regional trade. Perhaps for the first time such elements as skilled labor, traditions, and capital resources have been recognized by Soviet policy-makers as factors in industrial location—to be considered along with raw materials and markets. It is too early to judge the long-term impact of this policy and specifically, whether the weight of raw material pull (whose center is along the Urals) will be countered by these other factors. With the center of Soviet population currently along the Volga—and the agricultural center of gravity to the southwest (between the Ukraine and the Volga), there is at present an imbalance between these centers of gravity and those of heavy industry and industrial raw materials that lie several hundred miles to the east.

POPULATION DISPERSAL

If industry's march to the east should be slowed down by the above-mentioned factors, then the movement of population eastward may experience an unexpected lag. To date, however, the need for developing mineral resources and building factories, and the political drive to Russify the map of the U.S.S.R., intensified as they were by the events of World War II, show few signs of abating. True, the current center of population is only about 400 miles southeast of Moscow, and the absolute gap between population west and east of the Urals keeps widening because of the heavily-weighted western population. What is more important, however, is the qualitative impact of the move of hundreds of thousands of selected Russians into Siberia. The current migrants are not peasants—they are technicians, administrators, and agricultural pioneers. In their thrusts eastward, Great Russians, 60 per cent of the country's total population, have overwhelmed native minorities. Southward, in the Caucasus and Central Asia, progress has been slower, for Russian immigration has had to contend with both existing native populations and less favorable physical environments. Nonetheless, over the broad sweep of time the process of Russian dispersion throughout the land seems inevitable. The Middle Volga, once Asiatic, is now two-thirds Russian. The Lower Volga and Ural River valleys, still largely Asiatic, contain growing Russian industrial centers. North Kazakhstan, the contact zone between Siberia and Central Asia, is now mainly Russian, as are areas in eastern Central Asia, like Semipalatinsk and Alma Ata, which have recently been opened to development by the building of the Turksib Railway. Farther north, the mining areas of the Western Altai Mountains are mainly Russian. The Trans-Caspian railway, which traverses southern Central Asia, has touched off Russian settlement along the eastern Caspian Sea, at Ashkabad and at Samarkand.

While Western Ciscaucasia (the Kuban) has long been Russian and is part of the R.S.F.S.R., the Caucasus as a whole remains essentially native. There are, however, Russian enclaves in Dagestan and Baku.

Along the country's western frontiers, there have been significant population changes in Karelia and Kaliningrad (formerly northern East Prussia), which now have Russian majorities, and in Western Byelorussia, where, in the wake of the emigration of Poles and the extermination of Jews, White Russians now predominate. Even where Russians are not in the majority, the introduction of Russian settlers into selected localities where industry, mining, or farming is being developed injects a Russian influence that cannot be measured in mere numbers. Urbanization means Russian settlement throughout the Soviet Union—a phenomenon that Chauncy Harris first observed from his studies of Soviet census data over two decades ago.[3] For example, recent Soviet policy has stressed the dispersal of industry throughout the countryside, away from the major manufacturing centers. In many instances these new centers have replaced older market towns, whose function has long since

[3] Chauncy Harris, "Ethnic Groups in the Soviet Union," *The Geographical Review*, July 1945, pp. 466-473.

disappeared as a result of the collectivized agricultural framework. These new industrialized cores are Russian enclaves within the rural native habitat, setting the pace for the modernization that affects farming as well as the city.

Political and cultural recognition of the 169 nationalities was a far-sighted response by Soviet leadership to the problems created by the cultural diversity of Czarist Russia. The political-administrative framework that has evolved is based essentially upon this heterogeneity of nationality. But both strategic and economic needs motivate the Russians and their allied Slavic groups to continue to spread throughout the land. The very fact that the technical and administrative know-how needed to exploit the raw materials of the Soviet Union's frontier lands resides essentially in Russian minds and hands, makes immigration necessary and endangers the cultural position of national minorities. The construction worker, the foreman, the plant engineer, and the administrator are all needed to develop backward rural areas, and most of these are drawn from the older, industrial centers. The success of this exploitation of resources, in turn, makes the European Russian corelands increasingly dependent upon the frontier reaches. From this standpoint regional interdependence, rather than regional self-sufficiency, has been the inevitable result of Soviet planning.

Interdependence is something more than dependence, to be sure. Nonetheless, each day brings with it greater Russian need for raw materials and products of national minority lands. As a consequence, nationality distinctions and freedoms are likely to yield increasingly to the centralizing forces and pressures of Russification.

THE GEOPOLITICAL REGION—THE U.S.S.R.
AND EASTERN EUROPE

The most significant geopolitical fact of our times has been the division of Europe into East and West. Central Europe has become a mere geographical expression without geopolitical substance. The term, Eastern Europe, is used here to refer to the lands that extend from the borders of the U.S.S.R. to the Elbe River. When, in 1919, Halford J. MacKinder spoke of East Europe as the area from the Elbe to the Urals, he was warning against, but nonetheless anticipating, the time when East Europe strategically and economically would fall under a Moscow-imposed framework of unity.[4]

Under Soviet-imposed Communism three major changes have taken place to reshape the geopolitical map of Eastern Europe. First, while the states concerned were formerly heterogeneous mixtures of peoples, today as the result of war, mass extermination and boundary revision they are essentially homogeneous. Second is Eastern Europe's strategic dependence upon the U.S.S.R. Between the Black and the Baltic Seas, the Soviet Union has common borders with Poland, Czechoslovakia, Hungary, and Rumania. All of these countries are subject to pressures and the threat of instantaneous reprisals from Soviet soil. In addition, because of post-World War II boundary changes and population expulsions, Poland and Czechoslovakia seek security from future German demands; Bulgaria from Rumanian counter-claims in Dobruja; Czechoslovakia from Hungarian counter-claims in Slovakia; Yugoslavia from Hungarian counter-claims in Voivodina; and Rumania from Hungarian ambitions in Northern Transylvania. Even if local Communist parties did not require Soviet assistance to maintain their control over the satellite countries, the strategic dominance currently exercised by the Soviet Union would make independence of action in the face of Soviet opposition highly unlikely.

The third change affects the pace of industrialization and its character. Shortly after the Soviet take-over, the pattern of industrialization began to follow that of the Soviet Union, with its initial emphasis on national heavy industry. Steel was the guidepost, and production has been progressively increased to 20 million tons, 2/3rds from the Silesian-Moravian complex. More recently, there has been a Soviet-pressured shift from the policy of national industrial self-sufficiency to one of economic specialization within the framework of Comecon. From the U.S.S.R. come oil, iron ore, pig, steel, cotton, wheat, timber, metals and some types of machinery. To the U.S.S.R. go machinery, equipment, and consumer goods. Nearly 60 per cent of all Soviet trade is with East Europe (20 per cent alone with East Germany), certainly a testament to the significance of the latter as a trading partner. From the standpoint of individual satellites, 60 to 90 per cent of their trade is with

[4] Halford J. MacKinder, *Democratic Ideals and Reality,* New York, Holt, 1942, *passim.*

the Soviet Union and other Comecon countries, and there is little to suggest that basic alterations in this trade pattern will occur in the near future. The current resistance of Rumania to the Soviet policy of economic specialization and regional interdependence is, admittedly, a serious check on this grand strategy. But this clash can well be regarded as an evolutionary process within which the forces of regional interdependence and national self-containment must clash. There are doubtless minimum levels of national self-sufficiency which for reasons of prestige, national psychology, and economics will continue to be pursued by the Eastern European satellites, especially by those which possess a diversified raw-material base that might encourage greater self-sufficiency and trade with China and the West.

Thus in Eastern Europe, despite efforts of national Communism to take up more independent economic and ideological positions, the strategic vulnerability of the region to Soviet pressures appears to preclude any possibility of breaking away. Nor can the region aspire to become part of some genuinely neutral Central European buffer zone. The Soviet-dominated geopolitical region has, with the exception of Yugoslavia, Austria and Finland, expanded to its full continental European limits. This geopolitical unity was born of World War II. It is not likely to be broken in the foreseeable future save with the consent of the Soviet Union or through the cataclysmic force of a Third World War.

THE GEOSTRATEGIC REGION—THE EURASIAN CONTINENTAL WORLD

The regional hierarchy that has been postulated includes the national state, the geopolitical subregion, and the geostrategic region. In this sequence are included: (1) the U.S.S.R., (2) the Soviet Union and Eastern Europe, and (3) the Eurasian Continental World, consisting of the U.S.S.R., Eastern Europe, and East Asia.

To speak of the Eurasian Continental World as including Mainland East Asia may appear to some as an overweighting of an ephemeral element, like the ideological unity of World Communism, in the face of cultural, racial, and physical environmental differences. To others, this may appear to be an underweighting of the impact of the internal ideological rift between the two Communist nuclei.

We may not be able to prove or disprove the thesis that the gulf between a Westernized, Christianized Russia and Oriental China is too great to be bridged by Marxism. Nor can we predict the length to which the ideological conflict within the Communist camp is likely to go. But we can challenge the thesis that China and the Soviet Union are too far apart to be able to operate within a unified geostrategic framework.[5] While the distance from Canton to Riga is about 5,000 air miles, and that from Shanghai to Moscow is about 3,700 miles, the gap between Lanchow, China's "Chicago of the West," and Alma Ata, Kazakhstan's scientific university center, is only 1,500 miles. Paotou, the new steel city of North China, is but 900 miles from Irkutsk.

Admittedly, there are vast empty areas between the two states. Semipalatinsk, a site of Soviet nuclear testing, lies exactly midway between Peking and Moscow and is surrounded by empty reaches. However, the true test of proximity in space is the distance that separates the two nations' industrial heartlands as well as the channels of movement that bind them together. Novosibirsk, a city of nearly one million people, and now the eastern edge of the Soviet heartland, is 1,800 miles from Peking, the focus of the North-Northeast Chinese core area. Moreover Sinkiang, China's "New Frontier" of the Northwest for mineral and industrial development, adjoins one of the Soviet "New Frontiers," Kazakhstan.

In viewing the ties of the East Asia Mainland geopolitical region to that of the Soviet Heartland-East European region, we can draw some useful parallels from the relations currently prevailing in the Anglo-American region. Just as the North Atlantic regions have become increasingly interdependent strategically and economically, so have the two Eurasian Continental geopolitical units. Traditionally, the U.S.S.R. has feared the pressures upon its Siberian lands that might be exerted from Chinese Turkestan, Outer Mongolia, and Manchuria. In recent decades these pressures originated from Japan or even from the more distant Pacific-held bases of the Western World. In the future, whatever pressures are exerted will emanate from Mainland Chinese areas that are within the strategic reach of Soviet land power.

As Soviet agriculture and industry continue to spread into

[5] George F. Kennan, *Russia and the West under Lenin and Stalin,* Boston, Little, Brown, 1960, p. 276.

Russian Central Asia, Central Siberia, and the Far Eastern provinces, the U.S.S.R. will surely become more vulnerable to Chinese pressures. At the same time, the greater Soviet stake in Asia and increased Siberian self-sufficiency will both force and enable the U.S.S.R. to find a *modus vivendi* with its neighbor. Extension of the Chinese frontier northeastward (Manchuria) and northwestward (Chinese Mongolia and Sinkiang) is bound to have the same effect upon Chinese relations with the Soviet Union. The result is likely to produce a reconciliation of present differences and, somewhat surprisingly in view of the contradictory political forecasts, a greater interdependence between the Soviet Union and Communist China. Such an interdependence may yet be achieved precisely because of their conditions of mutual vulnerability.

THE EURASIAN CONTINENTAL WORLD
AND THE HEARTLAND THESIS

It was Halford J. MacKinder who first suggested that unified control of interior Eurasia (the "Heartland") would spell domination of all of Eurasia and Africa (the "World Island") and consequently of the world.[6] The emergence of the Soviet Union as a strong, unified national state with strategic control of Eastern Europe to the Elbe River represents the unity of the Heartland that MacKinder foresaw. However, such a unity has not brought to the Heartland a command over either Maritime Europe or over other parts of the Eurasian Rimland. Even with respect to East Asia, Heartland unity has not resulted in automatic dominance of the latter by the former.

Centrality as a feature of the Heartland location and control of the Eurasian pivot are factors which make it possible for the U.S.S.R. to bring to bear various forms of pressure along the Rimland. On the other hand, the unity of the Heartland has not brought with it a command of Maritime Europe because of the processes of unification which have increasingly characterized Western Europe during the same period. Moreover, the size and diversity of the Heartland is such that much of it is not an effective base for threatening the Middle East or South Asia save with the

[6] Halford J. MacKinder, "The Geographical Pivot of History," *Geographical Journal*, 1904, pp. 421-444.

weapons that are also available to the more distant, but equally accessible, maritime powers. Finally, the mutual vulnerability of Central and Eastern Siberia and East Asia forces the Heartland into strategic partnership with East Asia, rather than one region becoming the captive of the other. Thus we regard the historic Heartland not as a strategic entity of its own, but as part of a greater geostrategic region, the Eurasian Continental World.

The drawing of sharp and rigid boundaries around the Eurasian Continental region (the Iron Curtain, the Tibeto-Indian border, the Burma- Chinese border, Vietnam, Taiwan, South Korea, Japan) has been an act of the utmost geopolitical consequence. To achieve a global equilibrium, sharp local lines have had to be drawn, and others may yet be drawn. The world as it is now constituted is intolerant of political vacuums; even the physical barrier-zones that fringe the Eurasian Continental World cannot substitute for clearly defined lines of political influence. A heartlandic location does, indeed, present the U.S.S.R. with certain Cold and Limited War advantages against the Rimland, but these are countered by the disadvantages of land movement friction, of wastelands, and of a sparsity of population. Land movement friction seriously hampers foreign trade contacts, and population sparsity contrasts with the high density and specialized skills of much of the Rimland.

In the aggregate, the Soviet Union's position in Eurasia through a control of the Heartland spells not world control, but an ability to stand as the dominant power element within the Eurasian Continental Geostrategic region—a region whose inherent positional and spatial qualities, in turn, make it a major but *not the dominant factor* in this Divided World.

SUGGESTED READING

Books:
Baransky, N., *Economic Geography of the U.S.S.R.*, translated by S. Belsky, Moscow: Foreign Languages Publishing House, 1956.

Cohen, S. B., *Geography and Politics in a World Divided,* New York: Random House, 1963.

Cole, J. P. and F. C. German, *A Geography of the U.S.S.R.*, London: Butterworths, 1961.

Jackson, W. A., *Russo-Chinese Borderlands,* Princeton: Van Nostrand, 1962.

Jorre, G., *The Soviet Union,* translated by E. D. Laborde, London: Longmans, 1960.

MacKinder, H. J., *Democratic Ideals and Reality,* New York: Holt, 1942.

Shabad, T., *Geography of the U.S.S.R.,* New York: Columbia University Press, 1951.

Articles:

Gyorgy, Andrew, "International Relations: Concept and Application," in *Geography and Politics in a World Divided,* by S. B. Cohen, pp. 291-318.

Harris, Chauncy, "Ethnic Groups in the Soviet Union," *The Geographical Review,* July 1945, pp. 466-473.

MacKinder, Halford J., "The Geographical Pivot of History," *Geographical Journal,* 1904, pp. 421-444.

9. Contrasting Economic Patterns: Chinese and Soviet Development Strategies*

by Nicolas Spulber

Comparing the economic policies adopted by Communist China with those of the U.S.S.R., this essay stresses the similarity of their ultimate goals and the basic differences in strategy. It points out a number of important divergencies in "subjective interpretations." In addition to these psychological variants, China has been concerned with an entirely different set of economic and geopolitical problems; consequently, it could not have used in the course of the first decade and a half of its "post-takeover" economic development the same tactics and methods employed by the Soviet Union over a period of nearly five decades.

Throughout its recent economic and manpower mass-mobilization, Communist China had come to depend increasingly on the resources of the considerably more advanced Soviet Union. Thus it was badly hurt by the wholesale withdrawal of Soviet aid and technicians during the current controversy in the U.S.S.R. Its problems were compounded by two or three disastrous harvests as well as the failure of certain irrational industrial experiments. One of the few alternatives open to a Maoist leadership, which had grossly miscalculated its economic planning processes, is capital investment from more highly developed countries. This investment could supply the necessary foundations for the current drive for modernization and industrialization. In view of the bitter dispute with Russia, Chinese Communist leaders have been forced to make

* Reprinted, with editorial changes, from *Soviet Studies*, Vol. XV, No. 1, July 1963, pp. 1-16. Permission granted by the editors of *Soviet Studies*, University of Glasgow, Scotland.

overtures to capitalist France, Japan, Canada, and even to such fellow-Communist nations as Rumania in the Balkans. So far, these attempts to develop profitable economic relationships have not paid off adequately. Nicolas Spulber's conclusion that the Chinese economy, still tied to its backward agriculture, "now depends almost exclusively on its own national resources to carry out further industrialization," is strongly supported by recent world political events.

STRATEGIES ARE WAYS OF ALLOCATING RESOURCES IN ORDER TO reach a long-run objective, political, economic or military. A common objective for all underdeveloped areas is industrialization in the shortest possible period. But this objective is always accompanied by a number of proximate ends, each of which may be furthered or hindered according to the ways in which each and all of the other ends are pursued. For instance, since the mid-1920s the Soviet leaders have set for their backward economy the bold objective of "catching up with and surpassing in the shortest possible historical period the highest indices of capitalism." Simultaneously the Russians aimed at the liquidation of the rich peasants, the rapid collectivization of agriculture and the elimination of market relations in certain sectors—objectives which in certain ways impeded their main goal. Their economic strategy was thus shaped not only as a function of the ultimate goal, but also as a function of a number of proximate goals, each of which reflected both objective possibilities and subjective interpretations of what was necessary and feasible for reaching the main goal.

Since the early 1950s, the leaders of Communist China have decided to aim high and boldly: their first goal is to surpass Great Britain's industrial development, but they add their intention "to leave Britain and even the whole capitalist world behind" once a "socialist industrial China, mighty, prosperous and unshakeable" has been established.[1] While taking Britain's outputs as their first target, the Chinese naturally and continuously compare their own problems, solutions and achievements with those of the U.S.S.R. during its own industrialization drive.

Both countries are vast in size, both started from very low levels

[1] Niu Chung-hang, *China Will Overtake Britain* (Peking, Foreign Languages Press, 1958), p. 66.

of development, and both have the same ultimate goal. But if the ultimate goals of the two giant Communist powers are identical, their strategies differ significantly. This is due not only to crucial differences in factor endowments but also to subjective interpretations concerning the utilization of peasant manpower in the process of industrialization, the "optimal" correlation between the growth rates of industrial and agricultural outputs, the ways of spreading modern technology in a vast and extremely backward economy, and planning principles and methods. The rationale of the two strategies is of interest for those who follow not only developments in the Communist bloc, but also the efforts at industrialization of all newly emerging nations.

When the U.S.S.R. was launched on the path of all-out industrialization in 1928, the United States was producing 16.9 times the U.S.S.R.'s coal output, 11.8 times its pig-iron output, 12.2 times its steel and 20.0 times its electricity. In agriculture the United States also exceeded the Soviet output of such staples as wheat, rye and barley. The Soviet per capita outputs ranked even lower because the U.S.S.R. had a population of over 150 million as against less than 120 million in the United States; the per capita income was probably 5.3 times higher in the United States than in the U.S.S.R.

Not being plagued by insuperable problems of natural resources —except locational problems—the Soviet Union could rapidly erect a new, modern industrial and military structure on a rather limited domestic foundation. In 1928 its industrial plant consisted of a total of 9,190 "large" enterprises with an installed capacity of 2.5 million horsepower and a gainfully employed total of some 2.2 million. Within these totals, the producer goods industries (fuel and power, iron and steel, machine construction, chemicals and building materials) employed 1.2 million, while small industry, including handicrafts, employed some 3.9 million workers, 76.2% of whom were in rural areas. On this foundation only, and for a long time with very limited imports of machinery and equipment from abroad, the Soviet leadership built a respectable industrial and military power in only 12 years (1928-1940).

While the rural population was 4.4 times as large as the urban population, the Soviet leaders placed the former, from the early 1930s on, within the tight organizational framework of peasant collectives, a framework which made the peasant a residual claimant to his own output and allowed both a sharp step-up in the rate of savings in agriculture and the channeling of most of these savings by the state into the planned expansion of heavy industry. The Soviet leaders regarded the peasants as a passive element to be dragged along while the process of industrialization proceeded to reach full speed. The peasants were to be a docile ally, patiently cooperating with the state, while a growing army of industrial workers erected a powerful industry—a mighty industry of producer goods. After the development of industry on a large scale, peasant agriculture and the villages would be deeply changed: the expanding domestic producer goods industry would mechanize fully all agricultural work, while cheaply re-equipped consumer goods industries would cover all mass-consumption needs.

Notwithstanding the general acceptance of the idea that the peasantry could not change in any significant way through its own efforts, divergent views arose as to what was both feasible and appropriate in order to accelerate the industrialization of the country. Three main positions emerged during the Soviet debates carried on during the mid-1920s regarding the rate of growth, the intensity of industrialization, and the principles and methods of planning.

Some economists affirmed that in a backward country like the U.S.S.R. the most rapid industrialization would be achieved through a rapid rise of agricultural productivity. Massive channeling of investment into this sector, and the ensuing expansion of output, would guarantee rapidly increasing savings which could subsequently be channeled into industry. The growth of agriculture would expand capabilities for importation of equipment from abroad and would at the same time secure adequate raw materials for domestic light industry. All this would prevent the disruption of trade between town and countryside, would further the processes of urbanization and industrial growth, and would in time allow the growth of a domestic heavy industry, providing for uninterrupted and harmonious development.

The second position on the way to achieve industrialization was formulated by N. Bukharin, leader of what later became the Right wing of the party. Bukharin stressed the need of developing industry (light as well as heavy) and agriculture simultaneously. According to him, industry and the towns depended both on agricultural supplies and on the rural market; since agriculture needed producer as well as consumer goods from the towns, Bukharin rejected the postponement of the development of producer goods industries.

The third position taken in the debate was propounded by the so-called Left wing of the party. The Left emphasized, for both political and economic reasons, what it called "the dictatorship of industry" and the absolute primacy of heavy industry in any rapid, autarkic economic development. In a crucial document of the 1920s E. A. Preobrazhenski, the economic spokesman of the Left, affirmed that the rapid industrialization of the country and the mechanization of its agriculture could be achieved only if a massive and sustained effort was made to develop the domestic producer goods industries. Asserting that the existing underdevelopment forced a skewed type of growth—with industry expanding faster than agriculture, and heavy industry expanding faster than light industry—Preobrazhenski affirmed that for a long period agriculture would have to pay a "tribute" to industry as the lever for the rapid economic transformation of the country as a whole.

After hesitating between the Right and the Left position, Stalin finally chose to implement the latter, while simultaneously smashing both factions politically. In order to force the peasants to cooperate with the bureaucracy and the industrial workers, Stalin's party-state machine forcibly collectivized the peasants within a few short years. At the height of the drive, during the first three months of 1930, millions of peasants were forced into collectives, and in the process an enormous amount of rural capital was annihilated.

The basic characteristics of the Soviet strategy of development are by now quite familiar. Throughout the all-round planning era opened at the turn of 1928, the Russians systematically allocated from 40% to 50% of all their investible resources to industry, 80% of which were in turn concentrated in heavy industry and particularly in the "key" group of electricity, iron and steel and machinery construction. The most advanced technological processes were introduced on a large scale in this group, while the lowest priorities in investment were assigned to light industry and agriculture. The Russians did introduce tractors into agriculture when they proceeded to collectivize it—in part to offset the losses of draft animals killed by the peasants during this forced drive; but even after the introduction of tractors on a large scale, many aspects of agricultural work and of livestock husbandry remained highly labor intensive and farming continues to absorb, up to now, close to half of the total labor force.

Since 1928 no debates on this path of development have taken place in the U.S.S.R. While at certain times—in 1953 particularly —the rate of investment has briefly been brought into question, a massive shift in the basic pattern of investment chosen in the late 1920s has never been advocated. The Soviet literature on growth presents this pattern of allocation as the embodiment of "universal laws" of economic development, and presents the Soviet economic strategy and planning procedure as a model valid for any under-developed area—a fortiori for Communist-led backward countries.

Compared with China at the beginning of its industrialization drive in 1952, the U.S.S.R. produced at the inception of its acceler-ated industrialization process, in 1928, 1.7 times China's pig-iron output, 3.3 times its steel, 1.5 times its coke, and 29.0 times its oil output. In relation to the production levels of the industrial giants, China's industrial posture was even more precarious than that of Russia in the 1920s.

It is interesting to note, however, that in the early 1950s China had an apparently larger industrial and handicraft plant than that of Russia in 1928. China counted in 1952 some 27,000 "large" and 140,000 small plants with a combined labor force of 12 mil-lion, 5.1 million of whom were gainfully employed in industry and 6.9 million in handicraft production. China had, moreover, signifi-cant help from the U.S.S.R. and the other bloc countries in the form of imports of fully equipped plants and technical assistance; thus it took her only three years to reach, in the mid-1950s, some of the main output levels reached by the U.S.S.R. at the beginning of its all-out industrialization. But the Chinese achieved these results with an industry heavily concentrated in the country's coastal areas, disposing of a poor transport system, handicapped by the lack of some key raw materials—such as oil—and hampered by the ab-sence of a diversified machine-building industry capable of manu-facturing machine tools, power generating equipment, metallurgical, mining and transport equipment, tractors, trucks or aircraft. Even though China caught up rapidly with the Soviet industrial output of the 1920s, it ranked far lower than did Russia in the 1920s in rela-tion to the levels reached by the main industrial countries.

With a total population four times larger than that of the U.S.S.R.

in the late 1920s, and with an agricultural labor force more than four times as large, China's total grain output was in the early 1950s only twice as large as that of the U.S.S.R. China's overpopulated, poverty-stricken countryside yielded a lower capital accumulation than Russia's for sustained industrial growth.

Only a small part of China's land is under cultivation. In the vast expanses of Sinkiang, Kansu, Tsinghai, Inner Mongolia and Tibet, only 2% of the land is cultivated. In the northeast, north, east and central-south China, 20% of the land is under cultivation. A vast tract of fertile wasteland could be reclaimed—in China just as in the U.S.S.R.—but China lacked the necessary machinery and oil, and its transport facilities were very limited. Now as in the past, in Chinese agriculture, manual labor is the main factor in operation, animal power is the main factor in cultivation and natural fertilizer is the main factor in fertilization.

In launching simultaneously both collectivization and industrialization, the Soviet leadership aimed at obtaining from the collectives the increased marketed share of grains and the additional manpower needed to sustain industry. When the Chinese started to industrialize in 1952 and when they started to prepare the conditions of "cooperativization" in agriculture, they had in view the same aims; but there was a significant difference of degree in the goals and achievements of the two countries, in respect to both the size of the marketed share and the amount of manpower freed from agriculture.

In most of the late twenties and early thirties, the marketed share of grains rose in the U.S.S.R. both relatively and in absolute terms, even in the face of a falling output. China's massive and growing population rendered such a performance impossible. The state collection and purchase of grain fluctuated there in the 1950s between 25% and 38% of total output; but a large part of this grain had to be sold back to the farmers. Even if the Chinese leaders had wanted to follow blindly the Soviet strategy of development, they could not fail to notice that in these conditions their specific problem was to find ways of massively employing rural manpower in capital construction both inside and outside agriculture. Although China's agriculture was using the most primitive techniques—the sickle, hoe, pick and shovel were the basic tools in the countryside— the accelerated cooperativization of the peasants carried out during

the mid-1950s, after a short period of widespread private ownership of land, was bound to release an appreciable amount of manpower. And the Chinese leaders did not stop with the formation of
agricultural producers' cooperatives (the Soviet kolkhozy); they
rapidly pressed further than the Russians toward the formation of
the so-called communes, a form of peasant organization intended
not only to increase the marketed share of grains but also to release
more manpower for labor other than field work. Paradoxically, no
matter how much labor was forthcoming, China's leaders always
seemed to need more: the Chinese viewed the full mobilization of
their rural manpower for a variety of labors, including the building
of an industrial structure, as their only means for industrialization.

At the start of its long-term plan in 1953, China seemed to follow the Soviet strategy of development as far as the pattern of its
investment was concerned. It allocated four-fifths of its investments
to heavy industry. Light industry and agriculture received low
shares of investment. But the Chinese planners, unlike the Russians
in the 1920s, asserted that (a) substantial unused capacities were
still available in light industry and in its auxiliary handicraft industry, and that the latter would be further expanded to meet the
peasants' demand for farm tools and consumer goods; and (b)
that appropriate measures for the development of agriculture had
to be taken immediately in order to avoid the danger of a gap between industrial and agricultural production. For this purpose the
planners stressed the need of improving farm techniques, and
organizing the peasant on a wider scale for capital construction in
agriculture, i.e., for irrigation, draining, water and soil conservation,
etc.

During the Chinese civil war Mao had emphasized the joint role
of the bloc of the working class, the peasantry, the urban small
bourgeoisie, and the national bourgeoisie; unlike the Russian Bolsheviks, he relied on the peasants' organization rather than on the
urban workers for conquering the towns and establishing the party
in power. In carrying out the first and most arduous phase of
China's industrialization, Mao and the Chinese Communists again
assigned to the peasants an active role. In June 1950 Mao declared:
"The majority of China's population are peasants. The revolution
was won with the help of the peasants, and the industrialization of
the country must again depend on their assistance for its success."
In 1956 he formulated the so-called policy of "walking on two

legs," stressing the need of a "correct balance" between the development of industry and agriculture and the development of heavy and light industry.[2] Again and again Chinese documents stressed the importance of the country's peasant masses both as suppliers of industry and as buyers of its products—the latter aspect seldom, if ever emphasized by the Russians after the rejection of Bukharin's approach to industrialization.

From the beginning of the Chinese First Five Year Plan, the organization of the peasantry and the mechanization of agriculture were viewed as following one another and as each consisting of two stages: cooperativization of the peasantry should grow into collectivization, and semi-mechanization (extensive use of horse-drawn or ox-drawn, double-wheel, twin-blade plows) should lead to large-scale mechanization (when the country would be able to produce tractors, pumps, oil and fertilizers). The form and scope of collectivization, however, took on new characteristics as the population pressure started to mount.

Between 1952 and 1957 China's urban population grew from 71 to 92 million people, 8 million of whom had come from the countryside. After 1957 the growth of the urban labor force exceeded 1 million per year, more than adequate to fulfill planned needs. In order to cut off the inflow of rural labor into the cities and sustain the growth of all sectors, the Chinese leadership decided to expand the use of rural labor in an unheard-of way. With the launching of the Second Five Year Plan, a new policy came into being: the so-called "big leap" policy, based on the use of peasant muscle to develop simultaneously large scale, medium scale, and small scale enterprise—in order to erect a widespread national iron and steel industry, to stimulate the spread of technological change from the developed coastal areas to the backward interior, and to provide for agriculture with meticulous care. The peasants were formed into a new kind of organization, the communes, whose role was to organize them simultaneously in agriculture, forestry, animal husbandry, fisheries and subsidiary occupations, including factories for repairing and making machines and for processing farm and subsidiary products.

By the beginning of the Second Five Year Plan, China's rural labor force was estimated at 260 million and was increasing by 4

[2] Yang Ling, "Agriculture: Foundation of the National Economy," *Peking Review* (October 18, 1960), p. 14 *et seq.*

million a year. Balancing human resources against planned needs on a wide front encompassing a variety of capital construction works in agriculture, the planners already foresaw in 1957—before the launching of the "Leap Forward"—increasing shortages of labor in the countryside. The ambitious "Leap Forward" and the ensuing overstraining of the available human resources, grave miscalculations in planning, poor incentives in the communes and a succession of poor harvest years forced the Chinese leadership to readjust their plans significantly by the end of the 1950s. This readjustment was done, for the most part, without abandoning their basic strategy, predicated on the utilization of rural manpower for a massive effort of capital construction in all directions.

The Second Five Year Plan, scheduled to be completed in 1962, was proclaimed fulfilled at the end of 1959. After two years of the "Leap Forward," China had increased its industrial plant to a significant degree. A widespread network of small and medium plants was established in a number of fields ranging from metallurgy to chemicals, machinery, instruments and farm tools. An integrated industrial system based on the production of iron, steel and machinery, and combining large, medium and small enterprises with a broad geographic distribution, took shape by the end of the 1950s.

Before 1958 capital construction in the steel industry had centered on the building and expansion of the capacity of three giant steel centers. After the "Leap Forward," by the end of 1959, some 1,400 iron and steel enterprises of different sizes, and another 3,000 small iron and steel units employing indigenous methods, had sprung up in all the provinces, municipalities and autonomous regions (except Tibet), enabling all the areas of the country to produce their own iron and steel. A considerable number of chemical plants based on local resources and operating for local needs started to produce fertilizers, paints and drugs, giving a substantial boost to the country's chemical production. Some 20,000 factories produced tools, building materials, and processed foods in the vast rural areas. The simultaneous development from east to west of the links of a chain of large, medium and small enterprises allowed the rapid introduction of new techniques and their integration by various indigenous methods. Products manufactured by modern plants were reproduced with new and old techniques in small plants operating with indigenous style machines.

In the process of this mass mobilization to expand capital construction in several competing directions, the Chinese leadership overreached itself. On the basis of scattered official data, it is estimated that in the late 1950s from 50 to 90 million peasants were drawn daily into the campaign for building "back-yard" iron and steel plants. Some 55 million women were drawn into the kitchens, nurseries and laundries of the communes. In agriculture the small irrigation projects occupied 77 million, and the deep plowing movement employed daily some 100 million peasants.

However, agricultural output fell far below the level required for sustaining such a vast mobilization of labor outside the agricultural sector. 1958 had been an excellent harvest year, the best since the Communist conquest of the mainland. But overestimating the result and believing that high yields were thenceforth definitely assured, the Chinese planners reduced the grain acreage. Then, severe calamities struck in 1959, 1960, and 1961, sending the output of grain below the 1957 level. The fall in agricultural product, coupled with an expansion in population by 40 million since 1958 and the stepped-up investment effort substantially reduced consumption levels after 1958. Industry was affected by the dwindling supplies of agricultural raw materials; the mass mobilization in all directions led to an enormous waste of resources and in certain cases to patently poor results. The 1958 steel campaign led to rapid expansion in capacity and in output of iron and steel, but in many instances the products obtained were of extremely low quality and of limited use, hardly justifying the immense amount of human and material resources drawn into this mass campaign all over the country.

Faced by a crisis of enormous magnitude, from 1961 on the Chinese leadership organized a vast retreat, more ample than the *New Course* attempted in Eastern Europe after 1953, following the first round of long-term plans. The Chinese leadership cut back the scope of capital construction, lowered the planned rate of industrial development and started to divert a far larger share of the output of the so-called sector I (producer goods industries) to light industries and agriculture (in the form of more tractors, drainage and irrigation equipment, chemical fertilizers, insecticides and transport means). The commune system was readjusted to allow a larger play of incentives in agriculture: members of the communes were allowed to produce vegetables and other crops on their personal plots, to raise pigs and poultry and to engage in handicraft production for personal use; rural trade fairs were reinstituted to provide additional supplies and a better circulation of goods in the countryside. Furthermore, the basis of agricultural levies was changed from predetermined quotas to actual production; and, notwithstanding shortages of foreign exchange, in December 1960 China shifted from imports of machinery and raw materials to imports of grain.

The need to retreat further than was first anticipated became imperative. By 1962 the party's spokesmen had to affirm that the general policy of developing the national economy with agriculture as the foundation and industry as the leading factor henceforth implied specifically that top priority would be given to the restoration and development of agricultural production, because the latter "still cannot meet the demands of national construction and the people's livelihood." [3] All references to a Third Five Year Plan were dropped, and no yearly plan data were released.

The Chinese leadership is thus marking time in its effort to push rapidly the expansion of certain heavy industrial branches. It has been forced to come to the aid of agriculture. But it has by no means abandoned its basic strategy of industrializing through mass mobilization of rural labor, nor has it revised its commitment to expand heavy industry. The *New Course* does not imply a *new strategy*.

The Chinese Communists shaped their strategy of industrialization not in open debates—as did the Russians in the mid-1920s—but in closed meetings of their top leadership. We cannot, therefore, ascertain the alternatives which were rejected. Scattered references to "impatience of leftists" and to "conservatism of rightists" indicate the existence of divergences and strains, but there is as yet no way of examining the proposals and views of the defeated.

In terms of the Soviet debates on strategy of development, the Chinese approach comes closest to Bukharin's preoccupation with both agricultural supply and peasant demand, his insistence that the countryside needs both agricultural machinery and manufactured goods of mass consumption, the products of both heavy and light industry. But the Chinese have acted to further industrial and agricultural output simultaneously in a way not clearly perceived in

[3] "On to New Victories," *Jenmin Jibao*, abridged in *Peking Review*, January 4, 1963, p. 7.

the 1920s. They opted for technical dualism, i.e., for simultaneous development of two industrial sectors, a modern, capital-intensive one and a small-scale, labor-intensive one. Conditions for implementing these plans were in preparation ever since the early 1950s.

Throughout the 1950s the Chinese hoped that the small-scale sector would be able to cope with the needs of agriculture for both implements and consumer goods, so that the largest part of the centralized investments could be fed massively into the modern sector. For a while the two emphases—on heavy industry and on multi-purpose developments in agriculture—were not in conflict, since the scarce inputs they claimed were in many respects dissimilar. But the Chinese could not seriously hope either for a continuous orderly advance on all sectors or for a lasting separation between the modern sector and the rest of the economy. A small-scale industry could not be expected to provide the machinery with which to mechanize agriculture.

Notwithstanding their over-ambitious goals, their ruthlessness, their uncoordinated advance in several competing directions, and their gross miscalculations in planning, the Chinese leaders' approach to economic development exercises today an unmistakable impact particularly in the densely populated, backward Asian or African areas. Their approach may be summed up as a reliance on the mobilization of vast masses of labor for capital construction work in heavy industry, light industry and multi-purpose projects in agriculture; a simultaneous expansion of a modern and a small-scale industrial sector; postponement of the mechanization of agriculture until the domestic industry is able to supply a substantial quantity of tractors and fuel. Despite their tight organizational set-up, the Chinese have probably not reached the rates of savings achieved by the Russians—or for that matter, more recently, by other Asian countries with special advantages such as Japan or Burma. The crux of the problem is the growth of population and the fact that the planners continue apparently to believe that on balance an expanding population is an asset for a country relying on a massive mobilization of its under-employed rural labor. The failure of agricultural output to grow rapidly may force the planners to become aware of the mounting pressures which the population growth puts on the country's slim savings from current output.

In spite of significant strides, China is still far removed from its goal, and is far behind the main industrial countries. While pushing vigorously ahead in the development of certain basic intermediate products, China still has to catch up with Great Britain, not to speak of the U.S.S.R. at the latter's level of 1940. Moreover, China is far behind in some crucial modern industries, such as nucleonics, electronics, and plastics. In agriculture, despite a turn toward mechanization, by the beginning of the 1960s China had only as many tractors as Russia had possessed in the early 1930s. But the Chinese leadership does have the ruthless power to rely on massive mobilization for carrying out the further industrialization of the country.

The Chinese profited from Soviet errors: they avoided pushing the peasants into collectives before an active psychological and organizational campaign had been undertaken. But they have committed new and no less disastrous errors of their own, particularly in terms of overstraining and physically exhausting their human resources, blunting agricultural incentives, overestimating the results achieved, and drawing erroneous sowing plans. However, the current New Course is not likely to cripple indefinitely their advance. Growth will necessarily continue to be both unstable and subject to periodic setbacks, because the Chinese economy is still strongly tied to a backward agriculture and now depends almost exclusively on its own national resources to carry out further industrialization.

SUGGESTED READING

Books:

Nove, Alec, *The Soviet Economy: An Introduction,* New York: Praeger, 1961.

Spulber, Nicolas, *The Soviet Economy: Structure, Principles, Problems,* New York: W. W. Norton & Company, Inc., 1962.

Wiles, Peter, *The Political Economy of Communism,* Cambridge: Harvard University Press, 1962.

Articles:

Jones, Edwin, "Peking's Economy," *Problems of Communism,* January-February 1963, pp. 17-25.

Mosely, Philip E., "Soviet Myths and Realities," *Foreign Affairs,* April 1961, pp. 341-354.

Perkins, D. H., "Centralization v. Decentralization in Mainland China and the Soviet Union," *Annals,* September 1963, pp. 70-80.

Schurmann, Franz, "Economic Policy and Political Power in Communist China," *Annals,* September 1963, pp. 49-69.

PART IV

World Communist Areas of Weakness

Introduction to Part IV

THIS PART OF OUR STUDY FINDS THAT THE PATTERNS OF WORLD Communist weakness are essentially threefold:

a) Irrational economic experiments have considerably weakened the foundations of Communist economies, particularly those of the Soviet Union and Communist China;

b) There is no provision under Communism for a peaceful transition of political power from one totalitarian leader to the next. Each case of "succession" becomes a struggle in which constitutional formalities are disregarded and the cleverest, most opportunistic or luckiest leadership-aspirant usually wins. In the October 1964 succession battle in the Soviet Union, Nikita Khrushchev was summarily and unexpectedly replaced by a new dual leadership. The mysterious circumstances of his removal, after approximately eight years (1956-1964) of single-handed rule, again emphasized the seemingly permanent characteristic of a totalitarian dictatorship: its inability, both in theoretical and practical terms, to formulate preliminary, but binding constitutional arrangements for an orderly transition of power. Despite Khrushchev's efforts, ably analyzed in Myron Rush's essay, it seemed impossible in the Soviet Union of 1964 to provide for a political machinery which could have brought about the selection of a future leader (or leaders) in a peaceful and systematic manner; and

c) A major area of world Communist weakness is highlighted by the fascinating story of abortive Communist revolutions. Of thirty-eight Communist revolutions, over a 47 year period, only fourteen have been successful while twenty-four have proved to be failures.

The three analytical articles explore the major facets of Communist crisis-situations.

10.   Marxism and the Soviet Economy*

by Joseph S. Berliner

Considerable debate is currently taking place with regard to the relevance of Marxian theory to the "real operating principles" of a socialist economy. Joseph Berliner's excellent essay reaches the forceful conclusion that classical Marxian theory has had very little influence upon the solution of Soviet economic problems. The author is convinced that the "relative economic under-development" of the countries which have first adopted the socialist system can be traced to this inevitable divergence between original theory (the economic "laws of socialism") and latter-day Communist practice.

A related point, stressed by the author, is the basic question as to just what areas of a "planned" economy should be planned. Is centralized planning of the type presently practiced in the Soviet Union an essential part of a socialist economy? He also raises the important issue whether such centralized planning is more or less difficult to operate in an advanced industrial economy, more specifically, in a capitalist "bourgeois democracy," such as the United States. It is probably the key conclusion of this thoughtful essay that the "convergence theory," pointing up similarities between the U.S.S.R. and the United States in their long-run development, makes sense in the field of large-scale industrial management. By patterns of comparison, the reader is informed that in the United States "the process of socialization has extended to the several millions of persons who hold directly or indirectly the shares of the corporations," while in socialist countries "socialization is already universal so that there is no need to take the trouble of issuing

* Reprinted, with editorial changes, from *Problems of Communism*, Vol. XIII, No. 5, Sept-Oct. 1964, pp. 1-11. Permission granted by the Editors of *Problems of Communism*, U.S. Information Agency, Washington, D.C.

shares of stock." At any rate, for both types of economies it is a clear-cut fact and a dominant industrial principle of the mid-nineteen sixties that effective management control remains firmly in the hands of small groups of people: their truly selective and self-perpetuating economic elites.

THERE IS A CURIOUS THING ABOUT THE WAY IN WHICH TREATISES on the development of the Soviet economy handle the subject of Marxism. One is likely to find a chapter on the "historical and ideological background" dealing with such matters as surplus value, the falling rate of profit, and the industrial reserve army. The chapter on prices will have a section on the labor theory of value and why it is all wrong. But once the author gets down to a serious discussion of Soviet economic organization and policy, little more will be said about Marxism.

Surely this is cause for some puzzlement. For where, if not in the field of Soviet economic organization and policy, ought one to look for application of Marxian economic theory? And yet not only is the search mostly barren, but the question is often raised whether Marxian theory has any relevance at all to the understanding of Soviet development. It is with this problem that the present study is concerned.

Let us suppose that a political party that identifies itself as Marxist comes to power in a capitalist country. To what extent is Marxist theory relevant to the interpretation of its policies? The term "relevant" may be understood in the normative and in the analytical sense, and, accordingly, the question may be rephrased as follows: First, to what extent does the party's knowledge of and commitment to Marxism determine its decisions regarding economic policy? And secondly, if we view the party itself as governed by the prevailing social forces, can we find in Marxism analytical tools that would help us explain and predict the party's behavior? This is the issue to which the last part of this article is devoted.

If we are to take the notion of Marxian "influence" seriously, we must at the outset reject the trivial meanings of the word—that is, the identification of "influence" with name-labels. We would learn little if we proceeded on the assumption that any "Marxist" party must by definition base its policy on Marxian principles. If the discussion is to be of any interest it must be possible for us to accept, at least at the outset, the hypothesis that a "Marxist" party may, in its concrete policies, reveal very little or no influence of Marxian theory. If Marx himself could declare that by certain standards he was not a Marxist, it is surely appropriate to raise a similar question today with respect to "Marxist" parties.

VOLUNTARISM AND MARXIAN THEORY

In the case of Marxian economics there is particularly good reason to suggest that the hypothesis not only merits consideration but may in fact be valid. There is the question, first of all, whether a theory consisting of a set of *objective* social laws can serve as the basis of policy for a party with the power to *make* and enforce decisions. Secondly, there is the question of whether a set of propositions defined in capitalist categories can be appropriate to a socialist system. And third, there is the matter of the relevance to an underdeveloped country of a theory that presupposes a high level of economic development.

Let us begin with examining the relevance of Marxian theory to a party that wields the power to allocate the nation's resources. Few would dispute the statement that, at a minimum, the policy *goals* of a Marxist party are influenced by its Marxist heritage. The nature of the influence, however, is socio-psychological, rather than scientific. A party that professes to be Marxist will accept as its own certain ends which are implicitly defined as good within the context of the Marxian system, such as social ownership of the means of production, industrialization, welfare of the masses, elimination of urban-rural differences, and the eventual withering away of the state.

Besides such broad goals, however, there are also certain specific policy issues, particularly those discussed by Marx in his *Critique of the Gotha Program,* which a Marxist party could be expected to endorse. But the more detailed the issue about which a decision has to be made, the greater the role of cultural and psychological factors and the smaller the role of Marxian theory. Should the land be nationalized? Should planning be centralized or decentralized? Should factories be under one-man management or worker control? How high should be the rate of investment? As the USSR Academy of Sciences textbook, *Political Economy* (3rd ed., p.

331), put it in discussing the nationalization of land, the matter must be decided

> in accordance with the concrete conditions of each country. In Russia, where the peasant traditions of private property in land were weaker than in the West, the Soviet state, in accordance with the needs of the peasant masses, carried out the total nationalization of land at the very beginning of the revolution. . . . In those countries where small-scale peasant property in land has existed for a long time and where the tradition of private property is therefore strong, the working class, on coming to power, does not carry out the total nationalization of land.

In other words, the effective basis on which the decision is made is not Marxian theory, but specific cultural and historical traditions.

The difficulty in employing Marxian theory as a guide to policy is due also to the fact that Marxism is a true "sociological" rather than a "psychological" theory. It purports to analyze the social consequences of specific social arrangements and individual forms of behavior. As a true social theory, it deals with the order "that arises as a result of individual action, but without being designed by any individual," as Friedrich von Hayek once put it. It deals with Engels' realm of necessity, the realm of the unconscious social consequences of conscious individual action. Like the theory of "perfect competition," the Marxian model applies to a society in which no decision-making unit possesses the power to influence the major economic variables, such as the price level, the rate of investment or the wage rate. And yet these are precisely the kinds of variables which a governing Marxist party must determine. What is required, therefore, is a theory that lends itself to normative use, one that can provide a basis for answering policy questions such as, "What should I do?" Marxism is rich in propositions explaining the behavior of economic variables that are determined by objective social processes, but is not concerned with the problem of finding optimal solutions and choosing among alternatives.

But, it may be argued, as a scientific theory Marxism does contain propositions of the form, "if X, then Y." It contains a model of an economic process which provides a basis for predicting the consequences of alternative courses of action—even though it does not provide a theoretical apparatus for evaluating the relative efficiency of the alternatives—and for a Marxist party this is surely a highly relevant feature of the theory. However, the economic process with which Marxian theory was concerned was that of a capitalist system. It is not at all self-evident that the same theory can deal with economic processes under socialist conditions. Our next question, therefore, is whether the capitalist and socialist economic systems have a sufficient number of common properties—whether, in other words, Marxian propositions about the former are relevant to decision-making in the latter.

SOCIALISM IN SEARCH OF MARXISM

No respectable social theory presumes to be so general as to apply under all conceivable conditions. Classical Marxian theory deals with the dynamics of a society conditioned by such phenomena as private ownership of the means of production, classes based on their relationship to private capital, certain socio-psychological characteristics that constitute part of the data of the system, and so on. The same may be said of the theoretical systems of Marshall, Schumpeter, Walras, or any social theorist. But the special property of Marxism (shared to some extent by Schumpeter's system) lies in the fact that as a dialectical theory of change it predicts the destruction of the conditions under which it operates. Hence it may be asked whether the theory is analytically relevant to the next stage, with its different conditions, when the dialectical process of historical change has been consummated, a Marxist party has come to power, and capitalist conditions have disappeared. How, in short, does Marxian theory apply to the post-capitalist stage?

One of the basic decisions the party must make is the choice of some substitute for the defunct market-system of coordinating the production of goods. However, in its search for new organizational forms it will find very little guidance in Marxian theory. Such views as Marx and Engels occasionally expressed about the organization of a socialist economy, whatever their merits, were not derived from their theory of capitalist development. The party's final decision will therefore be influenced by such factors as the cultural traditions of the nation, the level of social development, the psychological properties of the party leaders, the political conditions of the time—and not by any segment of systematic Marxian theory.

Another problem the party leadership will have to solve is the organizational form of the basic production units. Again the possible forms range from full one-man management to complete worker control. Methods of distribution of the social product, incentive systems, techniques for enforcing factory discipline, all provide a range of alternatives. Marxian writings contain much valuable material on the ways early capitalism handled these problems: one recalls the vivid historical treatment of capitalist methods to increase surplus value (so as to offset the tendency of the rate of profit to decline), as well as the description of capitalist techniques in recruiting and training rural labor for the discipline of factory work. But when Marx described the use of piece-rates as a device for increasing surplus value, he was obviously not advising a ruling Marxist party to adopt a similar system for the same purpose. Indeed, if the party does in fact adopt those techniques, it is not to be ascribed to the influence of Marxism as a scientific theory; it is simply a matter of the party selecting from the historical storehouse of available methods those that it regards as most suitable to its purposes.

Equally limited in relevance to post-capitalist institutions are the Marxian behavioral propositions. Marx may have been successful in predicting the response of a capitalist to a change in the price of a factor of production; but a socialist manager with different material interests and working in a different socio-economic environment cannot be presumed to react in the same way. On the other hand, the technical relations of production, such as the relationship between consumption and investment, are likely to be sufficiently similar under socialism and capitalism to permit the adaptation of Marxian analysis to socialist conditions.

In fact, this is one area in which Marxian theory was once highly relevant to the problems of Soviet economic policy. It may be remembered that Marx's analysis of the process of simple and expanded reproduction[1] was the point of departure in the vigorous discussion of Soviet growth policies during the 1920's. However, Marxian theory has little to say about how to make the most advantageous use of economic resources under conditions of scarcity,

[1] The model divides the economy into two sectors, one producing consumer goods and the other producing capital goods. Marx used the model to determine the relative amounts of consumer goods and capital goods that must be produced if the economy is to turn out the same output year after year (simple reproduction) or if it is to increase the output every year (expanded reproduction).

which is a crucial problem for any socialist economy. It is precisely in this area that non-Marxian economic theory has in recent years made the most significant advances, and a Marxist party that neglected these theoretical sources would hardly be doing justice to its responsibilities.

The third serious difficulty with the applicability of Marxian theory is the fact that Marxist parties have typically come to power in countries in which economic development had not reached the level predicted by Marxist theory. Marxism assigns to the epoch of capitalism the historic task of accumulating a massive stock of social capital and the training of the masses in the social behavior and experience appropriate to an industrial society. This very process leads at that same time to a sharpening of the prevailing social contradictions, and culminates in turn in a revolutionary change of the system itself. By the time the revolution occurs, an industrial society has come into being.

For a variety of reasons, history did not follow the path foretold by Marxian theory, and the party has repeatedly been confronted with the awkward task of completing the economic transformation that, according to the rules, should have been completed in the preceding epoch. Since the very existence of an underdeveloped socialist society is evidence of the imperfect predictive power of Marxism, it is perhaps not surprising that the Marxian theory has not been a fruitful source of theoretical guidance for the party's policies. Indeed, as will be argued presently, it is the very fact of economic underdevelopment, rather than Marxian theory, that helps explain the distinctive policies of the socialist countries.

THE ECONOMIC "LAWS" OF SOCIALISM

The observation was made at the outset of this article that economists writing about Soviet economic policy and institutions rarely find it necessary to refer to Marxian theory. In the pages above some of the reasons for this remarkable phenomenon were explored. It could be argued, however, that writers in the West, on whose works this conclusion was primarily based, neglect the role of Marxian theory because of their insufficient grasp of socialist economic practice. Let us therefore turn to a consideration of the treatment of Soviet experience by economists who have personally participated in the formation and interpretation of Soviet policy.

The 1959 edition of the textbook, *Political Economy,* published by the U.S.S.R. Academy of Sciences, serves as a good example. The book duly notes that with the establishment of socialism "the capitalist economic forms and their laws of development lost their governing power," and "new economic laws, appropriate to socialist conditions of production, arise and gradually expand the sphere of their influence" (p. 337). The authors then present the basic operating principles of the Soviet economy in the form of a set of socialist economic "laws." The new "laws," it is said, like the laws of capitalist development, are objective, in the sense that they "emerge and act independently of the will of men. . . . They cannot be created, transformed or abolished by the will of men" (p. 440). Let us examine the form and content of the "laws of socialist development" in order to discover their relation to Marxian theory.

The first and most general is the "Basic Economic Law of Socialism," the characteristic features of which are "the steady expansion and improvement of production on the basis of advanced technique with the aim of the fullest satisfaction of the steadily increasing requirements and the many-sided development of the members of society" (p. 450). It is difficult to construe this "law" as objective in the meaning defined above for, clearly, it cannot operate independently of the will of men as the genuinely Marxian laws of capitalist development do. The test of a law-like statement is the question whether the "law" under consideration was operative before being discovered. Marx's law of value *is* such a statement; commodities would presumably continue to exchange at their labor-values even if Marx had never discovered the law. But we cannot imagine the Soviet economy continuing to operate according to the "Basic Economic Law of Socialism" without that "law" having been discovered; for if the "law" holds at all, it is because the party sees to it that it does. Indeed, it is not the kind of law that one "discovers." It is rather like a law that one "legislates," which is to say that it is not a scientific or sociological law at all.

But if it is not a true law in the Marxian sense, it may perhaps be rescued as a proper law in the teleological, or functional, sense. A law of this kind defines the conditions that must be satisfied if a given system is to be maintained; it also describes the mechanism that restores the system when the latter is disturbed. Teleological laws in biology, for example, define the organ functionally, in terms of their contribution to the preservation of the organism of which they are a part. The heart does not *have* to beat, but if it fails to, the organism will cease being that organism. Similarly, the "Basic Economic Law of Socialism" could be construed as a teleological law: the party may, through error or will, act in ways contrary to the law, but if it does, either some social mechanism will correct its actions or the system will not survive. However, in order to defend this construction, it would have to be shown that there exist social forces which would tend to eliminate the erring party leadership or restore its policy to one that conforms to the law. Unfortunately, the history of socialism fails to provide any evidence for the existence of such forces.

It is probably more reasonable to follow the interpretation of those who view the "Basic Law of Socialism" not as a law at all, in either the causal or teleological sense, but rather as a statement of the economic goals that a Marxist party ought to pursue. As a statement of goals, it does indeed reflect the influence of Marxism. The more interesting question, however, is the extent to which Marxian theory provides guidance for the attainment of these goals, but here again little satisfaction is offered, for the goals in the "law" are stated so generally that there is little to be said about their implementation.

The second "objective law" is the "Law of the Planned, Proportional Development of the National Economy." This "law" requires that "the development of all branches of the economy be subordinated to a unified planned direction by the society, and that proportionality among all the parts and elements of the economy be preserved" (p. 416). Like the "Basic Law" discussed above, and unlike the genuine law-like formulations of Marxian theory, this "law" is also expressed in the form of a desideratum. It describes a state of affairs not as it necessarily is, but as it ought to be. It is doubtful that any candid observer of socialist experience would insist that disproportions cannot and do not occur under socialism. The statement that one ought to avoid them is not the kind of statement that we usually think of as law-like. Nor can this "law" be rescued by suggesting that it be interpreted as a teleological law. As long as the disproportions are kept within reasonable bounds, the failure to achieve proportionality is hardly likely to lead to the destruction of the system. Nor is there anything distinctively Marxian in the exhortation that there should be no waste.

There are several other economic "laws of socialism," but one in particular is worth considering, the famous "Law of Value." Here is a law taken directly from Marxian theory. That it is alleged to continue functioning under socialist conditions is due to a variety of reasons, chiefly because products continue to be commodities in the Marxian sense. The "Law of Value" under socialism requires that "the production and sale of commodities be carried out on the basis of the concomitant socially necessary labor outlays" (p. 517). In conformity with this "law," price policy should be oriented toward socially necessary labor, but it should permit certain departures for such purposes as bringing demand into line with available supplies.

Here is a clear case of the potential relevance of Marxian theory to socialist economic policy. In fact, however, Soviet economic policy makers have not found it expedient to fix prices according to the requirements of the "Law of Value," and for excellent reasons. As has sometimes been pointed out, whatever the virtues of a labor theory of value for the analysis of large aggregates, it contributes very little to the clarification of the problems of micro-economic theory, which happen to be very real problems in economic administration.

It is also quite apparent that while the "Law of Value" as defined in the Soviet textbook has substantially the same form as the Marxian law, its quality is quite different. In Marxian theory, the law of value is a genuine scientific law, formulating a relationship that occurs under capitalist conditions independently of the knowledge or will of men. But under socialism, the "law" is voluntaristic in origin. All it states is that it would be a good thing to exchange commodities according to their socially necessary labor inputs. Very likely Marx himself thought that there was something natural or moral, in any exchange economy, about valuing commodities in proportion to their socially necessary labor, although there is some dispute about this among Marxian scholars.[2] In any case, it is worth noting that even in this instance of direct relevance of

[2] Ronald L. Meek (*Studies in the Labor Theory of Value,* London, 1956, p. 260), quotes Marx's parenthetical remark about equating supply and demand under socialism. But he does not cite the fourth following sentence, in which Marx wrote that "The exchange, or sale, of commodities at their value is the rational way, the natural law of their equilibrium." *Capital* (Kerr edition), Vol. III, p. 221.

Marxian theory to socialist economic policy, the influence of the theory again asserts itself in the socio-psychological sense of an inherited attitude about what is good and just, rather than in the sense of a behavioral proposition or a social law.

In sum, the basic principles of Soviet economic policy, as interpreted by Soviet economists in their "economic laws of socialism," suggest that Marxian theory has had very little influence upon the solution of Soviet economic problems. The principal exceptions are Marx's growth model and his labor theory of value, which have had a substantial impact upon the thought, if not the practice, of socialist economics. It is becoming increasingly clear, however, that the labor theory of value has had rather unfortunate consequences for the Soviet economy since the fixation on labor time has inhibited the development of a more general theory of value that would take account of the scarcity of factors other than labor.

A THEORY OF CATCHING-UP

It is logically impossible, of course, to prove the absence of anything (how does one establish the non-existence of X?)—and that includes the absence of effective Marxian influence on Soviet economic practice. The evidence presented thus far should help to establish the *plausibility* of this proposition: to *prove* it beyond a shadow of a doubt would clearly be impossible. However, if it is true, as it is here alleged, that Marxian theory does not supply the basis of the real operating principles of the socialist economy, it may be useful to ask what in fact does? One may hope to support the case for the innocence of one man by establishing the guilt of another.

This brings us to a factor noted earlier, namely, the relative economic underdevelopment of the first countries to adopt the socialist system. It is the thesis of this article that the now widely-used slogan of "overtaking and surpassing" the advanced capitalist countries is in fact the most fruitful basis available for explaining the actual policy of socialist economic development. To present the argument most sharply, let us imagine a socialist party that came to power in a relatively underdeveloped country. Suppose the party is socialist in the minimal sense of being committed to the social ownership of the means of production as an economically and ethically superior form of social organization, but that it is otherwise totally ignorant of the theoretical structure of Marxism. Suppose, secondly, that it is motivated by the wish to overtake and surpass the leading capitalist countries in as short a period as possible.[3] And finally, suppose that the party is determined to maintain itself in power under all circumstances in order to attain its objectives. In the opinion of this author, the party would very likely introduce all the policies and forms of economic organization that have actually characterized Soviet economic development, and with no recourse at all to Marxian theory.

First, a long tradition of economic theory from at least Adam Smith on points to the accumulation of capital as the crucial factor determining the differences in the wealth of nations. We may therefore expect that our socialist party would strive to expand the capital stock as rapidly as possible and maintain a high rate of investment.

Second, the source of accumulation may be, in part, foreign lending. If this should not be available, capital accumulation would have to come exclusively from domestic savings. Since the level of living is low and the voluntary rate of savings is likely to be correspondingly low, some form of compulsion will have to be introduced to achieve the desired rate of saving. This can take the form either of inflationary financing, or of direct controls on the volume of consumption.

Third, since the population is overwhelmingly agricultural, the mass of savings must be sought in the agricultural sector. Hence a form of agricultural organization must be introduced that would generate a maximally large agricultural surplus. If the party's ideological commitment to social ownership is relaxed and pragmatic, the party may select some combination of small-scale private and voluntary cooperative agriculture, relying on peasant incentives to generate the increased production and marketings. If the dedication to social ownership is total and uncompromising, the party will introduce some combination of state-operated and collective agriculture, trusting that its political control over distribution will offset any disincentives in production. The decision will be heavily

[3] Either in order to defend the country against a "hostile capitalist world" or in order to enhance the "demonstration effect" of a successful socialist system. The conclusions will differ somewhat according to whether the one or the other motive is primary.

influenced by historical and cultural traditions, as the *Political Economy* textbook notes.

Fourth, the abolition of private ownership of the means of production and of the profit incentive requires that a substitute system of economic organization be introduced; the socialist managers of economic institutions must be provided with some basis for making production and investment decisions. The possibilities of alternative forms of economic administration vary widely. At one extreme, a form of decentralized market socialism may be adopted in which the state limits its participation to such functions as price setting and supervision, while managers make the production decisions according to some pre-established rules. At the other extreme, the state may concentrate all decision-making at the center and simply require the managers to fulfill the plans. Again the choice will depend heavily upon the cultural traditions of the country. If the tradition is one of centuries of strong central government, and if the supply of technically expert and politically reliable managers is small, the party is likely to be attracted to the centralized form. Furthermore, the attraction of centralization will increase in proportion to the economic and political pressures required to achieve the predetermined rate of savings. In other words, the smaller the rate of voluntary savings in proportion to planned savings, the more will the economic system gravitate toward centralized forms.

Fifth, having opted for central planning, the party must work out a set of rules to govern the procedure. The most rudimentary requirement of such a system—a requirement readily apparent even to those untutored in theory—is that the planned production of each commodity must be at least equal to the planned uses of that commodity for consumption or for further production. (The party may, if it wishes, refer to this requirement as the "law of the planned, proportional development of the national economy.") But if it wanted to look for theoretical sources, it would find an abundance available, starting with François Quesnay (1694-1774), the celebrated physiocrat who first analyzed the economy in terms of the flows of commodities among the major production sectors. Another, even more important source of theoretical guidance could be Leon Walras (1837-1910), one of the founders of the "marginal utility" school, whose "general equilibrium" system was the inspiration for the modern "input-output" analysis of Wassily Leontief. Walras would not only remind the party of the obvious need for a balanced plan—which the Soviets strive to satisfy with their method of "material balances"—but, more important, he would also call the planners' attention to the fact that many different balanced plans are possible, and that certain conditions must be satisfied if the best, or "optimal," plan is to be carefully selected. It is only in the last half-dozen years that the Soviet planning system has advanced beyond the naive stage of simple material balances.

Sixth, in the absence of the private-profit motive, some devices must be found for motivating managers to fulfill the planned targets and encouraging workers to exert themselves in their work and to improve their skills. A non-Marxist socialist party, uninstructed in the lessons of Marx's *Critique of the Gotha Program,* may resist introducing personal material incentives similar to those of individualistic capitalist institutions, but experimentation with other forms will quickly reveal that there is no other choice, at least for the time being. The commitment to a high rate of growth will exact the most effective incentive available.

The catalogue could be extended, but enough has been said to indicate the substance of the thesis here expounded: The influence of Marxian economics on the actual course of socialist economic policy may be tested by considering the probable behavior of a socialist government that has no knowledge of Marxism. It is reasonable to believe that such an imaginary regime would adopt policies similar to those actually pursued by existing socialist states. In sum, on the principle of Occam's razor, Marxian theory is redundant in interpreting the economic policy of these states.

One might pursue the argument further by considering the opposite case. Imagine a society with a highly developed economy in which power has been seized by a Marxist party. In other words, imagine that the historical dialectic had actually followed the course which Marxian theory predicts; namely, that the socialist revolution would appear first in the most advanced capitalist countries. It could surely be shown that in such a case the pattern of socialist economic (and perhaps social and political) development would be quite different from that which actually occurred. If this is so, then it follows that the truly distinctive explanatory factor in social-ist economic policy is not Marxism but the fact of economic under-development.

A MARXIAN INTERPRETATION OF THE SOVIET ECONOMY

So much for the usefulness of Marxian theory to a socialist party in a position of power. But what of its usefulness when applied as an analytical tool by those wishing to understand the course of economic policy in a socialist country?

As the point of departure, let us take Marx's and Engels' for-mulation of the sociology of knowledge. In their view it is the pre-vailing social situation that determines men's consciousness. This formulation of the problem, just like their labor theory of value, is based on an analysis of social systems characterized by property-based classes. And as in the case of Marx's theory of value, the question may be raised whether the Marxian theory of knowledge is sufficiently general to be applicable to other types of social systems.

Marx and Engels determined a person's class identification by his relationship to the means of production—as owner or non-owner. From a modern, more general sociological point of view, such a criterion is but one of many that may be used in the iden-tification of social groups. Thus in addition to biological criteria such as sex and age, there are other useful social criteria such as marital status, education, occupation, religion, and so on. Marx and Engels, of course, addressed themselves specifically to the relationship between consciousness and economic class—this on the theory that the latter factor is the unique or dominating deter-minant of ideas—and it would be rare to find a total denial of this proposition even today. Most of the current work in social psy-chology is devoted to the discovery of the ways in which member-ship in a group of any kind influences ideas, as well as how mem-bership in specific groups determines particular ideas. There is no doubt that if one wished to predict the responses of a sample of people to a variety of attitudinal questions, knowledge of their economic class would be a most useful indicator. At the same time, if one could incorporate into the equation additional data such as age, sex, national origin, religious identification, level of education, etc., the prospects for successful prediction would very much increase. Moreover, the relative importance of each of the group identifications would be different for different types of attitude. In certain communities in the United States, for example, knowledge of a person's religion may be more useful for predicting his political affiliation than knowledge of his economic status.

For the analysis of a capitalist society, which was Marx's main concern, economic-class identification is indubitably a significant determinant of the range of ideas and attitudes associated with political and economic policy. But what about a socialist society? What happens when private ownership of the means of production is abolished so that the economic-class distinction in the Marxian sense is eliminated? Under a narrow construction of Marx's meaning, the problem of the sociology of knowledge would vanish. But under a broader socio-psychological interpretation, it would mean that, although that particular class distinction had been eliminated, the new class distinctions which any complex society must maintain would continue to generate differences in men's consciousness.

It is indeed not difficult to discover a set of social categories under socialism that correspond to the categories found by Marx in capitalist society. The basic categories are still classes, defined by their relationship to the means of production. If we construe that relationship not in its historically-specific form of "legal ownership" of the means of production, but in the more general form of "effective control" over the means of production, then we have at hand the framework for a thoroughly Marxian analysis of the historic stage of socialism.

But a new stage in history and a new alignment of classes must be preceded by a major change in the mode of production. And there has in fact occurred a massive change of this sort since the days of Marx: it is the revolution that has taken place during the last half-century in the means of transportation and communication, and the ensuing revolution in industrial and social organization. Developments in radio, television, aviation, and automation have contributed to the possibilities of controlling human behavior on a scale and with an intensity undreamed of a century ago. Under the impact of this massive change, the class organization of the old society has given way to new forms, specific to the new material relations. To the ancient social-relationship categories of master and slave, patrician and plebeian, lord and serf, capitalist and worker, there has now been added the historically new relationship of the party and the masses. Under capitalism, effective control over the means of production by the capitalists takes the legal form of "private ownership"; under socialism, effective control over the means of production by the party takes the legal form of "public ownership." Bourgeois democracy, in the Marxist view, is the ideological form under which the capitalists disguise the fact of the class nature of the old society and justify the alienation of the workers from the product of their labor. "Democratic centralism," it may be said, is the ideological form under which the party disguises the class nature of the new society, and justifies the alienation of the masses from the product of their labor.

National differences, of course, continue to persist. In the United States, the process of socialization has extended to the several million persons who hold directly or indirectly the shares of the corporations; labor union pension funds alone now amount to billions of dollars, mostly invested in corporate stock. In the socialist countries, socialization is already universal so that there is no need to take the trouble of issuing shares of stock. In both instances, however, ownership is so thoroughly diffused that effective management control remains firmly in the hands of small groups of people.

OPTIMIZATION VERSUS DIALECTICS

But differences aside, the organizational revolution has led to an interesting convergence of development, namely, the emergence in both societies of a class of people who manage the resources of the nation, whose personal success depends upon the skill with which they manage their enterprises, and who are not themselves the lawful owners of the resources placed at their disposal. There is considerable evidence that the common class status of the managerial groups has led to a common form of consciousness, as manifested in various similarities of behavior exhibited under similar circumstances. There is a common consciousness of technical superiority, and resentment at dictation from the bureaucrats in Washington or Moscow who don't really understand local conditions, who never had to "meet a payroll," and who nevertheless presume to tell the managers how to run a business. There is the drive for personal success and the manipulation of the legal rules of the game in behalf of the special interests of one's own organizational unit. In short, there is enough evidence to suggest that the common features of industrialization and large-scale organization generate a significant degree of commonality in the attitudes and behavior of the managers. Thus the Marxian proposition that man's social environment determines his consciousness emerges as a useful tool of analysis of socialist economic organization.

It may be appropriate to conclude with a note on the relationship between men's interests and their perceptions of reality. One of the post-Marxian propositions of the sociology of knowledge is that men whose material interests are vested in stability and security incline toward a pluralistic view of social causation, whereas those whose material interests are vested in revolution and social destruction tend to view social causation monistically. The leaders of a socialist society who have made their revolution should therefore be expected to view the process of social change differently from the way it was viewed by Marx and the revolutionary generation. With the revolution accomplished, the task ahead is one of introducing stability and promoting economic growth. One is still committed to change, but it is change that is characterized by quantitative magnitudes, with no evident qualitative change (or revolution) at the end of the process. One views change as a linear rather than a dialectical process.

It may be suggested in this connection that economists are the most likely group to lead the way toward perceiving change as a linear rather than a dialectical process. This is so because of the central role played in economic theory by the concept of optimization. The appropriate size of the firm or rate of output is some optimal magnitude which in general is rather less than the maximum possible. One substitutes the scarcer factor for the more abundant not to the extreme point of complete replacement of one by the other, but to some intermediate point that has the characteristics of the optimal combination.

Now the practice of solving problems by the search for optima is in sharp contrast to the practice of the dialectician who views the process of social change as one working toward some maximal consummation. Consider, for instance, how he views the class struggle: as something that must be pushed to the maximum, for only thus does the "qualitative" revolutionary change occur. But what if the final degree of desired change brings us to a point where the end state differs from the beginning quantitatively only? If the heating of water from 99 to 100 degrees will produce steam, there may be compelling advantages in applying the final degree of heat. But if the change from 99 percent collectivization to 100 percent entails a consequence no different than the change from 98 percent to 99 percent or from 68 percent to 69 percent, the urgency in pressing the process to its culmination is much less.

Clearly then, the policy problems of a socialist nation with its revolution behind it involve the latter type of process more generally than the former. What proportion of real personal incomes should take the form of free goods? How far should decentralization of planning and administration proceed? To what extent should personal material incentives be substituted for moral incentives? How long should a usable but obsolete machine continue in service? People who view the world dialectically tend to value maximal solutions. In the end personal material incentives must give way entirely to moral incentives. Temporarily we may have to limit the free distribution to goods, but in the end we should promote the process of free distribution from 99 percent to the ultimate 100 percent.

However, the sociology of knowledge suggests that with the change from an interest in revolution to an interest in stability, these dialectical views vanish and in their place comes an optimizing view. As Lenin would say, life itself forces the change. The first goods freely distributed, such as water or local transportation, involve very few problems. The next ten percent involve somewhat higher social costs, as heralded by the case of the collective farmer who bought low-priced bread to feed to his hogs. Each additional percentage of freely distributed goods adds to the problems and the costs, particularly as one approaches goods with larger income elasticity. Eventually someone must raise the question of whether the gains from an additional percentage of freely distributed goods are greater than the mounting social costs; whether, in other words, there is not some optimal combination of free distribution and distribution by purchase. And similarly with an optimal level of decentralization, an optimal combination of material and moral incentives, perhaps an optimal combination of private and state enterprises in agriculture and in trade and possibly also in small-scale industry.

Thus, it is reasonable to expect that Marxian economics, reflecting the consciousness of a revolutionary society, should give way to economic theories of efficient resource allocation, reflecting the consciousness of stabilized society. The renewed interest in profit as an indicator of managerial success, the search for new bases of price formation, the turn to mathematical models of economic planning and similar recent developments in Soviet economic theory are therefore fully understandable in terms of the Marxian proposition that changes in the social situation entail changes in men's consciousness.

SUGGESTED READING

Books:

Baykov, Alexander, *Development of the Soviet Economic System,* New York: Macmillan, 1947.

Berliner, Joseph S., *Factory and Manager in the USSR,* Cambridge: Harvard University Press, 1957.

Brzezinski, Zbigniew, and Samuel P. Huntington, *Political Power: USA/USSR,* New York: The Viking Press, 1964.

Campbell, Robert W., *Soviet Economic Power,* Cambridge: Houghton Mifflin Company, 1960.

Granick, David, *The Red Executive,* Garden City, New York: Doubleday and Company, 1960.

Nove, Alec, *The Soviet Economy,* New York: Norton, 1962.

Nove, Alec, *Soviet Strategy for Economic Growth,* Bloomington: University of Indiana Press, 1964.

Schwartz, Harry, *Russia's Soviet Economy,* Englewood Cliffs, N.J.: Prentice-Hall, 1959.

Articles:

Crankshaw, Edward, "Neither Communism Nor Capitalism," *The New York Times Magazine,* October 6, 1963, pp. 36-37 *et seq.*

Goldman, M. I., "Economic Controversy in the Soviet Union," *Foreign Affairs,* April 1963, pp. 498-512.

Schaeffer, Harry G., "What Price Economic Reforms?", *Problems of Communism,* May-June 1963, pp. 18-26.

Smolinski, Leon and Peter Wiles, "The Soviet Planning Pendulum," *Problems of Communism,* November-December 1963, pp. 21-33.

11. Succession and Institutions in the Soviet Union*

by Myron Rush

The succession problem has for centuries preoccupied politicians and political observers alike in many large and small countries. Both democracies and dictatorships have their own peculiar succession crises, as the dramatic events of November 22, 1963 and October 14, 1964 have recently illustrated. The former date marked the ghastly murder of President John F. Kennedy and the transition of power, exciting in terms of the fateful developments of the day but constitutionally speaking smooth and dignified, while the latter denoted the swift and complete removal of Nikita Khrushchev from the dominant position in Soviet politics. Democracy, as one expert noted, has the virtue of accepting most forthrightly man's frailty and his fallibility in connection with the problem of succession to political leadership. Indeed, democratic forms of government can be viewed in this context as rule "not just of the majority, but of successive majorities for limited periods of time." [1]

In dictatorships, however, the succession issue looms large and central at all times, divorced from a majority of public opinion and unregulated in advance either in constitutional form or in political substance. Each round in leadership succession thus provokes crises, convulsions and usually a bitter and lengthy infighting among those members of the inner elite who feel they have a justified monopoly-claim to succeed the fallen leader. In Communist

* Reprinted, with editorial changes, from the *Journal of International Affairs,* Vol. XVIII, No. 1, Spring 1964, pp. 67-75. Permission granted by the editors of the *Journal,* Columbia University, New York.

[1] Professor Dankwart A. Rustow in his excellent article, "Succession in the Twentieth Century," in the *Journal of International Affairs,* Vol. XVIII. No. 1, Spring 1964, pp. 104-113, especially p. 113.

states this struggle has been particularly sharp and deadly. In the Soviet Union, Lenin's and Stalin's deaths have caused several years of instability, intense rivalries and finally a situation from which there emerged a single dictator with unlimited totalitarian powers.

Dictatorial forms of government, ranging from the "partial" dictatorships of the newly developing countries to those which have fashioned full-fledged totalitarian forms of rule, have been notoriously incapable of setting up formalized procedures ensuring an orderly and systematic transition of power for the next round of leadership. Although, as Myron Rush states in the following essay, Nikita Khrushchev had tried hard to provide for an orderly succession "by making the necessary institutional and personnel dispositions in advance," his pre-arrangements were arbitrarily swept away by the Central Committee of his Party in the course of the events of mid-October 1964. The dual leadership then decided upon and shared by Brezhnev and Kosygin, further compounded the leadership problems of the U.S.S.R. since it appeared, from its inception, as a temporary, innocuous and wholly transitional form of "collective leadership" which had been tried twice before (after both Lenin and Stalin) and which had failed every time.

Another one of Myron Rush's major conclusions is that if the basic institutions of the Soviet dictatorship will become involved in the factional struggle among future leadership aspirants, then a substantial weakening of the entire fabric of the Soviet political system may well be expected. Thus the author foresees succession crises in Communist societies as evolving along two parallel levels —the institutional and the personnel levels. The former, to borrow a Marxist-Leninist phrase, is the substructure of an organized political system: if it is not going to be disturbed in a substantial manner, then the political passing of the dictator will not inevitably produce a major crisis in the leadership. The latter is the superstructure of the Soviet dictatorship: the regime will have to face major and unexpected personnel changes first in the form of an immediately post-Khrushchev "collective leadership," and later in the well-established pattern of a single "total" dictator in the more commonly accepted meaning of the term.

For observant political scientists two significant conclusions emerge from the rapid and unexpected political liquidation of Nikita Khrushchev. One is the ineluctable fact that neither Brezhnev nor Kosygin are likely to occupy important seats of power for any length of time if past patterns prevail. As transitional and expedient choices, appearing in the midst of a crisis-situation, they are bound to fade away sooner or later. The second point to stress is the time factor which seems to prevail in connection with every Soviet succession crisis and will undoubtedly assert itself in the post-Khrushchev leadership era.

The time-span required to reduce the group pattern (or collective leadership) to one-man direction (total dictatorship) was about the same in both the Leninist and Stalinist succession crises. It took Khrushchev approximately five years, from Stalin's death in 1953 until 1958, to consolidate his hold over the Communist Party of the Soviet Union and the government of the U.S.S.R. A generation earlier, it had taken Stalin from Lenin's death in 1924 until 1929 to get rid of his major opponents. The five-year cycle of history between one dictator's disappearance and the full-fledged emergence of the next, may well repeat itself at the present time, after Nikita Khrushchev's political demise.

Speaking of the time factor, it is also worth noting that Stalin was 50 years old when he had finally won the struggle for power, while Khrushchev was 64 by the time he successfully completed his ascent to the top political position. Khrushchev's years of rule were thus destined to be considerably shorter than were Joseph Stalin's, and the Soviet political system is currently enmeshed in another disturbing power- and succession-crisis.

This crisis is not simplified or brought closer to a solution by the fact that practically the entire Soviet elite is composed of men in their fifties and sixties who will thus rule for only a few years, to be succeeded in turn by a much younger, subsequent generation. In countries where an older group wields political power (among the Communist countries this is the case in China, Yugoslavia and the U.S.S.R.), the habitual succession crises are compounded in their seriousness by the need for the sudden and wholesale replacement of one team by another group of political leaders. In such situations collective struggles for succession are bound to occur leading first to collective (or group) leadership, as noted above, and producing finally that single, much younger, and more charismatic leader who can be expected to resolve the succession crisis in a decisive manner.

Myron Rush has prophetically raised the right question, "Was there a Khrushchev Succession Problem?", in his excellent article. Indeed, there has been one—and the dramatic semi-secret events which have occurred in the Kremlin in late 1964 have not immediately contributed to a successful settlement.

THE PROBLEM OF SUCCESSION TO STALIN ENGAGED THE INTEREST of many observers almost from the beginning of the Cold War in the aftermath of Allied victory in 1945. Now the U.S.S.R. is studied far more than in those years, but not a great deal of attention has been given to the Khrushchev succession. Yet, it is as important as the succession to Stalin and could even produce far greater political effects. There are several reasons why the Khrushchev succession problem has been relatively depreciated.

Stalin's person amply filled the Soviet political scene when he ruled, and this was recognized by almost all qualified observers. On occasion, Presidents Truman and Eisenhower expressed the view that the true source of what was evil in Soviet foreign policy was to be sought not in Stalin but in the men around him, but this was certainly an aberration. Actually, Stalin so overshadowed his lieutenants that the West knew relatively little of their political character until after his death, and they may have been unsure of it themselves. With Khrushchev it was different. The extent of the power he held has been disputed among experts for more than six years, ever since his chief opponents were eliminated from the leadership in 1957. A large group of Western observers remain convinced that Khrushchev was but a spokesman for a collective leadership; he had to execute its will in the most important matters and was not a dictator in his own right. If his place in the leadership was so modest, then vacating it seemed unlikely to produce great consequences.

There is another reason why the significance of the Khrushchev succession has been depreciated. By the time Stalin died, he had brought rule by terror close to the limits of its possibilities. Despite his great accomplishments, changes were now required to overcome the bureaucratic inertia and personal alienation that were inevitable results of his system of rule. This was widely recognized in the West, and it was confirmed by the initial policies of his heirs. While they disagreed as to the character and extent of the changes required, they all accepted the need for radical change. In the decade since Stalin's death, his system of rule has been significantly altered, although not in the decisive respects. While many Western observers are disappointed that the Stalin succession did not lead to far greater and more beneficent changes in the Soviet political system, it is widely believed that the acute social and political problems that Stalin bequeathed to his heirs have been resolved. The Soviet political system has been stabilized, it is thought, and the Khrushchev succession is not likely to upset it.

In the realm of foreign policy, there has been a similar accommodation to the needs of the time. While Stalin continued to adhere to outmoded doctrines of the regime's early years, his heirs have come to terms with the Nuclear Age.

The elements of this argument contain much that is true, but the conclusion to which the argument leads is in error. In what follows, an attempt will be made to establish the following assertions, which controvert the above argument for depreciating the importance of the Khrushchev succession.

First, in the Soviet political system, the passing of the dictator inevitably produces a crisis in the leadership.

Second, since Khrushchev was a dictator in the commonly accepted meaning of the term, the regime is faced with a serious problem in the Khrushchev succession.

Third, the changes in Soviet politics and in Soviet society effected by Stalin's heirs have produced an equilibrium, it is true, but it is an unstable equilibrium. Soviet society is unlikely to preserve the basic features of its post-Stalin phase. This is not to say that progress in domestic liberalization is inevitable; such progress, or its opposite, will depend in significant measure on the outcome of the Khrushchev succession crisis. Similarly, the U.S.S.R. is confronted with great issues in international affairs, and its foreign policies are subject to radical change.

INEVITABILITY OF SUCCESSION CRISES

The chief reason why succession is a fundamental problem for the Soviet regime is that there is no established, recognized center of decision-making in the Soviet system. Supreme authority cannot be said to inhere in either the Government's Council of Ministers or in the Party's Central Committee. At times the small *Secretariat* of the Central Committee has been sovereign; at other times it has been the larger and more authoritative *Presidium*. Most of the time the power of decision has been in the hands of a dictator, although dictatorial power inheres in no particular office or title: it is unprovided for in the fundamental question of Soviet politics. Uncertainty as to the supreme authority is, of course, greatly alleviated when a dictator seizes effective power and makes himself the decisive authority, as Lenin, Stalin and Khrushchev have done. On the other hand, the question of supreme authority becomes acute in the absence of an established dictator; that is, during the succession crisis.

Since supreme authority inheres in no office or title, no rule for establishing the legitimacy of a successor or successors is possible in the Soviet system. To avoid a crisis, the transfer of power must be effected by the fiat of the dictator or of some collective leadership which might establish itself after the dictator's demise. But a dictator cannot transfer substantial powers to a designated heir without impairing his own, and it is difficult if not impossible in Soviet conditions for a collective leadership to seize power and exercise it effectively. In the U.S.S.R., then, the dictator or ruling group gains supremacy by arrogating power, not by an orderly transfer of legitimate authority. It is hard to see how such great powers can be seized against the certain opposition of personal rivals and hostile groups without producing a political crisis.

WAS THERE A KHRUSHCHEV SUCCESSION PROBLEM?

The question arises, however, whether Khrushchev's powers were so great that his political demise is upsetting the relative stability of the leadership and creating a major succession crisis. The question of Khrushchev's powers must be considered at some length, for it has a decisive bearing on the succession and is a subject of dispute in the West. As noted above, the view is widespread that Khrushchev was not a dictator but was only the most powerful figure in a collective leadership and held his power only at the sufferance of his colleagues.

The chief difficulty in this view is that one cannot readily identify the group of colleagues or oligarchical body to whom Khrushchev was supposed to be responsible. Such a body would need a stable membership. New members would have to be chosen by co-option, but at a slow rate so as not to dilute or undermine the power of the original members. Actually, the Party Presidium *was* such an oligarchy, or "collective leadership," in the years 1953-1957. Of the ten men who made up the Presidium after Stalin's death, the oligarchy purged one, Beria, who was a threat to the other members by reason of his control over the political police, and added two (Suslov and Kirichenko). The oligarchy was fundamentally unstable, however, being a transitional form of rule during the Stalin succession crisis, and was overthrown by Khrushchev in 1957. Of its members, besides Khrushchev, only Suslov and Mikoyan still remained at the time of Khrushchev's fall. There has been a considerable turnover even of new members during the last half dozen years. Khrushchev's chosen lieutenants had been brought into it, but some were later removed when they incurred his displeasure, either by failing to display the requisite zeal and competence or by overreaching the limits of their assigned powers.

As Khrushchev's former favorites were removed, new ones replaced them. After 1960, Podgorny, Polyansky, Voronov, Kirilenko and Kosygin were added to the Presidium. All but Kosygin were in relatively minor posts when Khrushchev became dictator in 1957, and there is no evidence that any of these five promotions originated other than with him. The October 1964 Presidium consisted— besides these post-1957 additions and Khrushchev himself—of a superannuated hack (Shvernik), two powerful young figures who were elected in 1957 (Kozlov and Brezhnev) and the above-mentioned holdovers, Mikoyan and Suslov. It is difficult to suppose that any of these men, or some combination of them, have controlled the composition of the Presidium during the past half dozen years. They, too, seem to have owed their positions and authority to Khrushchev.

While oligarchy requires stability in the ruling body, the composition of the Secretariat of the Central Committee, like that of the Presidium to which it is supposedly subordinate, has been markedly unstable. The eight-man Secretariat elected in June 1957 had grown to ten members by the end of 1959, but only three of the ten were still Secretaries in October 1964: Khrushchev, Brezhnev, who was removed from the Secretariat in 1960, but was subsequently restored to it after a three-year absence, and Suslov. After May 1960, when Khrushchev sharply reduced the size of the Secretariat by depriving members of the Bureau for the Russian RSFSR of their seats in it, he alone sat in both the Secretariat and the Bureau.

What of the Central Committee itself? Is it not possible that this body of several hundred men is the real ruler of Russia, the oligarchy on which the Presidium, the Secretariat, the Bureau, and even the First Secretary depend for their power? It is hard to believe this in view of Khrushchev's dictatorial demeanor at its meetings. In any case, the Central Committee, which is charged with directing all work of the Party between Congresses, is as much in flux as the executive bodies that it formally elects. Around half of the members and candidates elected following the Twentieth Party Congress (1956) were newcomers, as were roughly half of the next Central Committee elected in 1961. Moreover, the new Central Committee's capacity to deliberate was reduced by making it almost half again as large as its predecessor.

We are forced to conclude that none of these bodies constitutes the oligarchy to whom Khrushchev was supposed to be subject. They evidently were all subject to Khrushchev, being constituted according to his will. That Khrushchev was not accountable to the men around him for his conduct of affairs appeared most clearly from the fact that his power had been unimpaired by the failure of many of his chief policies. Khrushchev's blunders in agriculture, in relations with Communist China and Albania, in the matter of West Berlin, in the effort to further economic integration in East Europe—all of these visible setbacks have not shaken his power.*

Quite apart from the difficulty in identifying the organ or faction which was supposed to control Khrushchev, there was much positive evidence of his sovereign power. He alone was a member of all the chief organs of dictatorship: (1) the Presidium, (2) Secretariat,

---

* The reader must keep in mind that Myron Rush wrote this article in the Spring of 1964. It is to the author's credit that even one day prior to Khrushchev's forcible and mysterious removal in mid-October 1964, his statement to the effect that the Soviet leader's failures and numerous blunders could not shake his enormous power, appeared to be both incontrovertibly true and distinctly factual. The amazing events surrounding Khrushchev's retirement on October 14, 1964, have not yet been explained or fully justified by the post-Khrushchev Soviet leadership. Hence Rush's sophisticated analysis was neither disrupted nor brought up to date by the Editor. All thoughtful students of world Communism must be continuously aware of the pitfalls of long-range predictions in the exceptionally murky field of Soviet politics.

(3) Bureau (for the Russian Republic) of the Central Committee and (4) the Council of Ministers. No other leader used to sit on more than two of these bodies. He had the leading posts in the Party, the Government, and the army, having been First Secretary of the Central Committee, Chairman of the Council of Ministers and Supreme Commander-in-Chief of the Armed Forces.

Khrushchev legislated important reforms of the Soviet system. He succeeded in enacting the Party's new program, the first in over forty years, which formally establishes the pattern and direction of Soviet development for the next two decades, and is held up as a model for any nation that wishes to realize Communism. While the program may well be revised or abandoned as a result of Khrushchev's demise, until then it is fundamental. Khrushchev engaged extensively in personal diplomacy with the heads of Western Governments as well as with those of the newly emergent nations of Africa. He spoke for the U.S.S.R. both at the United Nations and at assemblies of the world Communist movement. His lieutenants credited him with initiative in establishing policies in their own spheres of activity and in the various divisions of statecraft: military strategy, foreign policy, agriculture, housing, industrial administration and Party affairs. Khrushchev has been the source of doctrinal change in the world Communist movement, modifying the official ideology, if not systematically, at least in accordance with the needs of practice.

The cult of Khrushchev was well established and had made steady progress, his pre-eminence being acknowledged in ritualistic formulas. The formula, "the Central Committee, headed by N. S. Khrushchev," advanced him above the position accorded him earlier, when he only "headed" the Presidium.

While Khrushchev commanded the levers of power and possessed supreme authority, as Stalin did in the early Thirties, he was not the autocrat the world came to know by the end of Stalin's reign. The chief limitation on Khrushchev's power stemmed from his incapacity, and perhaps disinclination, to deter opposition from his subordinates by the imminent threat of terrible sanctions. He reduced their power or even deprived them of it, but he evidently could not threaten his lieutenants with imprisonment or the loss of their lives. He was unsuccessful even in his efforts to apply further sanctions against "the anti-Party group" as an example to others who might similarly attempt to unseat him. Stalin also encountered in his lieutenants a reluctance to imprison, and especially to execute, his defeated rivals. Then, the outcome was the great purge. When Soviet society had changed radically and the regime was almost a half-century old, when Khrushchev's associates had been duly warned by History speaking with Khrushchev's own voice, and Khrushchev was past his seventieth birthday—so drastic an outcome was unlikely and Khrushchev was unlikely to insist on a blood purge. As a result, members of his entourage argued privately against particular proposals, and some were even emboldened to press against the limits of his power, testing his will and resolution in maintaining the power he had arrogated to himself. But there was no evidence of a faction opposed to his leadership.

THE KHRUSHCHEV SUCCESSION CRISIS

There is good reason, then, to believe that Khrushchev's passing from the political scene is giving rise to a succession crisis. Moreover, although his personal dictatorship was limited, unlike Stalin's virtually absolute despotism, it does not follow from this that the Khrushchev succession crisis will be less productive of political change than the crisis brought on by Stalin's death. On the contrary, certain differences between the present situation and the situation when Stalin died may make this succession crisis considerably more fluid than the last one.

The paralyzing fear of police repression that the Soviet people experienced under Stalin persisted after his death. This terrible legacy gave his heirs a needed period of grace in which to resolve the Stalin succession. In the past decade, however, an earlier and more permissive political atmosphere has evolved. Even in conditions of stability in the leadership, creative intellectuals have demanded more freedom for themselves, and some have even offered resistance in the face of dire threats. Factory and construction workers have gone on strike, meat-hungry city-dwellers have rioted, and the leaders of national minorities have repeatedly provoked Moscow's ire. Widespread reprisals have not seemed necessary, because the dissident groups clearly are not a present danger to the regime. They can be readily controlled by stable leadership such as existed under Khrushchev. In the absence of terror, however, the political resolution of these and other groups will probably grow. They may finally pose a serious problem to the top leadership if it loses its cohesion, as might well happen during this succession crisis.

Khrushchev's major achievement was to transform Stalin's system of rule based on terror into a relatively enlightened, though still totalitarian, despotism. The role of compulsion was considerably reduced while political stability and centralized control were maintained. It is not certain, however, that this newly established system can survive the shock of the succession crisis. It may prove to have been an interregnum which got its character from Khrushchev's leadership, but which his successors may be unwilling or unable to preserve.

Stalin so compelled his lieutenants to praise his person and policies that when he died these policies possessed an inertial movement that had to be slowed down, stopped, and then reversed in a prolonged effort extending over several years following his death. Khrushchev, on the other hand, relied chiefly on the rotation of his subordinates to obviate attempts to oppose his power. As a result, the men who have succeeded him are not so closely identified with his policies and may be disinclined to continue them. In general, Khrushchev's political personality played so large a part in his style of rule that his policies and reputation were likely to become subjects of controversy now that his vital presence is no longer there to sustain them.

Khrushchev bequeathed to his heirs a number of urgent and highly divisive problems, of which the following are only a sample.

Should the U.S.S.R. accept Yugoslavia's "market socialism" as a model or continue to improvise new ways of organizing a "command economy," a method which has produced manifestly poor results in recent years?

Should domestic agriculture be allowed to stagnate on the new plateau to which Khrushchev raised it in the first years after Stalin's death, or should agricultural investment be greatly increased? If agriculture is to receive much more capital, should it be used chiefly to raise yields or to increase acreage?

Alternatively, should the plans for sharply increased agricultural production be abandoned and necessary agricultural products purchased in world markets with Soviet industrial and other products?

Would the resulting loss of autarky impair the conduct of foreign policy?

Is it reasonable for the U.S.S.R. to try to exert sharp pressure against vital U.S. interests in the Cold War (as in Berlin) while failing to match the U.S. in intercontinental striking power? If not, is the solution to be sought in an accommodation with the West, or in stepped up efforts to overtake the U.S. in intercontinental nuclear delivery capabilities?

Related to these problems is the over-arching question of foreign policy: should the U.S.S.R. seek an accommodation with the West at the cost of intensified conflict with the Chinese People's Republic, or should it press the conflict with the West, either in conjunction or in competition with Communist China?

In the sphere of culture, Khrushchev's heirs face a fundamental problem that has been made acute by the absence of terror: how can the Party reduce its interference in cultural matters sufficiently to satisfy the intellectual's most persistent demands without endangering its own authority?

After Stalin died, the party apparatus, comprising full-time, paid party workers, soon united against the other major political and social groupings: the political police, government bureaucracy, economic managers and specialists, army leaders and creative intelligentsia. The disciplined unity of these party *apparatchiks,* which helped to ease the succession crisis and finally to resolve it, may be difficult to maintain since Khrushchev's demise. Khrushchev made the party apparatus sovereign, thereby raising the morale of its members and attracting able new men into its service. At the same time, however, he created important divisions in the party machine in order to assure the implementation of his will and to forestall efforts to limit his power. These divisions were of various kinds. The staff of the central organs were split geographically into a Russian and a non-Russian part. They were also divided functionally into bureaus and commissions for agriculture, industry, ideology, party organs (i.e., cadres), and Party-State control. Khrushchev's system of concentrating political power within the party apparatus, while dividing that power and balancing it against itself, could now lead to a serious fracturing of the party machine.

Khrushchev's de-Stalinization campaign, a necessary element in his program of transforming Stalin's system of rule, has had some undesired consequences. It has made deep rents in the close-knit fabric of ideology from which Communists derive their right to rule. In bold spirits, de-Stalinization has encouraged independence and disrespect to the Party and its top leaders. It has helped to create a chasm between the generation which, as adults, did what was necessary to survive the Great Purge of the Thirties, and the next generation which was taught in school to revere Stalin—only to be told, when grown to adulthood, that he had killed and oppressed countless Communist and loyal citizens. Only in a succession crisis in which the leaders are divided are these new sources of dissidence likely to gain full political expression.

While the changed circumstances enumerated above have tended to exacerbate the Khrushchev succession crisis, it is not possible to forecast its political consequences. These will depend on the course and outcome of the crisis. Khrushchev sought to arrange an orderly succession by making the necessary *institutional* and *personnel* dispositions in advance. He dealt with this double problem by trying to assure that the Party machine, its sovereignty firmly established, would pass at the decisive moment to the personal control of his designated heir. In his choice of an heir, Khrushchev was limited by the fact that few of the men around him had had long experience in the top leadership. In his last months he seems to have established a triadic relation, with himself as dictator, Brezhnev as heir-apparent (replacing the ailing Kozlov, who may also have been in disfavor), and Podgorny as the "counter-heir," charged with limiting Brezhnev's power. Should Khrushchev have wished to designate a more youthful successor, he had several candidates to choose from, including Polyansky and Shelepin.

Despite Khrushchev's efforts, the chances for an orderly transfer of dictatorial power remained small. The political consequences of the Khrushchev succession crisis may have been decisively affected by whether the inevitable factional struggle among the leaders would develop into a struggle between the institutions of dictatorship. What can be asserted, with some measure of confidence, however, is that dissidence in Soviet society is not likely to have great political effect unless the rulers have been substantially weakened. And the rulers are unlikely to be weakened except as the result of a succession crisis.

SUGGESTED READING

Books:

Brzezinski, Zbigniew, and Samuel P. Huntington, *Political Power: USA/USSR, Similarities and Contrasts; Convergence or Evolution,* New York: The Viking Press, 1964.

Fainsod, Merle, *How Russia Is Ruled,* rev. edition, Cambridge: Harvard University Press, 1963.

Gyorgy, Andrew, *Communism in Perspective,* Boston: Allyn and Bacon, 1964.

Leonhard, Wolfgang, *The Kremlin Since Stalin,* New York: Praeger, 1962.

Rush, Myron, *The Rise of Khrushchev,* Washington, D.C.: Public Affairs Press, 1958.

Serge, Victor, *From Lenin to Stalin,* New York: Pioneer Publishers, 1937.

Swearer, Howard R., *The Politics of Succession in the U.S.S.R., Materials on Khrushchev's Rise to Leadership,* Boston: Little, Brown and Co., 1964.

Wolfe, Bertram D., *Khrushchev and Stalin's Ghost,* New York: Praeger, 1957.

Articles:

Note: Of the innumerable magazine and periodical sources currently dealing with the succession-crises plaguing so many countries, two publications emerged with—in the editor's opinion—the most significant and durable contributions to the literature: one is the special issue of Columbia University's *Journal of International Affairs* (Spring 1964) dealing with "Statesmen and Succession," while the other is *The New York Times Magazine* in its recent issues. Particularly noteworthy are the following entries in the former:

Drachkovitch, Milorad M., "Succession and the Charismatic Leader in Yugoslavia," pp. 54-66.

Hoffmann, Stanley S., "Succession and Stability in France," pp. 86-103.

Klein, Donald W., "Succession and the Elite in Peking," pp. 1-11, and

Rustow, Dankwart A., "Succession in the Twentieth Century," pp. 104-113.

Important articles from the latter source are:

Bialer, Severyn, "Twenty-four men who rule Russia," *The New York Times Magazine,* November 1, 1964, pp. 26-27 and 104-105.

Neville, Robert, "Longo Tries Togliatti's Shoes," *The New York Times Magazine,* November 8, 1964, pp. 32, 129-130, and

Tanner, Henry, "How to Survive in the Kremlin," *The New York Times Magazine,* November 15, 1964, pp. 26, 122-124.

12. Failures in Communist Revolutionary Strategy

by Peter A. Toma

One of Toma's key assertions is that surveying Communist expansion throughout the world ever since 1917, its growth "was more effective through military conquest and occupation than through any other form of struggle." It is clear that immediately following World War II the might of the Red Army was directly responsible for imposing Stalin's Communism on the reluctant peoples of Eastern Europe. Compared to that expansionist wave of Communism, there have been few countries indeed where Marxism-Leninism has triumphed without an armed uprising, a civil war or a military intervention. To that extent, Lenin's call for a violent and protracted "revolutionary struggle" seems to have been more successful than the peaceful reinterpretation of the original call to arms offered, until recently, by the now repudiated leader of the Soviet Communist Party, Nikita Khrushchev. Violence thus becomes the handmaiden of modern Communism, while the insistence on "peaceful coexistence" and a peaceful transition toward Communism has actually weakened its fabric, structure and expansion-potential.

The author offers at least one surprising conclusion which may puzzle our readers. He states that: "Communism is less likely to succeed in countries where the degree of dedication, hard work and readiness to suffer for political ends is low than in countries where this degree is high." Unhappily, in view of the frequently cited prototype of the "hard-working, dedicated and fanatical" card-carrying and dues-paying Communist (the so-called "activist," in C.P. parlance), numerous illustrations can be found to support the author's assertion. An atmosphere of fanaticism, a willingness to suffer for certain political ends, a rigid enforcement of codes of party discipline have helped, for example, the Fidelistas of Cuba, the French Communist movement, or the Czech and East German Communist parties.

TODAY THERE SEEM TO BE three different versions of Lenin's theory of socialist revolution: the Maoist, the Titoist, and the Khrushchevist.[1] All three have declared themselves to be Lenin's loyal disciples. Yet, when confronted with the question of socialist revolution, they have viewed each other as heretics and enemies of international Communism.

LENIN'S DOCTRINE OF SOCIALIST REVOLUTION

Lenin considered the doctrine of socialist revolution the core of Communist ideology. "Without revolutionary theory," wrote Lenin in his treatise "What Is to Be Done?", "there can be no revolutionary movement." But Lenin also pointed out that "revolutionary theory is not a dogma," because it "undergoes final formulation when brought into close contact with practice." Thus, while retaining Marx's belief in the socialist revolution as a historical necessity, Lenin introduced the magic word "practice," which as a safety valve permitted more than one interpretation of revolutionary theory. As a result, Lenin saw in *practice* not *one* single threshold event (a great convulsive crisis, a political explosion of the oppressed class of proletarians), which would at one fell swoop end the rule of the bourgeoisie and thus all class societies, but rather a *protracted* struggle spreading over an entire epoch—a transitional period—extending from the time at which Communist forces organize, through both the bourgeois and socialist revolutions, into an indefinite duration of proletarian dictatorship. Hence to Lenin the dictatorship of the proletariat meant "a persistent struggle—sanguinary and bloodless, violent and peaceful, military and economic, educational and administrative—against the forces and traditions of the old society" which would bring about the transition from capitalism to socialism.

[1] Although Nikita Khrushchev has been personally repudiated by his Party's leadership in October 1964, his theory of revolution has survived so far as the official "line" of the current Soviet hierarchy.

Whereas Marx made a rigid distinction between the "socialist" and the "bourgeois-democratic" revolution (the latter preceding the former due to the "necessary" historical sequence of social systems), Lenin included the latter in the overall design of the protracted revolutionary struggle in which the proletariat should take the lead rather than the subordinate role prescribed by Marx. Lenin thus urged his fellow Communists to engage in any form of struggle that might weaken the system of "imperialist" capitalism. This struggle could be carried out, according to Lenin, in one single country or a number of countries—economically developed or underdeveloped—as long as it was led by the Communist party in alliance with the dissatisfied masses of workers, peasants and the petty bourgeoisie. Although peaceful revolution in the 1920s was not considered impossible—the Hungarian Soviet Republic, for example, was established in March 1919 without bloodshed—Lenin viewed such revolutions "extremely scarce" because the conditions for a revolutionary success were, in Lenin's time, not historical-evolutionary, but rather strategic ones. Lenin saw the proletarian revolution coming when

the decisive battle has fully matured . . . in such a way that (1) all the class forces hostile to us have become sufficiently confused . . . have sufficiently weakened themselves in a struggle beyond their strength; that (2) all the vacillating, wavering, unstable intermediate elements . . . have sufficiently disgraced themselves through their practical bankruptcy; and that (3) among the proletariat a mass mood in favor of supporting the most determined, unreservedly bold, revolutionary action against the bourgeoisie has risen . . .

Consequently, the question of the seizure of power was to Lenin something to be decided on military-strategic rather than on historical-evolutionary grounds.

The Leninist theory of socialist revolution was then a pragmatic appeal to the "world proletariat," dressed in ideological greens of Marxism, to save the Bolshevik Revolution in Russia by following the Russian example in countries where "the decisive battle" (rather than capitalism) "has fully matured." By changing Marx's single climactic event into a continuous class struggle; by replacing the historic mission of the proletariat with the "vanguard party"; by shifting the proletarian revolution from industrially advanced capitalist countries to economically backward colonial areas; and by substituting for the Marxist "proletariat" the combination of workers, peasants, toilers and small producers, Lenin elaborated a revolutionary theory which was a guide for his followers who continued, just as Lenin before them, to develop new interpretations and applications of this theory through *creative* Marxism. The Yugoslav Communists, for example, argue that modern capitalism differs so much from the capitalism of Lenin's day that it is time to abandon the old Leninist theory of socialist revolution in favor of the idea of gradual, spontaneous evolution of capitalism into socialism.

The Russian Communists, on the other hand, consider the establishment of a new world socialist system possible only through the application of the Leninist theory of socialist revolution. They insist that the major propositions of Lenin's theory of revolution continue to be entirely valid today, but that the epochal changes which have taken place in the world have faced the Communist movement with the task of further developing this theory. Therefore, at the Moscow conferences of 1957 and 1960 Lenin's theory had been reexamined in the light of certain fundamental changes that took place in the world during the past few decades. The conferences produced a modified Leninist theory of socialist revolution.

The peaceful socialist revolution, according to the Khrushchevian interpretation of Lenin's theory of revolution, takes place without an armed uprising, civil war or military intervention; whereas a non-peaceful socialist revolution involves one or another or all three of these elements (as was the case in Russia). Which type of socialist revolution is to be applied, peaceful or non-peaceful, is decided, according to the current Soviet hierarchy, on the basis of the revolutionary situation by the political leadership of the working class, i.e., the Communist party of the particular country involved, in coordination with the CPSU and other Communist parties. Operationally, this means that the Kremlin leaders establish the general scheme, while the local party echelons determine the particular form of the struggle.

Since the CPSU believes that the foreign policy of imperialism is based entirely on preparation for aggression, on balancing on the brink of war, and the domestic policy of imperialism is also imbued with the spirit of war: the military is assuming greater and greater influence on the government and the pressure of reaction is increasing in every sphere. Thus, the dialectical approach to capitalism prompted former party boss Khrushchev and his successors to revive the tactics of "peaceful coexistence," as part of the new Leninist theory of socialist revolution. Under the conditions of peaceful coexistence, the Kremlin assumes, "favorable opportunities are created for the intensification of class struggle in the capitalist countries, for the national liberation movement and democratic movements and socialist revolutions." [1] Such "opportunities" include the nationalization of certain "monopolized sectors of industry," the democratization of the management of public sectors of the economy, the development of the initiative and participation of the working people in all spheres of economic life, the creation of democratic control over capital investments in industry and agriculture, the carrying out of agrarian reforms, and others. These measures were discussed by the Rome conference of Communist party representatives of the European capitalist countries held in November 1959.

Peking, however, found the decisions of the Rome conference contradictory to Lenin's theory of class struggle and declared that the Moscow thesis of peaceful coexistence was almost the same as preaching class peace. This hard line of Mao's version of the Leninist theory of socialist revolution has also been supported by the Albanian Communist leaders. They charge that the CPSU "elevates the peaceful assumption of power by the working class to the status of an absolute" and thus follows the revisionist line of the Yugoslav Communists. In the meantime Moscow, of course, denies both charges by pointing out that the forms and methods of struggle the proletariat of one country or another would have to choose would be a matter for the Communist vanguard itself in each country to determine.

The gaining of power (the key to any type of revolution) without civil war, armed uprising or military intervention is, according to the Russian Communists, more probable than before for the newly-independent nations and some capitalist countries such as France, Italy and Chile. But this requires, the Kremlin analysis goes on to state, that the ruling classes be deprived of the possibility of putting weapons to use, of employing the police, army and

[1] *Pravda,* January 7, 1963.

state apparatus for suppressing the revolutionary movement of the masses. Can all this be achieved? Moscow is confident that it can be achieved through the weakening of militarism as a result of the success of a policy of disarmament, the transfer of a large part of the army and the state apparatus to the side of the people and through the complete realization by the ruling circles of the hopelessness of open struggle against the masses. If, however, such "favorable opportunities" do not exist in a country (such as Guatemala, Ecuador, Nicaragua, Portugal, and Peru) the revolutionary struggle will, according to the Soviet prophecy, inevitably assume non-peaceful forms.

In recent years the arguments between Peking and Moscow have reached a serious impasse. Quotations from Marx and Lenin are futile and the evidence, based on current Soviet and Chinese value judgments, proving or disproving the peaceful use of socialist revolutions in Eastern Europe after 1944, can no longer be subjected to examination by dialectics alone. Empirical evidence is imperative. Let us therefore turn now to a systematic examination of the socialist revolutions that took place from 1917 to 1964 and try to establish which, if any, of the interpretations of Lenin's theory of socialist revolution is valid.

BASIC TYPES OF SOCIALIST REVOLUTIONS

There have been thirty-eight socialist revolutions in the world since 1917. Fourteen were successful and twenty-four were unsuccessful. Of the fourteen successful socialist revolutions eleven had been accomplished non-peacefully (in Russia, North Vietnam, China, Korea, Yugoslavia, Albania, Bulgaria (1946), Poland, Hungary (1947), Rumania and East Germany) and three peacefully (in Czechoslovakia (1948), Outer Mongolia and Cuba). Of the twenty-four unsuccessful socialist revolutions, three were peaceful attempts (Hungary, India-Kerala, and San Marino), and twenty-one were non-peaceful attempts (in Russia-Petrograd, Finland, Germany (1919), Bavaria, Austria (1919), Germany (1921), Germany (1923), Bulgaria (1923), Estonia, Indonesia (1926), China: Shanghai, Wu-han, and Canton, Austria (1934), Spain (1934), Greece (1936), Spain (1937), Greece (1944-45), Burma, Malaya and Indonesia (1948)).

Of the eleven successful socialist revolutions that were accom-

TABLE I

Four Basic Types of Socialist Revolutions, 1917-1964

	Peaceful	Non-Peaceful	Total
Successful	3 (8%)	11 (29%)	14 (37%)
Unsuccessful	3 (8%)	21 (55%)	24 (63%)
Total	6 (16%)	32 (84%)	38 (100%)

plished non-peacefully six were usurpations imposed by the agents of the occupying Soviet army (in North Korea, Bulgaria (1946), Poland, Hungary (1947), Romania and East Germany); and five were guerrilla or civil wars (in Russia, China, North Vietnam, Yugoslavia and Albania). The form of struggle for the three remaining successful socialist revolutions—accomplished peacefully —two were *coups d'états* (in Czechoslovakia and Cuba) and one was a plebiscite in Outer Mongolia. Of the twenty-one non-peaceful socialist revolutions that failed sixteen were armed uprisings (in Russia-Petrograd, Germany (1919), Austria (1919), Germany (1921), Germany (1923), Bulgaria (1923), Estonia, Indonesia (1926), China: Shanghai, Wu-han and Canton, Austria (1934), Spain (1934), Greece (1936), Spain (1937) and Indonesia (1948); and five guerrilla or civil wars (in Finland, Bavaria, Greece (1944-45), Malaya and Burma). The form of struggle for peaceful socialist revolutions that failed was one *coup d'état* in Hungary in 1919 and two by electoral process in India-Kerala and San Marino.

It is perhaps significant that in many cases the form of struggle was not a single-factor affair. Overlappings of one form of struggle with another were frequent occurrences in the history of socialist revolutions. For example, in North Korea and Poland military intervention and in Czechoslovakia the *coup d'état* were all preceded by guerrilla wars which if not controlled were at least infiltrated by the Communist takeover at an opportune time.

TABLE II

Forms of Struggle of Four Basic Types of Socialist Revolutions, 1917-1964

| | PEACEFUL | | | NON-PEACEFUL | | | |
	Coup d'état	Plebiscite	Electoral Process	Military Interven.	Guerrilla Civil War	Armed Uprising	Total
Successful	2 (5.3%)	1 (2.6%)	0	6 (15.8%)	5 (13.2%)	0	14 (36.9%)
Unsuccessful	1 (2.6%)	0	2 (5.3%)	0	5 (13.2%)	16 (42%)	24 (63.1%)
Total	3 (7.9%)	1 (2.6%)	2 (5.3%)	6 (15.8%)	10 (26.4%)	16 (42%)	38 (100%)

Perhaps a more important factor affecting the outcome of socialist revolutions than the overlappings of guerrilla wars with the *coup d'état* and military intervention, was Communist military conquest and occupation. In fact, Communist expansion was more effective through military conquest and occupation than through any other form of struggle. Since October 1917, the following territories were acquired by the Communists through military conquest and occupation:

Estonia (from October 1917 to January 1918), the Ukraine (from December 27, 1917 continuously), Byelorussia (from December 30, 1917 continuously), Turkestan (from January 3, 1918 continuously), North Caucasus (from April 1918 continuously), Latvia (from December 1918 to April 1919), Lithuania (from January to May 1919), Slovakia (from June 16 to July 5, 1919), Azerbaidjan (from April 1920 continuously), Armenia (from November 29, 1920 continuously), Poland-Bialystok (from July 31, 1920 to March 18, 1921), Georgia (from February 1920 continuously), Mongolia (from March 13, 1920 to June 11, 1921), Poland: Polosk-Kamenetz-Podolsk line (from September 17, 1939 to June 22, 1941 and continuously after WWII), Finland-Karelia (from November 30, 1939 to June 22, 1941 and after World War II continuously), Romania-Bessarabia and Bukovina (from June 28, 1940 to June 22, 1941 and continuously after World War II), Lithuania (from August 3, 1940 to June 22, 1941 and continuously after World War II), Latvia (from August 5, 1940 to

June 22, 1941 and continuously after World War II), Estonia (from August 6, 1940 to June 22, 1941 and continuously after World War II), Iran-Azerbaidjan and Kurdistan (from October 6, 1941 to May 6, 1946), Romania (from August 1944 to May 13, 1955), Czechoslovakia (from October 1944 to December 1945), Subcarpathian Ruthenia (from February 1945 continuously), Bulgaria (from September 1944 to September 15, 1947), Tannu-Tuva (from October 11, 1944 continuously), Poland (from July 1944 to May 13, 1955), Hungary (from September 1944 to May 13, 1955), East Germany (from April 1945 to May 13, 1955), Austria (April 1945 to May 15, 1955), Northern Manchuria (from August 9, 1945 to February 15, 1946), North Korea (August 14, 1945 to January 1, 1949), Southern Sakhalin, Kurile Islands and Port Arthur (from August 15, 1945 continuously), South Korea (from June 25, 1950 to September 10, 1950), Laos (from June 1952 to March 1953), Cambodia (from March to July 1954) and Tibet (from March 1959 continuously).

With the exceptions of Slovakia in 1919, South Korea, Laos, Cambodia and Tibet, all other territories mentioned above were conquered and occupied at one time or another by the Soviet Red Army. In the case of Slovakia it was the Hungarian Red Army; in South Korea the Korean People's Army; in Laos and Cambodia the North Vietnamese People's Army and in Tibet the Chinese People's Army that enabled the spread of Communism.

Another interesting empirical finding in the study of socialist revolutions is the division of these revolutions according to duration of time and historical periodization. The longest-lived peaceful socialist revolution that failed took place in San Marino between August 14, 1945 and September 19, 1957, or roughly for twelve years; the shortest-lived unsuccessful socialist revolution achieved peacefully occurred in Hungary from March 21 to August 1, 1919, or 133 days *in toto*. The longest-lived non-peaceful revolution that failed took place in Finland from January 27 to April 12, 1918, or seventy-five days; the shortest-lived unsuccessful socialist revolution achieved non-peacefully was in Vienna, Austria, on June 15, 1919, lasting only a few hours.

After World War I, from 1917 to 1920 (the period of "international solidarity with the Soviet people"), there were seven revolutionary attempts of various types (military intervention excluded)

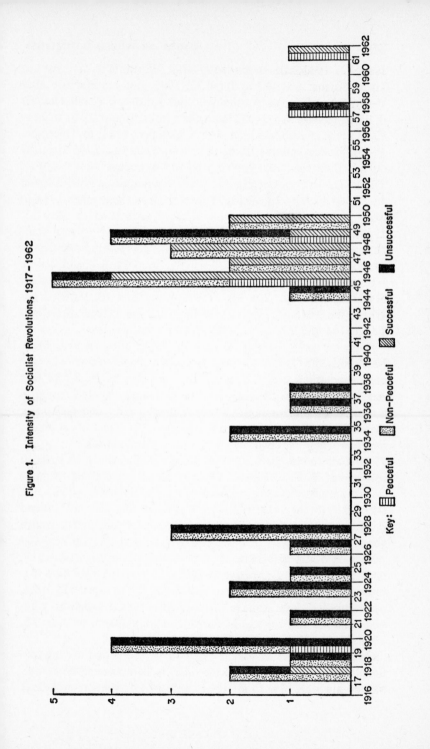

Figure 1. Intensity of Socialist Revolutions, 1917–1962

Key: ▦ Peaceful   ▨ Non-Peaceful   ▧ Successful   ■ Unsuccessful

trying to establish the dictatorship of the proletariat, but only one succeeded, that in Russia.

During the world depression years, 1929-1933, when strikes and lockouts, unemployment and demonstrations were higher than during any other period of Communist history, and when Communists all over the world were supposed to be guided by the program of the Sixth Congress of the Comintern (issued on September 1, 1928) calling for the creation of a "World Union of Soviet Socialist Republics" through the violent overthrow of bourgeois power and the substitution in its place of proletarian power, there were no revolutionary attempts anywhere and in many countries the membership in Communist parties declined rather than forged ahead. After World War II, during the 1945-1950 period, there were sixteen revolutionary attempts of various types (military intervention included), however, this time the ratio was almost reversed: there were twelve successful and only four unsuccessful socialist revolutions.

It appears obvious, on the basis of this empirical analysis, that the Communist Chinese argument for non-peaceful methods of socialist revolutions is historically justified. The immediate questions, then, are first, why the sudden change from unsuccessful to successful socialist revolutions and second, what are the reasons for this success?

Let us examine two peaceful socialist revolutions by *coup d'état:* one in Hungary (1919) that failed and the other one in Czechoslovakia that succeeded (1948).

THE HUNGARIAN EXAMPLE

There were four basic mistakes causing the collapse of the Hungarian Soviet Republic in 1919. The first mistake of the Hungarian Communists was the failure to maintain a monolithic, disciplined Communist party. The merger of the Communist party with the Social Democratic party into what on March 21, 1919, became known as the Hungarian Socialist party actually meant the self-liquidation of Communism in Hungary, since both the hard Communist core and the soft socialist periphery of the new party were made up of former Social Democrats. The small group of the Hungarian *Lumpenproletariat,* constituting the bulk of the four-month old, poorly organized and undisciplined Communist party was swallowed up by the Social Democratic party. The former Social Democratic party represented the political interests of the Hungarian trade unions and embraced a large disciplined following and an efficient bureaucracy.

TABLE III

Comparison of Social Democratic and Communist Strength in Hungary
(November 1918-March 1919*)

	No. of TU members (Potential Social Democrats)	No. of Unemployed (Potential Communists)
1918	721,437	67,061
1919	800,936	114,179

* Sources: International Labor Office, *Trade Union Conditions in Hungary* (Geneva: Atar, 1921) and L'Office Central Royal Hongrois de Statistique, *Annuaire Statistique Hongrois, Nouveau Cours* (Budapest: Athenaeum, 1925), vols. XXIV-XXX.

As the results in Table III indicate, the numerical strength of the Communists, in spite of their fast-growing popularity, was only about nine percent of the Social Democratic strength in 1918 and only about fourteen percent shortly before the merger in 1919. It is therefore not surprising to learn that when, on July 20, 1919, the hour of reckoning arrived, Communism in Hungary was first defeated from within by the powerful Social Democrats and shortly after that by the Rumanian mercenaries at the front.

The Hungarian Communists were always able to infiltrate—but never to control—the well-established Social Democratic trade unions. Countless Communist attempts to discredit Social Democratic leadership in the amalgamated party and the trade unions, through the tactic of pressure "from below," have usually ended in fiasco simply because the pressure "from above" was lacking strength. One reason for this was the alienation of the organized Hungarian workers. Constant Communist attacks on the trade unions drove many despondent labor leaders to find refuge in the Workers' Councils which soon after the Communist takeover became the local decision-making organs for the new Hungarian Socialist party. Béla Kun did not exaggerate when he wrote: "The

Communist as well as the Social Democratic party melted away into a number of workers' councils controlled by petty-bourgeois bureaucrats." That is why, ever since the collapse of the Hungarian Soviet Republic, it has been argued that Béla Kun and his associates committed a grave error when they decided to integrate the two parties in order to avoid further discords between the Communists and Social Democrats and in order to take power in Hungary without bloodshed.

The second mistake of the Hungarian Communists was that, once in power, they failed to carry out the long promised distribution of land: more than one-half of the population lived from agriculture and 80 percent of those were either totally landless workers or dwarfholders, owning 1-5 holds (1.43-7.15 acres) of land. One reason for this mistake is attributed to Communist logic: by preserving the large estates through socialization, the new, state-owned large farm industry would guarantee the uninterrupted production of agricultural products desperately needed for the industrial cities and the Hungarian Red Army. Another reason for the mistakes committed in the agrarian program was the deep-rooted Communist hatred for the peasant movement, which was essentially directed toward the ownership of the land. As a result, the Hungarian Communists failed to combine the socialist revolution with the agrarian one and, consequently, neglected to establish a strong alliance between the workers and peasants under the party leadership.

The third mistake rested in the fact that the Hungarian Communists failed to understand correctly the nature of the dictatorship of the proletariat. In all their actions, it is intimated, the Hungarian proletariat desired to establish socialism at one stroke and hence held the erroneous assumption that the transition from capitalism to socialism would take at most one or two years. This notion, it has later been charged, led to excessive centralization in government and mismanagement of the agrarian problem, the trade union organizations and the petty-bourgeoisie in the Hungarian Soviet Republic.

The fourth mistake is attributed to Béla Kun's egocentrism. As Commissar for Foreign Affairs, Kun's great ambition was to become a mediator between the Kremlin and the Entente Powers. His opportunity arrived in the middle of June 1919, when he actually fell into the trap set for him by George Clemenceau. On June 13, Kun received a radio-wire from Clemenceau composed in such a way as to give the impression that if the advancing Hungarian Red Army (in Slovakia and Ruthenia) would withdraw to the demarcation lines prescribed by the Entente, Paris would consider extending an invitation to Kun to come to Versailles to negotiate a Hungarian peace settlement. Without much hesitation, on June 15, Kun ordered the victorious Hungarian Red Army, only 80 kilometers away from the Bolsheviks in the Ukraine, to stop their further advance and withdraw to the new demarcation lines. On July 5, the Hungarian Red Army evacuated Slovakia and Ruthenia and on July 11, after having received the green light for negotiations with the Entente from Lenin, Kun wired Clemenceau that he had faithfully carried out the instructions received in the telegrams of June 13 and was now awaiting an official invitation from the Paris Peace Conference. Two days later Kun received an unsigned telegram from Paris informing him that the Peace Conference would not negotiate with him. Kun, enraged and humiliated, wired back to Paris asking for clarification of the unsigned telegram. Paris never replied. On July 20, Kun attacked the Romanians with a demoralized and undisciplined Hungarian Red Army. Within ten days the Romanian troops marched into Budapest and the Hungarian Soviet Republic fell.

THE CZECHOSLOVAK EXAMPLE

In Czechoslovakia, in February, 1948, the socialist revolution was successful because the Czech and Slovak Communists were diligent enough to learn from the mistakes committed by their Hungarian, German and other comrades.

The socialist revolution in Czechoslovakia, as the Communist historians view it today, began on May 27, 1946, one day after the first post-war parliamentary elections, and ended on June 27, 1948, the day when the Czechoslovak Social Democratic party was absorbed into the Communist party of Czechoslovakia. From April 1945 (when the basic principles to which the post-war Czechoslovak government professed allegiance were spelled out in a document known as the Kosice Programme) until May 27, 1946, the Communists in Czechoslovakia were engaged in a so-called national and democratic revolution. The primary task for the

Communists in this period was to build Communist strength in the nation. In practice this meant the organization of a mass Communist party controlled by a hard-core Communist elite; the assumption of power by the Communist-controlled national committees; the formation of a new people's security system and army; the prohibition of the revival of the political parties which had represented the reactionary interests in pre-war Czechoslovakia— (in this group was also included the largest pre-war political party, the Agrarian party), a systematic purge of the political, economic and cultural life of the country; the settlement of the relations between the Czech and Slovak nations on the principle of equality; the expulsion of the German minority, and other measures enabling the Communists to apply the "pincer" tactic against their enemies.

According to this technique, pressure is first created "from below" (the masses) through agitation, then it is combined with pressure "from above" (a Communist-dominated national and local government and parliament) through legislative initiative so that the opposition is constantly on the defense—moving in a Communist-activated area, which can be described as the jaws of a pincer. The aim of this scheme is to force the rivals to yield to exerted pressures by the National Front (representing the political unity) and by the workers and peasants (representing the national unity of the state) so that the adversaries can eventually be controlled and maneuvered into a desirable position for the final kill. In Czechoslovakia this final act was accomplished in the middle of February 1948. Until then the Communists were skillfully employing the "pincer" technique in a complex process of power struggle.

During the first stage—the national-democratic revolution— the Communists kept alive the struggle against former Nazis and collaborators, against black-marketeers and opportunists, against those hostile to the Kosice Programme and against opponents of the Czechoslovak-Soviet alliance. At the same time, within bounds, the Communists encouraged private capitalist enterprise and through their auxiliary organizations and left-wing Social Democrats rallied support for greater civil, political and economic rights in order to bring class antagonism into closer range. However, class struggle on such issues as "reactionary domestic forces," slow legislative work, "sabotage" by "the millionaires," the Marshall Plan, espionage for a "reactionary power" and the so-called "plot to overthrow the government" did not take place until several months after the parliamentary elections of 1946. The Communists in Czechoslovakia had decided first to legitimize their power through the electoral process and then to test it in a class war against the bourgeoisie involving "the revolutionary use of parliament."

The main ingredients of the Communist strength during the socialist revolution, which in February 1948 tipped the scales in Communist favor, were: (1) the ability to exploit the labor movement; (2) the monopoly over agricultural policy; and (3) the skill to transform the Social Democratic party into a front organization serving Communist interests.

Ever since the end of the war, the Communist-organized Revolutionary Trade Unions Movement (ROH) proclaimed itself the one and only trade union organization in Bohemia and Moravia. A similar organization, under identical circumstances, was established in Slovakia and on February 28, 1946, the two organizations merged into a single body called the United Revolutionary Trade Unions Movement of Czechoslovakia. In spite of the population loss of some 2.5 million since 1939, the strength of the new trade union movement in February 1948 stood at its pre-war peak of 2,250,000—eighty-six percent Czech and fourteen percent Slovak members. This membership made it the largest single organization in the country. By law, ROH was permitted to participate and to make suggestions in all legislative and executive matters affecting the workers; it had the right to representation on all public bodies not popularly elected; and it enjoyed a decisive position in management. Since ROH had a hierarchically centralized structure, decision making was vested in a twenty-member Board of Trustees of the Central Council of Trade Unions (URO)—both dominated by the Communist party. Thus, whenever the Communist strategists needed to exert pressure on their rivals from below, they could call on the trade unions; the leadership of the labor movement would see to it that labor support for Communist programs was available in noticeable measure. Unlike in Hungary during the Kun regime, the trade unions in post-war Czechoslovakia were controlled by Communists and not by Social Democratic bureaucrats.

The Communist scheme for the advancement of the socialist revolution in agriculture entailed the following steps. First, the members of the Peasants' Commissions discussed a draft proposal for land reform, submitted to them by the Communist-controlled Ministry of Agriculture; then, after voting upon it, they drew up petitions and passed resolutions in favor of the draft bill which was forwarded by thousands to Parliament where the Communists openly agitated and debated for passage of the program. M.P.s who were opposed to the measure were exposed as friends of "kulaks" and enemies of the people. Next, the Ministry of Agriculture announced even more drastic land reform proposals—thus exerting more pressure "from above," which in turn created greater intensity of the class struggle. In order to bring the complex process to a climax, delegations from the Peasants' Commissions—joined by representatives of other Communist-inspired organizations— stormed the Parliament building and shouted slogans demanding immediate implementation of the proposal—thus exerting more pressure "from below." Finally, the pressure from "above" and from "below" closed like the claws of a pair of pincers and the badly shaken opposition, suffering from political intimidation, gave way to the passage of the land reform laws which were interpreted by Communists and non-Communists alike as one more Communist victory.

Since it was imperative for the Communists in Czechoslovakia during the socialist revolution always to be on the offensive, pressures against the opposition, similar to those mentioned above, continued in full dosage until February 20, 1948. Twelve non-Communist party leaders in the twenty-six-member Gottwald government—demoralized, exhausted and unable to cope with such pressures any longer—resigned and thus prompted a Communist-engendered government crisis. While the disorganized opponents were still in shock, suffering from Communist "fair play," the proponents were displaying "mass support" for Premier Gottwald by organizing workers' and peasants' demonstrations and by parading armed militia-men in the town squares. Meanwhile, pressure had been mounted against a feeble old man, the President of the Republic, to accept the resignations of the twelve ministers and to appoint new ones (Communists and fellow-travelers)—hand picked long before the February crisis by the Presidium of the

Communist party. With the formation of a new government, suddenly the opposition disintegrated, opportunists from the opposite side of the aisles found new allies, and the Communist party seemed to be steadily moving toward the final stage of the socialist revolution. By February 25, 1948, the transfer from the old to the new government through the habit of obedience was for all practical purposes completed. The replacement of the capitalist with the Communist state's monopoly of power, however, had not become final until June 27, 1948.

The period between the February coup and the June *Gleichschaltung* was effectively used by the Communists to win to their side the "orphans" of capitalism and to consolidate the power of the dictatorship of the proletariat in the new people's democratic state. For these ends the Communists employed the following means: They initiated a third land reform which, as an overture to collectivization announced in November 1949, limited private ownership of the land to fifty hectares in size; permitted a new influx of members into the Communist party; introduced a new constitution which formalized the transmission belts of the new regime;[2] gradually removed all "enemies of the people" from responsible positions in the state; and on May 28, held a new election, this time with a single list of candidates receiving 89.3 percent of the votes cast (the rest were blank ballots indicating opposition), which legitimized the power they acquired in February, 1948. Hereafter the road was open for the Communists to travel with full speed toward the complete establishment of Communist monopoly of power in the state. It took them only one month to reach their destination.

On June 7, Edward Benes formally resigned his post as President of the Czechoslovak state and on June 27 the Communist party rejoiced over the incorporation of the expurgated rump of the Social Democratic party. According to Klement Gottwald, President Benes' successor, June 27 was as outstanding in the history of the Czechoslovak working class as May, 1945 and February, 1948. It symbolized the finale of a performance given by the left-wing members of the Social Democratic party under the "baton" of their leader, Zdenek Fierlinger.

[2] For details, see Edward Taborsky, *Communism in Czechoslovakia, 1948-1960,* Princeton: Princeton University Press, 1961, pp. 165-348.

With Social Democratic support in both the government and the legislature, the Communists were able to put through all their major proposals by simple majority. Since in the multipolar system of the national-front government the balance lay with the Social Democrats, the non-Communists, eager to win Social Democratic support, were also prepared to yield to Social Democratic demands which, in effect, represented Communist proposals advertently assigned for implementation to their front organization.

The post-war Social Democratic party, which was built vertically by the surviving left-wing leaders as an integral part of Communist power, served both as a Communist catalyst and a national solidifier in the political arena of new Czechoslovakia. Considering the strength of the pre-war Social Democratic party, especially in the labor movement, the reason for organizing two rather than one Marxist parties, at least in the Czech lands, becomes obvious. In order to capture the forty percent of all union members who before the war belonged to Social Democratic unions, and in order to prevent the right-wing leaders from usurping the potential Social Democratic power, the left-wing leaders, supported by the Soviet Red Army and Czech Communists, built a new Social Democratic party which in reality became a branch of the Communist party under a different label. Under left-wing management, the Social Democratic party had become an indispensable tool of Communist conspiracy. Without Social Democratic support, Communist pressure "from above" would have been a fiasco and the *peaceful* seizure of power in February 1948, unattainable.

After February, the Social Democratic party continued to function as a separate entity because, as Zdenek Fierlinger explained it, "the party had to be purged from all kinds of detrimental elements before it could be organizationally brought into the Communist party." On June 27, 1948, the purified and indoctrinated Social Democratic party, having fulfilled its purpose, was engulfed by the Communist party. The membership of the new Communist party swelled to over 2.5 million—the highest during the fifteen-year transition from capitalism to socialism.[3]

---

[3] For a penetrating analysis of Communist strength in Czechoslovakia and other East European countries, see R. V. Burks, *The Dynamics of Communism in Eastern Europe,* Princeton, Princeton University Press, 1961.

SUMMARY

Although the study of socialist revolutions is not a new undertaking in the social sciences, the study of unsuccessful socialist revolutions has been almost completely neglected in the West. Yet, as this study indicates, much is to be learned from the exploration of the 63 percent unsuccessful social revolutions. They taught Gottwald, Mao Tse-tung, Ho-Chi-minh and others how to avoid repeating the mistakes of Kun, Levine, Dimitrov and others; and for this they became glorified revolutionary theoreticians of our time.

In order to be predictive, it will be essential first to probe into the revolutionary state of mind of the Communist elite in a country where a socialist revolution is probable and secondly, to study the revolutionary mood of pressure groups in that country. Both steps are of equal importance (and complexity) and both lend themselves to different research techniques, including systematic public opinion analysis, decision-making, statistical analysis, multiple correlation analysis, content analysis and others.

As far as the indices for analysis are concerned, socialist revolutions can be studied through numerous phenomena. Such data as the strength of Communist parties, trade unions, unemployment, strikes and lockouts, demonstrations or the distribution of the national wealth can be useful measuring devices for tension, revolutionary opportunities, governmental stability, frustration, or tranquillity in a particular society. A systematic examination of socialist revolutions in the past should enable us to formulate certain uniformities which could then be empirically tested in correlation with a number of N factors inherent environmentally, attitudinally as well as analytically in socialist revolutions. The possibilities for exploration are numerous. For the time being a few hypotheses, yet to be tested, are offered here for consideration:

1. Socialist revolutions are most likely to occur in countries where the Communists have an even chance of seizing the monopoly of power at a time when a long period of gradual Communist build-up in strength is followed by a short period of sharp reversal. (The Communists then subjectively fear

that ground gained with great effort will be quite lost; their mood becomes revolutionary.)

2. If an established government is overthrown by guerrilla or civil war, the chances of a revolutionary situation prevailing long after the actual overthrow of the established government are much greater.

3. If an established government is overthrown by *coups d'état,* the transfer of the habit of obedience to the new regime tends to be automatic and brief.

4. If the revolutionaries have been successful in toppling an established government (by any means of struggle), yet unable to reestablish the monopoly of power in the state, the very dynamic of the state will prolong the contest.

5. Communist parties are less likely to be anti-religious and/or anti-nationalistic in countries where religion and/or nationalism touches life at every point and governs the whole social structure than in areas where religion and/or nationalism is an auxiliary phenomenon in social life.

6. Communism is less likely to succeed in countries where the degree of dedication, hard work and readiness to suffer for political ends is low than in countries where this degree is high.

7. A socialist revolution is more likely to be peaceful if it is a revolution against a liberal or moderate government with weak military and bureaucratic tradition rather than a conservative-reactionary government with strong militarism and bureaucratic support.

8. Socialist revolutions are more likely to succeed in countries where the Communist parties have a large membership with large parliamentary representation than in countries where the Communist parties are only small groups without any representation in government.

9. Socialist revolutions are more likely to succeed in countries where the Social Democratic party follows Communist lead-

ership than in countries where the Social Democratic party abstains from Communist leadership.

10. Socialist revolutions are more likely to succeed in countries with a high percentage of unemployment, strikes and demonstrations than in countries with low percentage of unemployment, strikes, and demonstrations.

11. Socialist revolutions are more likely to succeed in countries where trade unions follow Communist leadership than in countries where trade unions abstain from Communist leadership.

12. There were more socialist revolutions caused by political, social or economic injustice than by economic poverty.

SUGGESTED READING

Books:

Brzezinski, Zbigniew K., *The Soviet Bloc: Unity and Conflict,* Cambridge: Harvard University Press, 1960.

Fischer-Galati, Stephen, ed., *Eastern Europe in the Sixties,* New York: Praeger, 1963.

Modelski, George, *The Communist International System,* Woodrow Wilson School of Public and International Affairs, Princeton: Princeton University, Research Monograph No. 9, 1960.

Petersen, William (ed.), *The Realities of World Communism,* Englewood Cliffs, N.J.: Prentice-Hall, 1963.

Articles:

Brzezinski, Zbigniew K., "The Organization of the Communist Camp," *World Politics,* January 1963, pp. 175-209.

Laqueur, Walter Z., "The End of the Monolith: World Communism in 1962," *Foreign Affairs,* April, 1962, pp. 360-373.

London, Kurt, "The Socialist Commonwealth: Pattern for Communist World Organization," *Orbis,* 1960, pp. 424-442.

Shoup, Paul, "Communism, Nationalism and the Growth of the Communist Community of Nations After World War II," *American Political Science Review,* December 1962, pp. 886-897.

The Role of Goals
in the Communist System

by Betty B. Burch

PROMISES TO CONSTITUENTS AS A MEANS OF MAINTAINING POWER is a universal political device. Communist regimes, however, have institutionalized this device into an elaborate, articulated goal system which constitutes a major, though not the only, source of power. Simple promises of reward for political support become part of a system in which the promise of future reward is merged with the obligation on the part of constituents to make continual sacrifices to achieve goals. Both persuasion and coercion are based on the presumed need to reach certain goals at certain times, and the manipulation of goal content and goal timetables serves as a source of power. The system consists of conditions conducive to the maintenance of power and the means which operate to produce these conditions. The use of goals by governing bodies is a common political phenomenon, but their elevation into a pragmatic *system* for maintaining power is, at present, unique to Communist regimes. This concluding essay analyzes the Communist goal system and compares Soviet and Chinese practice in the use of goals as political instruments.

Two conditions are set up within the Communist goal system which are favorable to maintaining power. (1) The regime is able to call forth or exact from the people a high degree of present sacrifice for future, presumably rewarding, goals. By sacrifice is meant the giving up of cherished objects, attitudes or modes of behavior in order to achieve a higher objective. Goals are so structured as to evoke continual sacrifice and are so all-embracing in content that sacrifice in all realms of human life may be involved. Continual sacrifice in the form of tasks to be done to achieve goals enables the regime to establish standards for behavior which serve as a basis for reward and punishment; it creates a focus for a manipulated public consensus; and it acts as a motivating factor because promised rewards for goal achievement make acceptable the sacrifices demanded by the regime. Furthermore, it assists in legitimizing the power of the regime because it can point to accomplishments accruing from the efforts of the people. In sum, "the new authoritarians are more sensitive to the persisting gap between popular needs and national achievements, and also to the need for maintenance of enthusiasm and a spirit of sacrifice." [1] (2) The regime is able to concentrate power in the hands of a small elite. A series of goals is posited which necessitates continual, all-powerful guidance and leadership until the "last" goal is reached. The goals may be sold or imposed as being good for the people, but according to Lenin's elitist doctrine, those who have the deepest understanding of Marxian laws are best qualified to lead the people, determine the "good," and so to specify goal content. The first condition involves the nature and extent of power, while the second involves the organization and distribution of power.

By what means are these conditions achieved? How are goals manipulated so that power is total in scope and concentrated in the hands of a few? This is done by means of three factors which operate to produce and maintain the above conditions: a short-long range goal continuum, stress and ambiguity.

It is not surprising that the Marxian dialectic as an explanation of social change should give rise to the use of a goal continuum in Communist practice, although the former refers to the laws of history and the latter to acts of the state. While pragmatic in nature, the term "goal" as used in this essay should not be confused with "plans," such as Five- or Seven-Year Plans, which are detailed, working sheets for the former. Goals as used here are broader in scope and intent, involving political and social as well as economic objectives. The goal may be to enter the stage of Communism which involves the prior task of remolding man in relation to which the

[1] Manfred Halpern, *The Politics of Social Change in the Middle East and North Africa*, 1963, p. 228.

number of new school buildings to be built within a given time is an operational detail. Furthermore, while the ruling elite may have maintenance of power as their goal, what is under discussion here is the use of goals by the elite as a *means* for maintaining power.

The goal continuum consists of short- and long-ranged goals set up in a phased sequence. As soon as one set of goals is achieved, another looms on the horizon. What was long range becomes short range, and the continuum is kept open-ended by feeding in new future goals. The essence of the continuum as a political system is to maintain, or seem to maintain, a forward momentum along the continuum. To provide momentum incentives must be offered in the form of present satisfactions and future hopes. These satisfactions may be objective or subjective, material or non-material, a rising standard of living or national pride in the growing power position of the nation. Some immediate goals must be reached, and recognized as such by the people, to make the whole goal system credible. Sacrifices for the future can be maintained over a period of time only if the immediate situation provides enough satisfaction to make the more distant goals seem probable. (Neumann, in his comparative study of political parties, points out that the masses need visible rewards, and if they cannot have the fruits now, or at least reasonably expect that they will do so in the near future, they will leave the ranks.[2]

Lippitt, Watson and Westley discussing the leverage necessary to induce social change also point out the importance of an "immediate goal which will bring about a reasonably quick experience of success. Such a success will launch the change program smoothly and give it an immediate impetus." [3] The relation of present satisfactions to future hopes has an important effect on the ratio of coercion to persuasion used by the regime.). If there is sufficient present satisfaction to make more distant goals credible, persuasion, as a method of mass control, may be maximized and coercion minimized. Sacrifice may be called forth rather than exacted.

Furthermore, the scope of power in the goal continuum is kept broad by the nature of the goal content. In the Communist system

---

[2] Sigmund Neumann, "Toward a Comparative Study of Political Parties," *Modern Political Parties,* ed. by Sigmund Neumann, 1956, p. 399.

[3] R. Lippitt, J. Watson and B. Westley, *The Dynamics of Social Change,* 1958, p. 200.

the all-over goal is nothing less than the restructuring of society and the refashioning of the nature of man. Such an end is to be achieved by a step by step progress along the goal continuum, and its all-embracing content insures that no area of human life remains outside the range of controlled sacrifice. This aspect provides some insight into the nature of totalitarianism.

Stress, the second factor, is more self-evident. There must be continued stress to maintain continual sacrifice. The fruits of immediate goal achievement are to be enjoyed, but the people are urged to work even harder to push on to the next. Psychologically, people are uncertain of their roles and how to behave in stressful situations, and there is an increased desire for leadership to point the way to a future of less stress. "It seems that authoritarian leaders have a particular appreciation of the equilibrium acting to maintain their power in the high stress, highly structured goal situation." [4] Even democracies are aware of this propensity of wartime crisis situations when it is agreed that leaders must have powers not conceded to them in more normal conditions. However, a goal system institutionalizes stress by setting up a goal structure which makes stress continuous. Stress not only adds another motivating factor for producing momentum along the continuum, but it has the advantage of being easily manipulated by the regime which can increase or decrease intensity according to their evaluation of the situation.

This need for continual stress constitutes a serious problem. The degree of stress must not be so overwhelming that it exhausts the people to the point of apathy, as the People's Republic of China came close to doing in the Great Leap Forward, nor must it produce an attitude of "nothing to lose but our chains" as Stalin felt obliged to recognize in his *Dizzy From Success*, which called a temporary halt to the forced industrialization and collectivization drives of the early 1930s.

Ambiguity is the third factor in the goal-control system. It is obviously closely related to the short-long range continuum since short-range goals are likely to be less ambiguous than long-range. However, ambiguity in a goal system performs several positive functions. It contributes to the creation of stress because of the

[4] David C. Korten, "Situational Determinants of Leadership," *The Journal of Conflict Resolution,* Vol. VI, No. 3, September 1962, p. 224.

element of uncertainty. White and Lippitt refer to it as an operational device of authoritarian regimes: "Techniques and activity steps are dictated by the authority, one at a time, so that future steps are always uncertain to a large degree." [5] A more significant function is to provide freedom of action on the part of the ruling elite. By keeping the timing and content of future goals uncertain, the elite may justify their continued leadership and maintain flexibility in regard to policy content. Any direction in which the regime may choose to move must be encompassed in the ambiguity of future goals. By keeping future goals ambiguous, one yardstick for measuring the performance of the leaders is avoided. Ambiguous goals are allowed to become unambiguous only when there is reasonable expectation that they can be fulfilled. Furthermore, by keeping the content of future goals uncertain, any source of opposition is deprived of a specific basis for opposition. But the regime must exercise care not to be too ambiguous, for the utopia ahead must not be so lacking in content as to have no target value. Future goals must be specific enough to be recognized as goals by the people but ambiguous enough to leave freedom of decision to the leaders. A goal continuum necessitates passage of some aspects from ambiguous to unambiguous to maintain at least an appearance of momentum, but a proper judgment about when and what to convert into non-ambiguity is extremely difficult, and the cost of error is either the appearance of failure or the necessity of considerable ideological legerdemain to conceal the fact.

This need for ambiguity to provide freedom of action raises a special problem for Communist regimes because their goal structure must be posited within the confines of Communist ideology. The Marxian dialectic which culminates in the withering away of the state presents a dilemma for maintaining power. This aspect of Marxian "laws" gives a Communist regime three alternatives. First, it can accept the dialectic and abdicate its power when it is no longer functional. However, it appears that after nearly a half a century in power the current Soviet regime shows no sign of accepting this solution. Both Stalin and Khrushchev have devoted considerable effort to explaining why the regime must have more not less power as the final goal of Communism approaches nearer.

[5] R. K. White and R. Lippitt, *Autocracy and Democracy, an Experimental Inquiry,* 1960, p. 26.

It is conceivable that the regimes may be self-effacing in the future, but at present there is no such indication.

A second solution is to postpone indefinitely the entrance into the final stage of Communism on the grounds that the necessary pre-conditions have not yet been met. This seems to be the solution of the Chinese leaders, but it has the difficulty of creating a relatively static situation which loses the persuasiveness of seeming to move along the goal continuum. A third solution, and one followed by the Soviet Union, is to march along the goal continuum into the "final" stage of Communism, but upon approach to lay down a new series of phases or sub-goals within the new stage of Communism which will justify continued leadership, whether of state or party. This solution has the advantage of opening the possibility of continued controls even within Communism. It has the disadvantage in terms of social control of being ever more of the same with no relief in sight from the demands for sacrifice, a situation conducive to popular cynicism. Thus, there is no entirely satisfactory solution to the problem posed by operating a necessarily ambiguous goal system within a Marxian ideological framework. A brief comparison of Soviet and Chinese practice illustrates use of the system and indicates the similarities and differences arising from dissimilar objective conditions.

The need to sacrifice for future goals as well as the insistence on centralization of power are themes constantly reiterated in Soviet and Chinese official statements. Khrushchev in his Report of the Central Committee of the CPSU to the 22nd Congress of the Communist Party delivered October 17, 1961 (referred to hereafter as the Report), extols the achievements of the Russian people since 1949 but exhorts them to greater efforts in the present period so that they may realize the even more bountiful life of the future. Work is no longer simply a means of earning a livelihood, but a social calling, a moral duty. "The building of Communism requires a great labor effort on the part of the people, by literally every Soviet man and woman. Without labor there cannot be a prosperous society, there can be no well-being and happiness for man. The good things of life do not drop like manna from heaven. Every working man and woman must realize this and do his or her bit in the nation-wide cause of Communist construction.—Human society cannot be cleansed of that which prevents a happy and joyous life without a great deal of sweat and much vexation of spirit." Similar statements, though with a somewhat different tone, are made by Chinese leaders. The current tone of Soviet exhortation is self-confident, suggesting that additional work will produce even greater benefits, but that of the Chinese tends to be more negative, appealing to the basic revolutionary spirit of the people to overcome present difficulties and obstacles and emphasizing that conditions will get no better if the old order is not changed. As will be seen, the difference in length of revolutionary experience is only a partial explanation of the above. Liu Shao-ch'i in 1958 referred to the slogan "Hard work for a few years, happiness for a thousand." "Moreover, history shows that there never was a revolution which was able to achieve victory without zigzags and sacrifices. . . . Even if the guiding line of the revolution is correct, it is impossible to have a sure guarantee against setbacks and sacrifices in the course of the revolution. So long as a correct line is adhered to, the revolution is bound to triumph in the end. To abandon revolution on the pretext of avoiding sacrifices is in reality to demand that the people should forever remain slaves and endure infinite pain and sacrifice." [6] However, the call for hard work and sacrifice has been given even greater urgency since 1960 as a result of the failure of the Great Leap Forward and the cessation of Soviet aid. The new emphasis added to the long-standing theme is the necessity of achieving progress "by our own efforts."

On the whole, Chinese and Soviet leaders agree on the conditions necessary for the exercise of continuous power. Furthermore, practice indicates that both rely on a goal continuum, stress and ambiguity as means for achieving these conditions. Nevertheless, it is at the level of means or tactics that differences in the objective environment operate to produce modifications in the system. Differences in culture, material conditions, and length and nature of revolutionary experience raise different problems which affect the operation. An examination of Chinese and Soviet practice indicates both similarities and differences in the use of these means.

The Soviet goal continuum is structured into stages and phases, and since the lines of division are ambiguous, it is possible to make

---

[6] Central Committee of the CPC, "A Proposal Concerning the General Line of the International Communist Movement," *Peking Review*, No. 30, July 26, 1963, p. 16.

"ad hoc," subjective decisions as to when a phase is completed and so to point to another achievement. Each stage and phase has its own set of preconditions involving specific tasks which must be fulfilled before the next stage or phase can be entered. "Under socialism the principle 'From each according to his ability, to each according to his work' has been put into effect. In order to advance to the Communist principle 'From each according to his ability, to each according to his needs' time and certain definite conditions are needed.—The transition to Communist principles is possible, but not before the material and technical basis has been created, not before people have reached a high degree of consciousness, not before the potentialities of socialism have been revealed in full." The tasks and conditions necessary for passage into Communism are indeed formidable, especially since they must be achieved in twenty years: to surpass the economic level of the most advanced capitalist countries, the creation of the "new Soviet man," and the political and social transformation of society. These are tasks which obviously call forth a high intensity of work and sacrifice, and involve the full-range of human activity since even human nature is to be remolded according to specifications.

To justify the continuance of work and sacrifice after more than four decades, Khrushchev relied heavily on present satisfactions, greater rewards in the near future, and more distant hopes. Continued sacrifice may be necessary to reach Communism, but the goal of Communism is made credible by reference to present satisfactions. The Report dwelled at length on the subjective and material achievements already gained for the Soviet people, and while doubts may be raised as to the validity of the claims, nevertheless, the standard of living has risen sufficiently to be clearly apparent to the Russian people. Bauer, Inkeles, and Kluckhohn report: "That while the regime's objective is to extract from the citizen a maximum of effort with a minimum of reward,—most Soviet citizens appear to accept and approve the basic structure of the Soviet welfare state and do not seem profoundly troubled by the gross fact of extreme concentration of power in the U.S.S.R.; indeed they seem to regard it as inevitable if not downright proper." [7] This would indicate that the rewards to date have been sufficient to enable the

[7] Raymond A. Bauer, Alex Inkeles and Clyde Kluckhohn, *How The Soviet System Works,* pp. 250 and 261.

regime to make its manipulation of Soviet goals and so of Soviet society acceptable. However, additional effort will bring additional rewards in the near future. The Soviet people are told that if they continue to work hard, in the coming ten years they will be able to obtain consumer goods in abundance, and in the following ten years the consumer demand will be met in full. While the present leaders are able to base their goal-power system to a large extent on rewards in return for sacrifice, coercion is not lacking. The steady inveighing against "hooligans" and "parasites" indicate this. However, it is clear that because of readily apparent satisfaction, the present regime can rely increasingly on satisfaction as popular motivation for further goal achievement; whereas Stalin felt obliged to maximize coercion because he could offer so few material rewards.

Maintenance of continual stress as a stimulant to revolutional zeal is one of the most difficult problems which the Soviet leaders face. It is clear that every endeavor is made to prevent relaxation and a slackening of a sense of urgency. However, as the standard of living rises conspicuously in relation to previous conditions, a "bourgeois" attitude of enjoying the good things of life now and of preference for stability over change tends to appear.

This dilemma of conflict between increasing satisfaction and the need to preserve the ethos of a "permanent" or "uninterrupted" revolution may well be the Achilles heel of the Soviet goal system. When the Soviet leaders rashly set 1980 as an all too specific date for establishing in the Soviet Union the highest standard of living in the world as well as entering the final stage of Communism, they were motivated no doubt by the struggle with China for primacy in Communist leadership.

The Soviet leaders have preserved their leadership by allocating to themselves a monopoly of being able to see the first glimmers of light in the future, but they can see what they wish in the ambiguity they themselves created. However, by setting the unambiguous date of 1980 for entering the new historical period of Communism, the Soviet leaders created serious problems for their goal-power system. They can in 1980, of course, state flatly that the bowl *is* overflowing and each has all he needs, according to a standard of validity established by the regime. This would move the Soviet Union into the stage of Communism which holds that the state will wither away in the new historical epoch because it will be no longer functional. But at this point the problem arises of maintaining the power and freedom of action of the leaders within a Marxist framework.

The Soviet leaders attempt to resolve this dilemma by positing a series of phases within the new stage of Communism. The structuring of socialism into phases is projected into Communism for the same purpose of maintaining a sense of momentum and new opportunities for ambiguity. Communism also apparently is to have early and late phases. The first phase is the "beginning" of Communism which only later will become "fully-developed" Communism. This early phase, as described, seems little different from the last phase of socialism.

A corollary to the phasing of Communism is the newly expressed concept that the state is *not* to wither away at least in the first phase of Communism. "The state will remain long after the victory of the first phase of Communism. The process of its withering away will be a very long one; it will cover an entire historical epoch and will not end until society is completely ripe for self-government. For some time, features of state administration and public self-government will intermingle. In this process the domestic functions of the state will develop and change, and gradually lose their political character. It is only after a developed Communist society is built up in the U.S.S.R., and provided socialism wins and consolidates in the international arena, that there will no longer be any need for the state, and it will wither away."

The criterion of a "developed" Communist society is open to manipulation, and that of an all socialist world is reminiscent of Stalin's statement of 1939 that the state would be preserved so long as the Soviet Union was encircled by capitalist nations. But since it is conceded that the state is to wither away when Communism is fully developed and socialism is universal, the dilemma of maintaining power is merely postponed to an undetermined but certain future. To settle the problem of perpetual leadership, a final solution is envisioned. The state will wither away eventually but not the Party. The Party is equated with society itself. "Every organism consists of separate cells and is continually renewed as some cells die off and others are born. The Party and society as a whole are subject to the same process, to the same law of life. The natural process cannot be checked or violated without causing harm to the development of the organism of the Party and society as a whole."

Thus the Soviet system of goal manipulation is projected into the future. There is apparently to be ever more of the same. But is it a perpetual motion system? It is conceivable that sufficient satisfaction may be provided so that the Soviet people, content in enjoyment of their benefits, will also be content to be uninterested in the nature of political power. It is also conceivable that when a sufficient level of material satisfaction is reached, they will turn their attention to the process itself.

The Chinese leaders also use a goal continuum, stress and ambiguity to generate conditions conducive to maintaining their power. However, while the system is the same, the tactics differ because of different objective conditions. The Soviet Union has reached a self-sustaining phase of economic growth, while the Chinese are struggling desperately to achieve it, and must do so, as Zagoria points out, at a reckless speed or suffer stagnation and the failure of their revolution.[8] The shorter length of Chinese revolutionary experience is significant in this difference, but even more serious is the overwhelming problem of population and the comparatively adverse ratio of population to known resources.

It is within these conditions that the Chinese leaders operate a goal continuum. Liu Shao-ch'i says that the Chinese revolution has been able to advance at the opportune moment from one stage to another, scoring one victory after another. China is considered to be in the phase of constructing socialism, which is roughly equivalent to the first or Stalinist phase of the Soviet sequence. However, the Chinese are less insistent on phasing than the Russians, probably because their desperate need for quick economic development makes them impatient with the restraints of orderly phasing. Nevertheless, the tasks to be performed by the people before Chinese society can enter the era of Communism are similar and in many cases identical to those posed by the Soviet Union: higher production, restructuring of society, and the remolding of man. Like the Soviet Union, the tasks are so formidable and so broad that no limit is placed on the demands which may be made on society or the individual.

Having set the goals and the tasks, the Chinese leaders are faced

[8] Donald S. Zagoria, "Some Comparisons Between the Russian and Chinese Models," in *Communist Strategies in Asia,* ed. by A. Doak Barnett, 1963, p. 30.

with the problem of incentive. It is here that the tactics of the regime must necessarily differ from those used by the Soviet Union because they are not able to use present material satisfactions as a major incentive for continued sacrifice for future goals to the extent possible in the Soviet Union. While hunger has replaced starvation, and health, communications and education have improved, the increase in household and consumer goods which the individual is more likely to regard as an index of success has not been so conspicuous as to make future goals entirely credible, especially after the hardships resulting from the failure of the Great Leap Forward. The situation in this respect is not unlike that under Stalin but with the major difference that the Chinese ratio of population to resources makes it unlikely that China can duplicate the Soviet rise in standard of living in anywhere near an equivalent time. Since 1960 the regime has made some concessions to the need to revive effort by increasing material satisfaction. The target of a major industrial advance in heavy industry of the Great Leap Forward has been replaced temporarily by emphasis on agriculture and greater production of consumer goods. However, each reference to an improved standard of living is qualified by "gradual" and coupled with admonitions to be "thrifty" and "frugal." In any case, the shift from industrialization to agriculture and light industry as prime targets postpones the full socialist industrialization necessary for entrance into Communism.

Lacking a conspicuous rise in the standard of living, the Chinese leaders have had to rely on a series of non-material incentives for continued hard work and sacrifice in order to keep up momentum along the goal continuum. In addition to even heavier reliance on political and ideological education than the Soviet Union, three consistent Chinese tactics have been the use of external threat, a series of innovations, and an appeal to the pride and character of the Chinese people. Needless to say these devices are not lacking in the Soviet system, but at present they are less significant for the goal system than material rewards. The use of the threat of external enemies is a widespread device for controlling an internal situation.

The Chinese, then, like the Soviet leaders, appeal to satisfactions but with greater reliance on subjective, non-material incentives. National unity, ideological purity, and the rise of China to great power status take the place of housing and consumer goods. Stalin in an equivalent period made similar, though not necessarily identical, appeals but coupled them with the coercive force of purges. The Chinese have also used direct coercion in "rectification" campaigns but have preferred to keep coercion indirect in the form of thought reform as well as close military and police supervision. However, the Soviet Union was able to make a greater shift from coercion to persuasion in a shorter time than seems likely in China. While Chinese tactics have permitted the regime to exact heavy sacrifices from the "silent" people, the question is for how long without conspicuous material benefits? Here the problem of ratio between resources and population again arises. Are satisfactions such as national unity and rising national power, alone adequate to make future goals sufficiently credible so that continued sacrifices will be accepted? However, the use of stress as an operational device is clear from the above.

The Chinese leaders, like the Soviet, use ambiguity as a means for perpetuating power, but again with significant differences. The Chinese movement from the ambiguous to the non-ambiguous continues to be more jerky than the Soviet, with more "zigzags," double-takes, and second thoughts. To the ambiguity of future policies has been added the less desirable uncertainty and unpredictability of present policies. Future ambiguity properly proportioned, as seen above, is conducive to power retention, but undue uncertainty in current policies tends to produce a loss of momentum, incentive and sense of direction among the people. The necessity of restoring these losses places limitations on the freedom of policy decision of the leaders.

A case in point was the decision to make the Great Leap Forward into industrialization. Communes were introduced as part of the Great Leap with high optimism, and the attainment of Communism was no longer considered to be a remote future event. This early optimism in the autumn of 1958 was replaced in December by a more sober evaluation. Now the Central Committee warned that socialism must continue for a very long time, and will be realized on a national scale only after a considerable time. The failure of the "Great Leap" forced the Chinese leaders to abandon their preferred policy of rapid development of heavy industry, and to place greater emphasis for the time being on agriculture and light industry for consumer goods.

As a result the Chinese have been obliged to prolong the stage of socialism during which the preconditions for Communism are being laid down. While the Soviet leaders have preserved a forward momentum by setting 1980 as the date for entering the "final" stage of Communism, the Chinese have been obliged to postpone indefinitely entrance into the stage of "Each according to his needs." Some solace has been found in ideological purity. Mao Tse-tung set the "pure line" in 1949 when he said that the people and party must work hard to create the conditions in which classes, state power and political parties will die out naturally and mankind will enter the realm of Great Harmony. In 1963 the Central Committee of the CPC rebuked Khrushchev for his revisionism in maintaining that the Soviet Union in its present pre-Communist phase had already established a "state of the whole people," and insisted that as long as the state remains a state, it will have a class character.

In conclusion, both the Soviet and Chinese leaders have used the goal system as a significant component for maintaining power. The success of the system, while varied, has been sufficient so that neither gives any indication of abandoning it. As a practical device for governing, it fits very well with the spirit, sense of revolutionary movement, and explanation of social change provided in the Marxian dialectic. However, the system is not without flaw. The Soviet leaders are plagued by the slowing down of popular revolutionary zeal due to the considerable degree of both non-material and material satisfaction. While in democracies widespread satisfaction may slow down progress, it does not necessarily weaken the strength of the party in power; on the other hand, abundance is a mixed blessing to those in the Soviet Union basing their power on a goal system. As zeal is replaced by contentment, the regime is faced with the alternative of greater coercion, or more likely, with acquiescence in a less revolutionary role and a consequent modification of the system itself. Furthermore, Soviet abundance may appeal to the less developed areas as a source of bounty and a beacon of hope, but it can also reach a point where the Chinese model seems more relevant to their condition and experience. Yet, the Chinese system retains as a flaw its inability to provide enough material satisfaction. Consequently, the Chinese leadership must continue to rely heavily on such subjective satisfaction as increased international prestige, and search for new incentives to buttress its demands for continued popular sacrifice.

Index